Accounting for Non-Accountants

NINTH EDITION

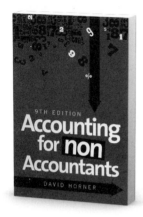

Accounting for Non-Accountants

David Horner

KoganPage

LONDON PHILADELPHIA NEW DELHI

First published by Kogan Page Limited in 1990
Ninth edition 2013

120 Pentonville Road	1518 Walnut Street, Suite 1100	4737/23 Ansari Road
London N1 9JN	Philadelphia PA 19102	Daryaganj
United Kingdom	USA	New Delhi 110002
www.koganpage.com		India

© Kogan Page, 2013

The right of David Horner to be identified as the author of this work has been asserted by him in accordance with the Copyright, Designs and Patents Act 1988.

ISBN   978 0 7494 6597 1
E-ISBN   978 0 7494 6598 8

British Library Cataloguing-in-Publication Data

A CIP record for this book is available from the British Library.

Library of Congress Cataloging-in-Publication Data

Horner, David, 1970–
    Accounting for non-accountants / David Horner. – 9th ed.
        p. cm.
    Rev. ed. of: Accounting for non-accountants / Graham Mott. 8th ed. 2012.
    Includes bibliographical references and index.
    ISBN 978-0-7494-6597-1 – ISBN 978-0-7494-6598-8 (ebook)   1. Accounting–Great Britain.
I. Mott, Graham. Accounting for non-accountants.   II. Title.
    HF5616.G7H67 2013
    657.0941–dc23
                                                                          2012034460

Typeset by Graphicraft Limited, Hong Kong
Printed and bound in India by Replika Press Pvt Ltd

CONTENTS

17   Accounting ratios 335

For Nancy Henwood

Thanks to Matthew Smith and Ian Hallsworth at Kogan Page for their enthusiasm and support.

Financial record keeping

Introduction

All businesses and many other types of organization will need to keep records of any financial transactions that take place. However, it makes sense to introduce some accounting terminology before we look at any system of recording financial transactions. We will begin by explaining some of the frequently used terms whose meaning may not be immediately obvious. These terms are **assets**, **liabilities** and **capital**:

- Assets are resources that are used within the business. These can take the form of physical resources used to facilitate production, such as premises and equipment. Assets can also include resources which are used as a part of the production process, such as materials that are going to be converted into goods, the cash used to purchase more assets and the outstanding amounts owed to the business by its customers.

- Liabilities are debts of the business that are outstanding. These are any borrowings which the business will repay at some point in the future. These can be short-term debts which are to be repaid in the next few days, such as an expense which has yet to be paid, but can also be long-term debts not to be repaid until many years in the future, such as a mortgage.

- Capital refers to the value of the owner's resources placed within the business. This can take the form of money invested in the business but can also take the form of owner's assets brought into business use, such as the owner's vehicle. The withdrawal of capital from the business by the owner is known as drawings.

The capital, along with the liabilities of the business, enables the business to acquire assets which can be used as part of the business operations. This leads us to the accounting equation, which can be simply stated as follows:

Assets = Capital + Liabilities

This equation must always hold true. To explain why the equation always holds, we must consider what the equation is telling us – that the resources in use within the business must have been financed either from the owner's resources or by borrowing resources. Once the business has become established and if the business is profitable, we can modify the equation to allow assets to be financed out of the profits of the business in addition to the capital and liabilities.

The process of recording and maintaining records of financial transactions is known as bookkeeping. However, there are two types of bookkeeping that are commonly practised by business organizations – single-entry and double-entry bookkeeping.

Single-entry bookkeeping

Very small businesses (usually one-person organizations known as sole traders) and other types of organization such as charities, clubs and other small not-for-profit organizations may keep their financial records through a process of single-entry bookkeeping where each transaction is recorded as one single entry.

This is bookkeeping at it simplest and often can be as basic as the maintenance of only a receipts and payments account. An example of a receipts and payments account is shown in Figure 1.1.

FIGURE 1.1   Receipts and payments account

2013	Receipts	£	2013	Payments	£
1 Feb	Capital	1,000	4 Feb	Purchases	230
8 Feb	Sales	320	6 Feb	Electricity	89
12 Feb	Loan: R Day	750	12 Feb	Purchases	195
20 Feb	Sales	275	28 Feb	Balance c/d	1,831
		2,345			2,345
1 Mar	Balance b/d	1,831			

This account shows all the monies received by the business and all the monies paid out by the business. The balance left over at the end of the month represents the current amount of money still left in the business bank account.

The receipts and payments account is more commonly known as a cashbook. The cashbook will record all transactions involving money either being received or being spent – either in the form of cash or as money taken from or paid into the firm's bank account.

If a firm maintains a receipts and payments account as its main financial record it will still need to keep records and details of the types of payment and types of receipt in each transaction. This will enable a firm to calculate the level of profit or loss generated. However, these extra details will often be kept in a memorandum form – meaning that they are not part of the firm's accounting system, but are there as financial records to provide information only.

A more detailed variation on the cashbook can be used if managers want to monitor and control the type of expenses paid out by the firm more closely. A multi-column approach to the cashbook would be well suited to a business that wanted to keep records that show the effect of VAT (Value Added Tax) separately from its overall purchases and sales. An example of a multi-column cashbook appears in Figure 1.2.

FIGURE 1.2 Multi-column cashbook

		Receipts					Payments			
2014	Details	Bank	Sales	VAT	2014	Details	Bank	Purchases	VAT	Other expenses
		£	£	£			£	£	£	£
1 Apr	Balance b/d	640			2 Apr	Insurance	99			99
11 Apr	E Mahoney	480	400	80	3 Apr	P Beard	300	250	50	
15 Apr	F Tindall	6			8 Apr	K Sutton	120	100	20	
					15 Apr	Wages	280			280

In Figure 1.2 the analysed columns enable a firm to keep records for VAT, which is necessary once firms reach a certain size (as measured by their sales turnover).

Problems with single-entry bookkeeping

Although popular with very small organizations, there are a number of limitations in relying on single-entry bookkeeping as a method of keeping financial records.

1 In the receipts and payments account, expenditure will appear but this does not allow the separation of expenditure on day-to-day running expenses and expenditure on assets. This is an important distinction for when a firm wants to calculate the level of profit for the period, assets would not normally be deducted as expenses.

2 Double-entry bookkeeping has a number of built-in checks, which means it is easier to spot mistakes with double-entry accounting (though mistakes still occur). Single-entry bookkeeping has no self-checking mechanism.

3 Attempting to control expenditure will require detailed records of where a business spends money. This is not easy unless there are separate records (ie individual accounts) maintained for each type of

expense. This limitation can be minimized through the use of a multi-column cashbook.

4 Lack of full accounting records will make theft from the business by business employees more likely. Obviously a one-person organization will not face this problem.

Double-entry bookkeeping

Once a business begins to grow beyond a certain size and certainly once the maintenance of financial records moves beyond the very straightforward, it will make sense for the financial transactions of the business to be recorded using the double-entry system of bookkeeping. It is widely believed that the system of double-entry bookkeeping was developed and formally set out by Luca Pacioli in the late 15th century.

The term 'double-entry' arises out of the fact that each and every financial transaction will require two entries. These are known as a *debit entry* and a *credit entry* and each will be recorded in a separate account. The account in which the transaction is recorded will depend on the nature of the transaction.

An example of how a double-entry account would appear is shown in Figure 1.3.

FIGURE 1.3 Example of double-entry account presentation

	Account name				
	Debit side (Dr)			Credit side (Cr)	
Date	Account details	Amount (£)	Date	Account details	Amount (£)

Given the 'T'-shaped appearance of the accounts they are often referred to as 'T' accounts.

Accounts will be opened and an entry made in the account for each different type of transaction that the business undertakes. This means that there will be separate accounts for each type of asset, each type of expense and each type of income. In addition there will be separate accounts opened for every individual credit supplier and credit customer of the business. All the transactions between the business and the owner will also be recorded in either a capital account or a drawings account, depending on whether the owner is adding resources to or withdrawing resources from the business.

There are different rules to be applied when making entries on the bookkeeping system to tell us which side of the account a transaction is to be entered. Many of the basic transactions would involve the rules for double-entry bookkeeping illustrated in Figure 1.4.

FIGURE 1.4 Rules used in double-entry bookkeeping

All asset accounts		All liability accounts		All capital accounts	
Debit	*Credit*	*Debit*	*Credit*	*Debit*	*Credit*
Increases entered HERE	Decreases entered HERE	Decreases entered HERE	Increases entered HERE	Decreases entered HERE	Increases entered HERE

All expense accounts		All income accounts	
Debit	*Credit*	*Debit*	*Credit*
Increases entered HERE	Decreases entered HERE	Decreases entered HERE	Increases entered HERE

These rules will make more sense if we see some examples of them in action.

Example 1.1

On 3 June 2013, the owner of the business places £2,000 of her own money into the bank account of the new business.

Bank

2013		£	2013		£
3 Jun	Capital	2,000			

Capital

2013		£	2013		£
			3 Jun	Bank	2,000

Explanation

Here the asset of 'bank' is increasing, which requires a debit entry, and the capital of the business (resources from the owner) is also increasing, which requires a credit entry. Notice how each account in effect cross-references the account containing the other entry for the double-entry transaction. This facilitates the ability to check that the system of bookkeeping is being correctly maintained.

Example 1.2

On 5 June 2013 inventory is purchased for resale on credit from Henwood Ltd for the value of £550.

Purchases

2013		£	2013		£
5 Jun	Capital	550			

Henwood Ltd

2013	£	2013		£
		5 Jun	Purchases	550

Explanation

Purchasing inventory means an increase in this asset, which requires a debit entry. Purchasing on credit from Henwood Ltd creates a liability account which is known by the name of the creditor, in this case Henwood Ltd. The increase in this liability requires a credit entry.

Example 1.3

Advertising of £80 is paid by cheque on 7 June 2013.

Advertising

2013		£	2013		£
7 Jun	Bank	80			

Bank

2013		£	2013		£
3 Jun	Capital	2,000	7 Jun	Advertising	80

Explanation

The payment of an expense means that we debit the expense account which is given the name of the type of expense generated by the business. The payment by cheque means the bank account will decrease and this requires a credit entry.

Example 1.4

On 17 June 2013 the account with Henwood Ltd is settled in full by cheque.

Henwood Ltd

2013		£	2013		£
17 Jun	Bank	550	5 Jun	Purchases	550

Bank

2013		£	2013		£
3 Jun	Capital	2,000	7 Jun	Advertising	80
			17 Jun	Henwood Ltd	550

Explanation

Settling a liability by payment will result in a decrease in the liability, which means the firm owes less and this requires a debit entry. In addition, the payment will reduce the funds in the bank and needs a credit entry.

Example 1.5

On 20 June 2013, the owner of the business takes £30 out of the business bank account for personal use.

Drawings

2013		£	2013		£
20 Jun	Bank	30			

Bank

2013		£	2013		£
3 Jun	Capital	2,000	7 Jun	Advertising	80
			17 Jun	Henwood Ltd	550
			20 Jun	Drawings	30

Explanation

Even though the business is owned and controlled by the owner, the financial records should always separate out the personal finances of the owner and the business finances. This is known as the concept of the **separate entity**. In this case, we are seeing a withdrawal of capital by the owner.

The rule for reducing capital is to debit the capital account. However, it is standard practice to show all withdrawals of capital in a separate account known as drawings. This follows the rules of the capital account. At the end of the period (or earlier if the owner so wishes) the balance on the drawings account would be transferred to the capital account and this transfer of drawings to capital would reduce the overall capital balance.

The bank account would be credited to show the reduction of the asset of bank.

Balancing accounts

Periodically the business will need to know the financial state of the business. A start in this process will be the balancing off of all the individual accounts. This process of balancing can be done at any point in time but is often done at the end of each month or at the end of the accounting period (usually the financial year end). Balancing an account involves calculating the net difference between the debit and the credit entries of that account. The balance on that account will be the overall difference in the two totals. Figure 1.5 shows an example of a balanced account.

FIGURE 1.5 Balancing of double-entry accounts

Bank

2014		£	2014		£
8 Jan	Sales	86	10 Jan	Purchases	690
15 Jan	Cash	112	14 Jan	Wages	380
17 Jan	Equipment	750	20 Jan	Balance c/d	1,878
27 Jan	Loan	2,000			
		2,948			2,948
1 Feb	Balance b/d	1,878			

In Figure 1.5, the total of the debit entries is greater than the total of the credit entries, meaning that there is a debit balance on the account by the difference on the two totals.

The term 'balance c/d' refers to the balance to be carried down on the account. This is not the balance on the account but it is the balancing figure (the amount needed to make the debit and credit columns total the same figure). The term 'balance b/d' refers to the balance brought down and this is the balance on the account.

This balancing process must be completed for each account. It will be the case that some accounts have debit balances, some accounts have credit balances and some accounts – where the totals of the debit and credit entries are identical – have no balance.

Example 1.6

Here is a worked example of how a firm would record its financial transactions for the month of January 2014. At the end of the month each individual account is balanced off with the balance on the account, ready for the following month.

2014

2 Jan	Owner places £5,000 from private resources into business bank account.
3 Jan	Rent paid on premises, £700 by cheque.
6 Jan	Goods purchased on credit for £800 from W Pierce.
9 Jan	Goods sent back to Pierce worth £150.
15 Jan	Goods sold for cash worth £450.
17 Jan	Goods sold on credit to S Nower for £300.
22 Jan	Nower sends cheque to us for £280 in full settlement (the difference represents a discount given).
24 Jan	We send Pierce a cheque for £400.
28 Jan	£100 Cash taken from bank for private use.

Capital

2014		£	2014		£
31 Jan	Balance c/d	5,000	2 Jan	Bank	5,000
			1 Feb	Balance b/d	5,000

Bank

2014		£	2014		£
2 Jan	Capital	5,000	3 Jan	Rent	700
15 Jan	Sales	400	24 Jan	W Pierce	400
22 Jan	S Nower	280	28 Jan	Drawings	100
			31 Jan	Balance c/d	4,480
		5,680			5,680
1 Feb	Balance b/d	4,480			

Rent

2014		£	2014		£
3 Jan	Bank	700	31 Jan	Balance c/d	700
1 Feb	Balance b/d	700			

W Pierce

2014		£	2014		£
9 Jan	Returns outwards	150	6 Jan	Purchases	800
24 Jan	Bank	400			
31 Jan	Balance c/d	250			
		800			800
			1 Feb	Balance b/d	250

Returns outwards

2014		£	2014		£
Jan 31	Balance c/d	150	Jan 9	W Pierce	150
			Feb 1	Balance b/d	150

Sales

2014		£	2014		£
Jan 31	Balance c/d	750	Jan 15	Bank	450
			Jan 17	S Nower	300
		750			750
			Feb 1	Balance b/d	700

S Nower

2014		£	2014		£
Jan 17	Sales	300	Jan 22	Bank	280
			Jan 22	Discount allowed	20
		300			300

Drawings

2014		£	2014		£
Jan 28	Bank	100	Jan 31	Balance c/d	100
Feb 1	Balance b/d	100			

Discounts allowed

2014		£	2014		£
Jan 22	S Nower	20	Jan 31	Balance c/d	20
Feb 1	Balance b/d	20			

Purchases

2014		£	2014		£
4 Jan	W Pierce	800	31 Jan	Balance c/d	800
1 Feb	Balance b/d	800			

If we look at the individual closing balances on all the accounts, we should find the following:

	Debit balances £	Credit balances £
Capital		5,000
Bank	4,480	
Rent	700	
Purchases	800	
W Pierce		250
Returns outwards		150
Sales		700
Drawings	100	
Discounts allowed	20	
Total	*6,100*	*6,100*

The totals of all the debit balances and of all the credit balances are the same. This may seem like an amazing coincidence. This is not a coincidence and should have been expected. This is explained in the following section.

The trial balance

Once the accounts have been balanced off it is normal to produce a trial balance. The trial balance is a list of all the outstanding balances found on the double-entry accounts. We are only interested in the balances on the accounts, not the totals for the accounts. A trial balance appears in Figure 1.6.

For the sake of convenience, in Figure 1.6 all the individual amounts outstanding by customers of the firm have been grouped together under the umbrella term of debtors. Similarly, all the outstanding amounts owing to the firm's suppliers have been combined into a single total for creditors.

The trial balance should always agree, that is, the totals of the debit and credit columns should be identical. Although this may sound like a coincidence, it is perfectly understandable why the trial balance totals agree. Remember that one of the basic principles of double-entry bookkeeping is that every transaction generates both a debit and a credit entry of an equal amount. Although entries will be made in different accounts and the balances on individual accounts will be different, the overall totals must always be the same. Hence the trial balance should agree.

FIGURE 1.6 Example of a trial balance

G Rayner
Trial balance as at 31 December 2017

	Dr £	Cr £
Sales		48,254
Purchases	29,500	
Insurance	340	
Lighting and heating	1,230	
General expenses	4,232	
Machinery	9,950	
Debtors	4,324	
Creditors		3,123
Bank	5,431	
Rent	11,280	
Administration expenses	890	
Drawings	14,200	
Capital		25,000
Loan (repayable in 2015)		5,000
	81,377	81,377

If the totals are not the same then mistakes must have been made in the double-entry bookkeeping. This check on the accuracy of the bookkeeping is one of the main uses of the trial balance. However, even if the trial balance agrees, errors may have been made. The trial balance cannot prevent the following types of errors occurring:

- transactions being missed out completely;
- incorrect amounts entered for both the debit and credit entries of a transaction;
- entering in the wrong type of account – such as entering an amount owing in the wrong personal account;
- debit and credit entries mistakenly reversed.

An additional use of the trial balance is that it helps a firm to produce a set of financial statements (often known as the final accounts of the business). These are the key financial documents produced by a business and consist primarily of a profit and loss account and a balance sheet. These are covered in the next chapters.

Daybooks and ledgers

In addition to the system of double-entry bookkeeping there are further procedures that firms will follow once they reach a certain size. These are not formal requirements but are sensible systems set up to make the tracing and monitoring of financial records easier.

Ledgers

A ledger is where the double-entry accounts are recorded. For a small firm, there may be only one ledger. It is simply a book containing these accounts. However, for firms with many transactions it makes sense to divide up the ledgers so that a ledger contains a specific type of transaction. It is fairly common practice to have three separate ledgers. These are as follows:

- sales ledger – for all the accounts of the firm's customers (the debtors);
- purchases ledger – for all the accounts of the firm's suppliers (the creditors);
- nominal (or general) ledger – for all other accounts.

Daybooks

Daybooks (often known as **journals** or **books of prime entry** or the firm's **subsidiary books**) are actually the first place in which a transaction is recorded. These daybooks are not actually accounts but are akin to diaries of business transactions. Each financial transaction is categorized and then recorded initially in one of six daybooks. Only after the entry is made in the daybook is the transaction then posted to the double-entry accounts in the relevant ledgers. Six daybooks are used:

- sales daybook – for recording all credit sales of goods to customers;
- purchases daybook – for recording all credit purchases of goods from suppliers;
- returns inwards daybook – for recording returns of goods back to the firm;
- returns outwards daybook – for recording all returns of goods sent back to the original supplier;
- cashbook – for all bank and cash transactions;
- the journal – for all other transactions; likely to be transactions that are more unusual.

Although the cashbook is a daybook it also functions as one of the accounts contained within the ledger. A cashbook is a combination of the cash and bank account and it is the only one of the daybooks to have this dual function as an account as well. Occasionally the cashbook is subdivided into a main cashbook and a petty cashbook which will record cash transactions of small amounts.

The journal is mainly used for unusual types of transaction. Buying assets to be used within the business on credit would be an example of a transaction which is initially recorded in the journal. In addition, the journal may also be used to record the initial setting up of the business, or the correction of errors. Most normal accounting transactions will be covered in the sales, purchases and cashbooks.

Modern double-entry bookkeeping

It is likely that all but the smallest business will use a computer to assist with financial record keeping. There are plenty of accounting software packages that can be used for double-entry bookkeeping. Accounting software will often complete the double-entry bookkeeping, balance off the accounts, and produce a trial balance as well as a set of full financial statements simply through entering the initial transactions. This increase in speed and potential increase in accuracy will help prevent mistaken accounting entries.

Although 'T' accounts are useful for grasping the basic rules of double-entry bookkeeping, it is more likely that modern bookkeeping will be performed via a computer package. In this case, it is likely that individual accounts will take the form of a three-column account. A three-column ledger account appears in Figure 1.7.

FIGURE 1.7 An example of a three-column account

B Street		Debit	Credit	Balance
2015		£	£	£
1 May	Sales	590		590 (Dr)
7 May	Bank		500	90 (Dr)
15 May	Sales	250		340 (Dr)
21 May	Returns inwards		90	250 (Dr)
24 May	Bank		250	0

In Figure 1.7 the account of B Street (who is a debtor of the business) uses the same rules of double-entry as we have considered earlier but this time the account is 'balanced' up after each transaction. This is useful as it enables a business to know exactly how much is outstanding on the account at any time. As we can see, the amount B Street owes the business varies throughout the month until the account is settled in full on 24 May.

Review questions

1 Ian Levinson is setting up his own business as a gentleman's barber. He has some of his own money and is going to borrow as well in order to get the business running. He wants you to construct a receipts and payments account for October 2020 based on the following data:

1 Oct	Started business with £5,000 of own money.
5 Oct	Paid £1,500 for rent on property for two months.
8 Oct	Borrowed £2,000 from bank in the form of a loan.
11 Oct	Paid £650 for equipment to be used.
12 Oct	Paid £100 for advert in local newspaper.
14 Oct	Paid £200 for leaflet drop in local area.
20 Oct	Paid £400 for business insurance.
22 Oct	Took £980 out of business for personal living costs.
26 Oct	Paid decorator for business sign (£405).

Answer

Receipts and payments account

		£			£
1 Oct	Capital	5,000	5 Oct	Rent	1,500
8 Oct	Loan	2,000	11 Oct	Equipment	650
			12 Oct	Advertising	100
			14 Oct	Leafleting	200
			20 Oct	Insurance	400
			22 Oct	Drawings	980
			26 Oct	Decorator	405
			31 Oct	Balance c/d	2,765
		7,000			7,000
1 Nov	Balance c/d	2,765			

2 Open and maintain the ledger accounts of P Shortland based on the following transactions:

1 November	Paid £2,000 of own money into bank.
4 November	Bought second-hand car for business use on credit from J Bellwood for £1,800.
7 November	Withdrew £200 out of bank for use as petty cash.
12 November	Paid Bellwood cheque £500 towards car purchase.

Solution

Capital

		£			£
			1 Nov	Bank	2,000

Bank

		£			£
1 Nov	Capital	2,000	7 Nov	Cash	200
			12 Nov	J Bellwood	500

Car

		£	£
4 Nov	J Bellwood	1,800	

J Bellwood

		£			£
12 Nov	Bank	500	4 Nov	Car	1,800

Cash (or Petty cash)

		£	£
7 Nov	Bank	200	

3 The following transactions relate to H Taylor, a customer of the firm, for February 2015. Construct the ledger account of Taylor for the following transactions and calculate the balance on his account by the end of the month.

    1 Feb   Sell goods on credit to Taylor for £560.

    6 Feb   He returns £25 of goods.

    9 Feb   A further £280 of goods is sold to Taylor.

    15 Feb   We receive a cheque from Taylor for £500 in full settlement of the goods sold on 1 Feb (the difference in the amounts represents a discount we allow Taylor as a prompt payer).

    20 Feb   Taylor returns £20 of the goods sold on 9 Feb.

Solution

H Taylor

		£			£
1 Feb	Sales	560	6 Feb	Returns inwards	25
9 Feb	Sales	280	15 Feb	Bank	500
			15 Feb	Discounts allowed (*)	35
			20 Feb	Returns inwards	20
			28 Feb	Balance c/d	260
		840			840
1 Mar	Balance b/d				

(* this discount is calculated as £560 – £25 – £500)

4 Construct the double-entry accounts for the following transactions of a sole trader and balance off each account at the end of the month:

1 Jul	Started own business by placing £3,000 into the bank account and immediately transferred £400 into the cash box.
3 Jul	Bought inventory on credit from K Atkinson for £231.
7 Jul	Paid insurance by cheque £500.
10 Jul	Bought inventory for £87, paying by cash.
16 Jul	Sold inventory on credit to H Taylor for £450.
19 Jul	Taylor returns £80 of the inventory.
27 Jul	Paid sundry expenses £120 by cash.
31 Jul	Taylor pays his account in full by cheque.

Solution

Capital

		£			£
31 Jul	Balance c/d	3,000	1 Jul	Cash	3,000
		3,000			3,000
			1 Aug	Balance b/d	3,000

H Taylor

		£			£
16 Jul	Sales	450	19 Jul	Returns inwards	80
			31 Jul	Bank	370
		450			450

Returns inwards

		£			£
19 Jul	H Taylor	80	31 Jul	Balance c/d	80
1 Aug	Balance b/d	80			

Sales

		£			£
31 Jul	Balance c/d	450	16 Jul	H Taylor	450
			1 Aug	Balance b/d	450

Purchases

		£			£
3 Jul	K Atkinson	231	31 Jul	Balance c/d	231
10 Jul	Cash	87			
		318			318
1 Aug	Balance b/d	318			

K Atkinson

		£			£
31 Jul	Balance c/d	231	3 Jul	Purchases	231
			1 Aug	Balance b/d	231

Bank

		£			£
1 Jul	Capital	3,000	1 Jul	Cash	400
31 Jul	H Taylor	370	3 Jul	Insurance	500
			31 Jul	Balance c/d	2,470
		3,370			3,370
1 Aug	Balance b/d	2,470			

Cash

		£			£
1 Jul	Bank	400	10 Jul	Purchases	87
			27 Jul	Advertising	120
			31 Jul	Balance c/d	193
		400			400
1 Aug	Balance b/d	193			

Insurance

		£			£
7 Jul	Bank	500	31 Jul	Balance c/d	500
1 Aug	Balance b/d	500			

Sundry expenses

		£			£
27 Jul	Cash	120	31 Jul	Balance c/d	120
1 Aug	Balance b/d	120			

5 State the balance on the following types of account (debit, credit, or either):

(a) Capital

(b) Sales

(c) Purchases

(d) Returns outwards

(e) Equipment

(f) Loan from bank

(g) Bank

(h) Rent received

(i) Rent (as an expense)

(j) Creditors – amounts owing to suppliers.

Solution

(a) Credit

(b) Credit

(c) Debit

(d) Credit

(e) Debit

(f) Credit

(g) Either

(h) Credit

(i) Debit

(j) Credit.

Income statements

02

Introduction

Generating as much profit as possible (known as profit maximization) is often seen as the main objective for many businesses. It is possible that a business has other objectives, such as growth or survival, but it is likely that profit will feature in the minds of the managers of a business when asked what they would like to achieve. Calculation of this profit will be important for the following reasons:

- A business may need to raise external finance (eg in the form of a bank loan) and the lender will want some reassurance that any debt will be repaid and may want to see if the business is currently profitable or is likely to be profitable in the near future.
- Profit allows a business to grow. Profits mean more funds can be reinvested within the business over time and expansion will take place.
- Tax paid by a company will be based on the level of profits earned for a year (though a sole trader will pay income tax rather than a tax levied purely on profits).

The overall profit of a business is calculated in an income statement. An income statement is one of the financial statements produced by a business at the end of the financial year (though it can be produced for shorter periods if the owners of the business so wish).

Calculating profit

Although the overall profit or loss earned by the business is calculated in the income statement, it makes sense first of all to explore what we mean by the term 'profit'.

In these examples we will make the assumption that the accounting records we look at are those of a 'trader'. A trader will generate profits through the buying and selling of finished goods which require no further production.

Any profit would be calculated as the difference between what a firm earns in income after the deduction of all its expenses for a specified period of time. Obviously profit would be generated if the total of income were greater than the total of expenses. A loss occurs where expenses total more than the level of income. The profit would mean that the firm had earned more than it spent and is therefore left with more than it started the period of time with. This means that the firm has grown (it is possible that a profitable firm does not grow if the owner withdraws the profit, but this will explored when we look at balance sheets).

For most businesses, the income would be the revenue earned from sales made during that period. This may be supplemented by other forms of income, such as rent received, commission earned or income from investments made by the firm.

Although overall profit is important, it is also important to know the size of the profit made on the actual sales that have been made before any other expenses are deducted. As a result, there are two measures of profit which are commonly used and understood. These are:

Gross profit   Profit earned by the firm's trading – through buying and selling goods

Net profit   Profit remaining after all expenses have been deducted

Gross profit

Gross profit is the profit earned by the firm on its main trading operations. The section of the income statement where gross profit is calculated is known as the **trading account**. Gross profit is measured by the difference between the sales revenue earned by the firm and the cost of the goods sold.

Gross profit = Sales revenue – Cost of goods sold

Sales revenue
Sales revenue simply measures the amounts that the firm has received or is owed for goods sold during the year. It may also appear simply as 'Sales', 'Turnover' or even 'Revenue'.

Cost of goods sold
The cost of goods sold is calculated by comparing the value of goods sold by the firm with how much those goods actually cost the business. This is not the same as the amount spent on purchasing inventory, because the firm is likely to have unsold inventory left at the end of the period. Any unsold inventory is not counted as part of the cost of goods sold.

Example 2.1

During the year to 31 March 2013, a firm earns £50,000 sales revenue. During the year it spent £24,000 purchasing goods for resale. Inventory as at 1 April 2012 was valued at £8,500 and by the end of the year this had risen to £9,900.

Trading account for year ended 31 March 2013

	£	£
Sales		50,000
Less Cost of goods sold:		
Opening inventory	8,500	
Purchases	24,000	
	32,500	
Less Closing inventory	9,900	22,600
Gross profit		27,400

Given that the gross profit is calculated as the profit made only on the buying and selling of goods, it is possible that a firm earns a gross profit but still ends up with a net loss. It is also possible but unlikely that the business makes a gross loss, which would make it highly unlikely that they would make anything other than a net loss.

Further complications

A new business will not have any inventory on hand at the start of the period. However, any business which has existed for more than one trading period will have inventory on hand at the start of the period as well as at the end. This opening inventory will need to be added on to the amount for purchases in the cost of goods sold calculation.

It is perfectly normal that a business will find that inventory purchased is not suitable and will be returned either to the business by customers or by the business to the original suppliers. In either case, these returns will need deducting from the respective sales or purchases figure in the trading account. **Returns inwards** (or Sales returns) would be deducted from the sales figure. **Returns outwards** (or Purchase returns) would be deducted from purchases. Both of these deductions would appear in the trading account.

In addition, costs for the transportation of goods into the firm, known as **carriage inwards,** may also be included in the cost of goods sold calculation. **Carriage outwards** – the cost of transporting finished goods to customers – would appear along with all other expenses as it is not connected with the purchase of the goods themselves. The following example incorporates these further adjustments to the trading account.

Example 2.2

The following data relates to the year ended 31 December 2019.

	£
Sales	99,200
Purchases	65,100
Returns inwards	1,190
Returns outwards	550
Carriage inwards	1,975
Opening inventory	11,230
Closing inventory	13,460

The trading account would appear as follows:

Trading account for year ended 31 December 2019

	£	£
Sales		99,200
Less Returns inwards		1,190
Net turnover		98,010
Less Cost of goods sold:		
Opening inventory	11,230	
Add Purchases	65,100	
	76,330	
Add Carriage inwards	1,975	
	78,305	
Less Returns outwards	550	
	77,755	
Less Closing inventory	13,460	64,295
Gross profit		33,715

Net profit

The net profit of the business will be found once all further incomes and expenses have been dealt with. Although income from sales revenue will be the main source of income for the business, it is perfectly normal for there to be other sources of income which would count towards the overall profits of the business. These incomes will be added on to the gross profit.

Other expenses incurred by the business will be deducted at this stage to give the net profit for the business. These expenses will be connected with the operations of the business, such as the costs relating to the staffing costs, power costs and general administration of the business.

The income statement

As stated earlier, the income statement is the financial statement which calculates the overall profit or loss earned by the business for a particular period of time. It is also commonly known as a **profit and loss account** (and is increasingly being called a **statement of comprehensive income**).

It is commonplace to produce a full income statement based on a trial balance. The trial balance consists of the balances from the double-entry ledger accounts. However, we will not use all the items in the construction of the income statement. At this stage we are only interested in the balance from the accounts that correspond with either an income for the firm or an expense.

The other balances listed in the trial balance (shown in light grey in Example 2.3) are not needed for the income statement but will be used in the construction of another financial statement – the balance sheet. A full income statement is illustrated in the following example.

Example 2.3

Trial balance as at 31 December 2014

	Dr £	Cr £
Sales		124,500
Purchases	76,800	
Inventory as at 1 January 2014	8,940	
Machinery	15,000	
Fixtures and fittings	8,450	
Trade receivables	9,876	
Trade payables		5,676
Bank overdraft		5,344
Electricity	1,630	
Wages and salaries	21,340	
General expenses	3,450	
Advertising	274	
Capital		35,000
Drawings	11,500	
Maintenance	2,890	
Commission received		2,130
Equipment	12,500	
	172,650	172,650

Inventory on hand as at 31 December 2014 was valued at £7,652.

Income statement for the year ending 31 December 2014

	£	£
Sales		124,500
Less Cost of goods sold		
Opening inventory	8,940	
Add Purchases	76,800	
	85,740	
Less Closing inventory	7,652	78,088
Gross profit		46,412
Add: Commission received		2,130
		48,542
Less Expenses		
Electricity	1,630	
Wages and salaries	21,340	
General expenses	3,450	
Maintenance	2,890	
Advertising	274	29,584
Net profit		18,958

As we can see, the firm makes an overall profit of £18,958. This is the surplus of overall income over the expenditure for the same period. This does not mean that the firm has money available equivalent to this amount. This idea, that profit and cash are identical, is a common misunderstanding made by students new to the subject.

The profit that the firm has made could easily have been already spent on buying inventory to generate further sales and profits. It could also have been used to acquire new assets to help the firm become more productive. The differences between cash and profit are explored in Chapter 16.

Classification of expenditure

One of the reasons why cash and profit are not identical is covered by the decision made as to what to include when constructing the income statement. It is important that only the relevant incomes and expenses are included in the calculation of profit or loss. We want the statement to show the true incomes and expenses that were incurred by the firm in this period. The correct recording of expenses is easy with some examples. For example, wages, insurance and heating costs can be easily linked to the correct accounting period; for instance, wages are specifically paid for a period of time. However, for some expenses this is less obvious. To solve this issue, expenses are classified into two categories: **revenue expenditure** and **capital expenditure**.

Revenue expenditure

Revenue expenses are those which are incurred on a day-to-day basis and are related to the running of the business. These expenses are 'used up' in the accounting period and do not add value to the non-current assets of the business. Common examples of revenue expenditure would include purchases of inventory, wages and salaries, advertising and other general expenses associated with running the business.

Capital expenditure

Capital expenditure involves the purchase or acquisition of non-current assets and some of the costs associated with getting the assets into working condition. These assets will normally be expected to last for a number of accounting periods and will not therefore belong to one period in particular. As a result, this expenditure will not appear directly in the income statement in the way that revenue expenditure does. This may seem odd – how can an item of expenditure not appear as a deduction against the revenue earned by the firm? Capital expenditure will appear in the income statement but it is dealt with through the process of depreciation, which is covered in Chapter 4.

Capital and revenue receipts

Incomes can be classified in the same way. Capital receipts and capital incomes are those which are not generated in a particular period of time (in that they are one-offs rather than earnings from a particular period). Examples of capital receipts would include loans taken by the firm, share issues, and sales of fixed assets. Revenue incomes are the incomes generated which relate to a particular period of time. Sales would be the main example of revenue income. Other examples of revenue income would include rent received and commission received.

Review questions

1   From the following data, produce a trading account for the year ended 31 December 2016.

	£
Opening inventory	8,750
Closing inventory	9,230
Purchases	64,300
Sales	97,400

Solution

Trading account
for the year ended 31 December 2016

	£	£
Sales		97,400
Less Cost of goods sold		
Opening inventory	8,750	
Add Purchases	64,300	
	73,050	
Less Closing inventory	9,230	63,820
Gross profit		33,580

2 From the following data, produce a trading account for the year ended 31 December 2017.

	£
Opening inventory	12,181
Closing inventory	31,905
Purchases	76,878
Sales	154,544

Solution

Trading account
for the year ended 31 December 2017

	£	£
Sales		154,544
Less Cost of goods sold		
Opening inventory	12,181	
Add Purchases	76,878	
	89,059	
Less Closing inventory	31,905	57,154
Gross profit		97,390

3 From the following data, produce a trading account for the year ended 31 December 2018.

	£
Opening inventory	8,130
Closing inventory	10,120
Purchases	65,800
Sales	84,000
Carriage inwards	320
Returns inwards	110
Returns outwards	255

Solution

Trading account
for the year ended 31 December 2018

	£	£
Sales		84,000
Less Returns inwards		110
		83,890
Less Cost of goods sold		
Opening inventory	8,130	
Add Purchases	65,800	
	73,930	
Add Carriage inwards	320	
	74,250	
Less Returns outwards	255	
	73,995	
Less Closing inventory	10,120	63,875
Gross profit		20,015

4 The following data relate to the year-end balances for the business of
   J Holloway. From this data construct the income statement for the year ended
   31 December 2015.

	£
Sales	100,000
Purchases	68,000
Opening inventory	5,400
Closing inventory	7,250
Carriage inwards	460
Rent	7,000
Insurance	2,100
Wages and salaries	18,500
Heating and lighting	870

Solution

J Holloway
Income statement
for the year ended 31 December 2015

	£	£
Sales		100,000
Less Cost of goods sold		
Opening inventory	5,400	
Add Purchases	68,000	
	73,400	
Add Carriage inwards	460	
	73,860	
Less Closing inventory	7,250	66,610
Gross profit		33,390
Less Expenses:		
Rent	7,000	
Insurance	2,100	
Wages and salaries	18,500	
Heating and lighting	870	28,470
Net profit		4,920

5 The following data relate to the year-end balances for the business of J Fowler. From this data construct the income statement for the year ended 31 March 2018.

	£
Sales	56,490
Purchases	24,654
Opening inventory	8,903
Closing inventory	6,563
Returns inwards	321
Returns outwards	450
General expenses	3,190
Commission received	2,100
Maintenance expenses	1,340
Wages	23,000
Office expenses	995

Solution

J Fowler
Income statement
for the year ended 31 March 2018

	£	£
Sales		56,490
Less Returns inwards		321
		56,169
Less Cost of goods sold		
Opening inventory	8,903	
Add Purchases	24,654	
	33,557	
Less Returns outwards	450	
	33,107	
Less Closing inventory	6,563	26,544
Gross profit		29,625
Add:		
Commission received		2,100
		31,725
Less Expenses:		
General expenses	3,190	
Maintenance expenses	1,340	
Wages	23,000	
Office expenses	995	28,525
Net profit		3,200

The balance sheet

03

Introduction

The financial statements (also known as the final accounts) of a business consist of an income statement, a balance sheet and a statement of cash flows. Whereas the income statement measures the performance of a business over a period of time, usually one year, the balance sheet focuses on the business at a particular moment in time.

The balance sheet is constructed from the remaining balances found in the trial balance which have not already been used for the construction of the income statement. These balances are from the double-entry accounts of the business. The income statement used balances relating to the incomes and expenses of the business; the balance sheet uses the balances relating to the assets, the liabilities and the capital of the business.

The balance sheet can be thought of as a statement of the resources used by the firm and how those resources were financed – either by the owner(s) of the business, or by borrowing. In this way, the balance sheet will always balance in that the resources of the business must have been financed by resources either from within the business or from outside the business.

In recent accounting standards, the alternative name of 'statement of financial position' has been used instead of the established name of 'balance sheet'. In this book we will stick to the long-established balance sheet name (though using some of the more recent terminology for items appearing on the balance sheet).

It is often thought that the balance sheet would be put together only after the income statement has been produced. The items remaining on the trial balance would then be used to produce the balance sheet. The thinking behind this is that the profit figure will need to be calculated first. Without the profit figure for the most recent period, the balance sheet would not balance. However, more recently there has been a reversal of this thinking. Limited companies following international accounting standards have been encouraged to think of the balance sheet as a statement of the firm's assets, with the increase in the net value of these assets between one period and the next used to represent the profit generated by the firm over that period.

Content of the balance sheet

The balance sheet can be thought of as a more detailed presentation of the accounting equation we came across in Chapter 1:

Assets = Liabilities + Capital

Each of these terms will have a corresponding section on the balance sheet. It is common practice to subdivide the assets into two district classifications – that of **non-current assets** and **current assets**. Likewise, liabilities are also subdivided into two classifications – **non-current liabilities** and **current liabilities**. This means that the modern balance sheet for nearly all types of organization will consists of five separate sections.

Assets

Assets are the resources that are used within the business. These can either be owned outright by the business or have been purchased and financed by borrowing. As stated earlier, assets are divided into two categories: non-current assets and current assets.

Non-current assets

Non-current assets (often referred to as fixed assets) are long-term assets that are likely to be held by the business for at least one year. They have normally been acquired specifically to add value to the business. They are not normally acquired to be sold (although they may well be sold at some point in the future, this wasn't the reason why they were acquired). Non-current assets are further divided into **tangible assets** and **intangible assets**.

Tangible assets

These are assets that have physical substance. They are likely to be the assets that are used by the business to facilitate the production of goods or the provision of a service. For most businesses, non-current assets will comprise mainly the tangible assets. Common examples of tangible non-current assets would include land, buildings, machinery, equipment, fixtures and fittings, and vehicles. These are usually stated on the balance sheet at their cost value (known as **historic cost**) less the accumulated depreciation (which is explained in the next chapter). The cost less accumulated depreciation is known as the net book value or carrying amount.

Intangible assets

These assets are without physical form. They are owned by the business and will normally lead to the generation of revenues and profits for the firm. Often these intangibles arise out of a firm that is long established and has built up either successful brand names or customer loyalty and these enable the business to generate profits.

Valuing these intangible assets, such as brand names, has proved difficult. Where these are internally generated, it is prudent not to include these values on the balance sheet as their value may be uncertain. If the brand name has been externally acquired, it is permissible to include a value for this on the balance sheet. The value for the intangible asset may be **amortized** (similar to the process of deprecation) over the expected life of the asset. However, if an intangible asset is expected to have an indefinite life, it is acceptable to leave its value unaltered over time.

Goodwill is another intangible asset. This occurs where a firm or part of a firm is acquired by another firm. If the purchase price exceeds the net value of those assets purchased, then the difference is defined as the creation of goodwill. This can be valued in the same way as the external acquisition of a brand name or any other intangible asset.

Investments

Investments may also be included within the non-current assets. A firm may use its resources to acquire a variety of financial assets. These investments may include debentures issued by other companies, bonds issued by governments (basically the same as a debenture), and shares purchased in public limited companies. The reason for the acquisition of debentures and bonds is usually that they provide financial return for the business in the form of interest on debentures and also dividends if the investment is in another company's equity.

When a firm purchases shares in another company there are rules that need to be followed when showing these investments on the published accounts of companies. The size of the shareholding in relation to the size of the other company's total issued share capital will be significant here. In the case where a firm has acquired over 50 per cent of a company's voting shares it will have control over that company. This is covered later in the book in Chapter 13 on limited companies. When we are dealing with the internal accounts of businesses, these investments will not need any further detail and will simply appear at their cost value as either 'investments' or 'financial investments'.

Current assets

These assets form part of the firm's trading cycle. They are used as part of the ongoing cycle of buying and selling goods. As a result, the current assets of the business are likely to be in a state of constant change. Although the firm will hold the same types of current assets, their values will be fluctuating on an ongoing, usually daily, basis. The current assets are seen as liquid assets. Liquidity is a measure of how quickly assets can be converted into cash (without any significant loss in value).

Common examples for current assets are as follows.

Inventory

Often referred to as stock, this represents the firm's holdings of products which are either ready to be sold or are to be used in the production process and will be turned into finished goods. For a firm that manufactures the goods that it sells there are likely to be three different types of inventory, which are as follows:

- finished goods;
- work-in-progress (partly finished goods);
- raw materials.

For a firm which is a trader (one that buys and sells inventory without adding anything to the products in terms of production), the only type of inventory likely to be held is that of finished goods.

It is prudent for the inventory held to be valued at its original cost. Finished goods are valued at the lower value of cost or **net realizable value**. Net realizable value refers to the expected selling price of the inventory less any costs involved in getting the inventory ready for sale, such as repaid costs. Given that a firm will normally expect to sell goods for a higher value than that paid to purchase them, we would normally expect inventory to be valued at cost.

Trade receivables (or debtors)

Amounts owing to the business for any credit sales made would be included under the heading of trade receivables. These are likely to be paid in the near future (average credit periods offered by firms will often vary between one and three months). If a firm has decided that some of the debts are unlikely to be collected, these may have been written off as bad debts. In this case, the amount of trade receivables will have been reduced by the value of the bad debts.

In addition, it is prudent for a firm to recognize the likelihood of future bad debts by subtracting an amount from the trade receivables referred to as the **provision for doubtful debts**. This will be covered in the following chapter; suffice to say that this is meant to reflect an estimate of future bad debts. The income statement will show an entry for the adjustment made to any provision that exists.

Other outstanding balances

Prepayments and revenue accrued (ie expenses paid in advance and revenue still owing to the firm) will also appear under current assets as they represent either amounts or services owing to the firm.

Bank and cash balances

Cash is the ultimate liquid asset. This amount comprises both any cash in hand held on the business premises and also any bank deposits that are available on demand (ie for which there is no period of notice is required for withdrawals). Although these balances will probably change several times a day (in a normal business), it is the amount on hand and on balance at the close of trade at the end of the financial period that will appear on the balance sheet.

Short-term investments

If a firm has sufficient cash balances to meet any short-term needs, then it is an option for the business to invest these cash balances in short-term investments, such as treasury bills. These investments will earn the firm a higher rate of interest than if they remained in a bank account. These investments are very liquid and can be converted into cash very quickly.

Liabilities

These represent amounts outstanding (ie owing) by the firm. As with assets, they are spilt into two categories: current liabilities and non-current liabilities.

Current liabilities

These are essentially short-term debts. The short-term nature of these debts means it is likely to be settled (ie repaid) by the firm within the next 12 months. Another name for current assets, mainly used in the UK (usually smaller businesses), is 'Creditors: Amounts due within less than one year'.

The following items are likely to appear under the heading of current liabilities.

Trade payables

These are amounts owing in relation to the credit purchases made by the firm. In the same manner as trade receivables, these amounts are likely to be settled by the firm within the next few months. They are commonly referred to as trade creditors (or even simply as creditors).

Bank overdraft

If the firm has an overdrawn balance on its bank balance (ie it has a negative bank balance where it has withdrawn more from the bank than it actually has in its account), then this will appear under current liabilities.

The overdraft is repayable on demand if necessary. However, as long as the firm appears solvent (able to pay its short-term debts), it is likely that a bank will allow an overdraft balance to exist on a semi-permanent basis. A firm should treat an overdraft as a short-term source of finance as the interest rate charged by most banks is likely to be significantly higher than that charged on short-term bank loans (ie it would be worthwhile a business taking out a short-term loan if it is believed that the overdrawn balance will remain for a prolonged period of time). Most firms that rely on an overdraft as a source of finance are more likely to rely on this only for sporadic periods of time (eg on a few days every month).

Accruals

These balances represent expenses owing at the end of the financial period. It is almost certain that these expenses owing will be repaid before the end of the next accounting period.

Taxation owing

A firm will be unlikely to pay its taxation owing exactly at the time at which it is due. Given that the balance sheet is normally drawn up at the exact date of the close of trade, the taxation owing will almost certainly appear as a current liability until it is paid sometime during the following financial year. For example, in the UK self-assessment of taxation means that an individual can wait 10 full months after the end of the financial year before they settle the amount owing with HM Revenue and Customs (as long as their assessment for tax is completed online).

Non-current liabilities

These are the long-term debts of the firm which have a repayment date of at least one year away. For sole traders and other unincorporated organizations, these non-current liabilities are likely to take the form of bank loans and mortgages.

Mortgages are loans taken by the firm solely to acquire property. The mortgage will be secured by the lender on the value of the property. If the firm fails to meet repayments when due, the lender has the option of repossessing the property. Given property prices generally increase in value over time, the mortgage will represent a low-risk loan by the lender. As a result, the interest rate charged by mortgage lenders (usually banks) is relatively very low and is usually only a few percentage points higher than the central bank's interest rate. The interest rate charged can often be fixed for a period of time. Although fixed interest rates on mortgages are generally higher than what they would average on a variable rate mortgage, the certainty of the payments that will be made on a monthly basis may prove attractive to firms that prefer to know how much they will be paying out each month.

Other names for the non-current liabilities section of the balance sheets are 'Long-term liabilities' and also, in the UK, 'Creditors: Amounts falling due after more than one year'.

Debentures

For limited companies, the possibility of issuing debentures exists. These are loans issued by a company in a similar way to the issue of shares. The debenture issue will aim to borrow a certain amount of money. However, the value of the loan will be divided into smaller-size portions of debt, which allows investors to purchase the debentures without committing to lending the company the full amount. The debenture will carry a fixed rate of interest and a repayment date. The debentures held by investors can be traded and their value will vary with the current interest rate relative to the interest rate on the debenture (which will not change).

Other non-current liabilities that exist for companies will be covered in Chapter 13.

Capital

Resources from the owner (or owners) which are used within the business are known as the capital of the business. This capital may consist of non-current assets which will be available for business use, such as vehicles and equipment. It can also consist of cash introduced into the business when it is set up. The crucial distinction is that the resource will come from the owner of the business. The capital of the business can be measured, using the accounting equation, as the difference between assets and liabilities.

For a sole trader, the capital balance that appears on the balance sheet will be increased by the net profits generated in the most recent trading period. This would enable the value of the capital to grow over time. Likewise, any net loss made by the business would be reducing the firm's overall capital balances. A further balance sheet adjustment to capital will be for any drawings that are made during the most recent trading period. Drawings are a withdrawal of business resources made by the owner. Given that the firm and the owner are, as far as the law is concerned, identical, the sole trader can withdraw any of the business resources at any time (keeping in mind that the owner of the business must ensure that they can repay any debts incurred by the business).

Capital of a limited company

The capital of a limited company that appears on the balance sheet will be different from that of a sole trader. A limited company is likely to have multiple owners who have contributed amounts of capital to the business. Most people are familiar with the term 'shareholders'. Each of these shareholders will hold a share of the firm's overall capital.

On the balance sheet, the money raised through issuing (selling) shares will appear as issued share capital. There are different types of shares which are all covered later in this book. Profits that are earned by the company are not added directly to the capital but are recorded separately on the balance sheet as reserves. Reserves represent increases in the firm's capital that arise from different sources and will appear on the balance sheet alongside the issued capital. Again, these are covered later in the book in Chapters 13 and 14.

The combination of issued share capital and the reserves of the company is often referred to as equity. They are also known as shareholder's funds.

Format of the balance sheet

The balance sheet will always balance. There is no exception to this rule. Any change in the value of the assets of the business will be matched by an equal change in either liabilities or the capital of the business. As mentioned earlier, the balance sheet can be thought of as an expanded version of the accounting equation. If we accept the reasoning of why the accounting equation must hold, then we should be able to accept that the balance sheet will always balance.

As mentioned earlier, there are five major building blocks that will appear on nearly all balance sheets and these have been covered within this chapter. These would be the assets (both non-current and current), the liabilities (non-current and current) and the equity (capital plus any reserves if we are dealing with the accounts of a limited company).

Traditionally, the balance sheet was presented in a 'horizontal' format. In this format, the assets of the business would appear on the right-hand side of the balance sheet, with the liabilities and the capital of the business on the left-hand side. In the UK, a balance sheet presented using the horizontal format would often have these positions reversed – with assets appearing on the left-hand side instead. Today, firms generally prefer the 'vertical' presentation for the balance sheet, which is the format that will be used throughout this book. However, even this vertical style of presentation has evolved over the years.

If using the vertical method, there are two main ways of presenting the balance sheet. These appear in Figure 3.1.

FIGURE 3.1 Alternative methods of presentation for balance sheets

Non-current assets	Non-current assets
Add	*Add*
Net current assets (current assets less current liabilities)	Net current assets (current assets less current liabilities)
Equals	*Equals*
Total assets less current liabilities	Total assets less current liabilities
	Less
Non-current liabilities	Non-current liabilities
Add	Equals
Capital (plus any reserves if a company)	**Net assets**
Equals	
Capital employed	**Capital (plus any reserves if a company)**

The right-hand balance sheet format is the one which has grown in popularity over the past 20 years. However, for limited companies that follow international accounting standards when preparing their financial statements, the format of the balance sheet will follow a different form of presentation. This is outlined in Chapter 15.

FIGURE 3.2 A typical balance sheet as at year end

	£	£
Non-current assets		
Premises		150,000
Fixtures and fittings		25,000
		175,000
Current assets		
Inventory	7,500	
Trade receivables	3,500	
Bank and cash	2,000	
	13,000	
Current liabilities		
Trade payables	2,500	10,500
		185,500
Non-current liabilities		
Mortgage (2035)		90,000
Net assets		95,500
Capital		
Opening balance		80,000
Add Net profit		20,000
		100,000
Less Drawings		4,500
		95,500

This balance sheet represents a simplistic business organization. In the following chapter, there will be further amendments made to the balance sheet.

Review questions

1   From the following data, construct a balance sheet for A Jarvis as at
    30 June 2015.

	£
Property	95,000
Equipment	14,500
Inventory	10,312
Trade receivables	6,545
Bank	892
Trade payables	5,999
Capital	102,311
Net profit for year	37,118
Drawings	18,179

Solution

A Jarvis
Balance sheet as at 30 June 2015

	£	£
Non-current assets		
Property		95,000
Equipment		14,500
		109,500
Current assets		
Inventory	10,312	
Trade receivables	6,545	
Bank	892	
	17,749	
Less **Current liabilities**		
Trade payables	5,999	11,750
		121,250
Capital		
Capital		102,311
Add Net profit		37,118
		139,429
Less Drawings		18,179
		121,250

2 From the following data, construct a balance sheet for J Amy as at 30 April 2016.

	£
Fixtures and fittings	43,450
Equipment	9,800
Inventory	3,413
Trade receivables	4,340
Bank	432
Trade payables	3,487
Cash	141
Capital	39,500
Net profit for year	21,904
Drawings	8,315
Long-term loan	5,000

Solution

J Amy
Balance sheet as at 30 April 2016

	£	£
Non-current assets		
Fixtures and fittings		43,450
Equipment		9,800
		53,250
Current assets		
Inventory	3,413	
Trade receivables	4,340	
Bank	432	
Cash	141	
	8,326	
Less Current liabilities		
Trade payables	3,487	4,839
		58,089
Less Non-current liabilities		
Long-term loan		5,000
		53,089
Capital		
Capital		39,500
Add Net profit		21,904
		61,404
Less Drawings		8,315
		53,089

3 From the following trial balance produce an income statement for the year to 31 December 2018 and a balance sheet as at that date.

B Wheen
Trial Balance as at 31 December 2018

	£	£
Sales		124,000
Purchases	78,000	
Opening inventory	6,790	
Premises	95,000	
Vehicle	13,500	
Trade receivables	6,756	
Trade payables		3,544
General expenses	2,918	
Office expenses	4,231	
Wages	22,410	
Insurance	540	
Mortgage		40,000
Capital		75,000
Drawings	15,000	
Bank		2,601
	245,145	245,145

Inventory held by the business as at 31 December 2018 was valued at £8,113.

Solution

B Wheen
Income statement for year ended 31 December 2018

	£	£
Sales		124,000
Less Cost of goods sold		
Opening inventory	6,790	
Add Purchases	78,000	
	84,790	
Less Closing inventory	8,113	76,677
Gross profit		47,323
Less Expenses		
General expenses	2,918	
Office expenses	4,231	
Wages	22,410	
Insurance	540	30,099
Net profit		17,224

B Wheen
Balance sheet as at 31 December 2018

	£	£	£
Non-current assets			
Premises			95,000
Vehicle			13,500
			108,500
Current assets			
Inventory		8,113	
Trade receivables		6,756	
		14,869	
Less Current liabilities			
Trade payables	3,544		
Bank overdraft	2,601	6,145	8,724
			117,224
Non-current liabilities			
Mortgage			40,000
			77,224
Capital			
Balance as at 1 January 2018			75,000
Add Net profit			17,224
			92,224
Less Drawings			15,000
			77,224

4 From the following trial balance produce an income statement for the year ended 31 March 2020 and a balance sheet as at that date.

L Blackmore
Trial balance as at 31 March 2020

	£	£
Sales		75,543
Purchases	45,342	
Opening inventory	5,341	
Business premises	195,000	
Fixtures and fittings	27,800	
Trade receivables	8,768	
Trade payables		10,641
Returns inwards	434	
Returns outwards		991
Rent and insurance	6,451	
Office expenses	4,990	
Salaries	18,090	
Heating and lighting	1,721	
Loan repayable in 2025		165,000
Capital		95,000
Drawings	23,430	
Bank	9,808	
	347,175	347,175

As at 31 March 2020, inventory was valued at £6,101.

Solution

L Blackmore
Income statement for year ended 31 March 2020

	£	£
Sales		75,543
Less Returns inwards		434
		75,109
Less Cost of goods sold		
Opening inventory	5,341	
Add Purchases	45,342	
	50,683	
Less Returns outwards	991	
	49,692	
Less Closing inventory	6,101	43,591
Gross profit		31,518

Less Expenses:

Rent and insurance	6,451	
Office expenses	4,990	
Salaries	18,090	
Heating and lighting	1,721	31,252
Net profit		266

L Blackmore
Balance sheet as at 31 March 2020

	£	£
Non-current assets		
Premises		195,000
Fixtures and fittings		27,800
		222,800
Current assets		
Inventory	6,101	
Trade receivables	8,768	
Prepayments	9,808	
	24,677	
Less Current liabilities		
Trade payables	10,641	14,036
		236,836
Non-current liabilities		
Loan repayable in 2025		165,000
		71,836
Capital		
Balance as at 1 April 2014		95,000
Add Net profit		266
		95,266
Less Drawings		23,430
		71,836

5 Why is a bank overdraft classified as a current liability despite many businesses using the overdraft for more than one year?

Solution

If a business uses an overdraft for a more than a one year, then it would be advised to obtain a loan instead to finance the business, as the interest rate charged on the loan is likely to be lower than that charged on the overdraft. However, many businesses will use an overdraft because on a more ad hoc basis the bank balance may not be continually overdrawn. The overdrawn balance may vary over time from small amount to a large balance. In this case, the business may rely on the overdraft, owing it possessing greater flexibility than a loan.

Further adjustments to the income statement

04

Introduction

The concept of profit as the surplus of income over expenses should not be too difficult to understand. However, in this chapter we are going to extend the idea of what we mean by income and expenses beyond those that were covered in Chapter 2. We have already seen that profit is more complex than simply the difference between money coming in and money going out, but we are going to look at further entries that will be made in the income statements of an organization.

Underpinning the construction of the income statement are a number of **accounting concepts and conventions**. These are rules (not strictly speaking always in the legal sense of the word 'rule') that are to be followed when constructing the financial statements of the business. It is seen as good practice to apply these concepts and conventions at all times and to have a good reason if they cannot be applied. A crucial concept to be applied in the construction of the income statement is the accruals concept. Accounting concepts are covered in more detail in the following chapter.

Accruals concept

The accruals concept is centred on ensuring that the income statement includes all the relevant expenses and incomes generated for a period of time and that these are correctly recorded. This sounds straightforward until you realize that this still applies even if the expense or income remains outstanding – that is, hasn't been settled.

We have come across this idea already; sales and purchases that are included in the income statement relate to credit sales and credit purchases – meaning we are already including incomes which have yet to be received and expenses which have yet to be paid. The receipts and payments in accordance with these sales and purchases may well not be settled until the next year (especially if they occur at a time close to end of the financial year).

This idea was also applied in the cost of goods sold calculation when we deal with inventory. We account for the cost of the goods that have been purchased only when they are actually sold. This means that we adjust for any inventory remaining on hand at the start of the period (ie opening inventory) as well as deducting the value of any purchases remaining unsold at the end of the accounting period (ie closing inventory). The same will also apply to other incomes and other expenses that are generated during the period of time.

Accruals and prepayments

It is perfectly possible that a business will not pay all its expenses (such as bills for heating) exactly on time. Some expenses will be paid later than the period in which they are due and, similarly, some expenses will need to be paid in advance of the period in which they are due. Any expense which is incurred by the firm during the accounting period should be charged to that period's income statement regardless of whether the business has paid the expense in full or not.

Any amounts remaining outstanding at the end of the period represent expenses owing and are known as **accruals** or **accrued expenses**. These accruals should be added to the amount actually paid when charged to the income statement.

Example 4.1

The annual rent charge for a business is £6,000. This is paid in equal instalments every three months (ie £1,500 a quarter). Payments are made on 30 June, 30 September, 31 December and 31 March. However, the payment due on 31 December 2014 was not paid until 12 January 2015.

If the business has drawn up its income statement for the year ended 31 December 2014, the ledger account for Rent will appear as follows:

Rent

2014		£	2014		£
31 Mar	Bank	1,500	31 Dec	Income statement	6,000
30 Jun	Bank	1,500			
30 Sep	Bank	1,500			
31 Dec	Balance c/d	1,500			
		6,000			6,000
			2015		
			1 Jan	Balance b/d	1,500

We can see that the mismatch between the amount paid by the end of the year (£4,500) and the amount due for the year (£6,000) is dealt with by carrying forward a credit balance on the account which represents the amount outstanding, that is, the accrual.

Similarly, a firm may pay expenses which are meant to cover this and some part of a future accounting period; that is, the business has paid some of the following period's expenses (even if only in part). This expense paid in advance is known as a **prepayment**. In this case, the prepayment must not be included in the current charge for the expense and should be subtracted from the total amount paid.

Example 4.2

A business arranges insurance for a vehicle purchased on 1 October 2016. The charge for insurance of £1,000 is to cover a six-month period starting on 1 October. Given, with a financial year-end following the calendar year, that half of this charge belongs to the next financial year, the account for insurance would appear as follows:

Insurance

2016		£	2016		£
1 Oct	Bank	1,000	31 Dec	Income statement	500
			31 Dec	Balance c/d	500
		1,000			1,000
2017					
1 Jan	Balance b/d	500			

The debit balance on the insurance account on 1 January 2017 represents the prepaid amount for this year which was paid during 2016.

This application of the accruals concept also applies to incomes, as well as expenses. Thus any income which is received in advance – known as **prepaid income** – and really relates to the next (future) accounting period should not be included as current income in the income statement. Likewise, incomes which are still owing – known as **accrued income** – to the business and have not been received by the end of the period should be included as income – that is, should be added in the income statement for the current period.

The same reasoning for both incomes and expenses will also apply to outstanding balances remaining from the earlier accounting period. Any expenses belonging to the previous period that is settled (ie paid) in the current period should not be included as a current period expense. Similarly, any incomes received in the current accounting period which relate to incomes generated in the previous period must not be included in the current accounting period.

Example 4.3

The annual charge for business rates is £2,000. However, in the year ending 31 December 2015 a business had paid £314 in advance for 2016. By 31 December 2016 the business had paid £275 in advance for 2017.

The account for business rates would appear as follows:

Business rates

2016		£	2016		£
1 Jan	Balance b/d	314	31 Dec	Income statement	2,000
31 Dec	Bank	1,961	31 Dec	Balance c/d	275
		2,275			2,275
2017			2017		
1 Jan	Balance b/d	275			

For illustrative reasons we have simplified the account by grouping all the firm's payments for business rates and entering them on 31 December.

Balance sheet adjustments

After adjusting the incomes and expenses for accruals and prepayments we will also need to make an adjustment on the balance sheet. The rationale for this is as follows: imagine two businesses with identical financial records with the exception that one of the businesses has not paid one of its expenses. If we apply the accruals concept then we might reasonably expect their profits to be identical. However, when constructing the balance sheets, we would find that the business which has unpaid expenses has more cash available than the one that has paid its expenses on time. How can the balance sheets be expected to balance in this case? The answer is that each accrual or prepayment generates an adjustment on the balance sheet. These adjustments appear in Figure 4.1.

FIGURE 4.1 Accruals and prepayments on the balance sheet

Adjustment in income statement	Appears on following section of balance sheet
Accrued expenses	Current liabilities
Prepaid expenses	Current assets
Accrued incomes	Current assets
Prepaid incomes	Current liabilities

It may help if we think of accrued expenses and accrued incomes as a variation of debtors and creditors.

Depreciation

As covered in Chapter 2, expenditure on non-current assets is classified as capital expenditure and will appear in the income statement through the process of depreciation. Given that the business will hopefully benefit from the non-current asset over a number of accounting periods, it makes sense that the cost of the asset is matched – a further application of the accruals concept – to the periods of time in which the business benefits from the use of the asset. For example, if a machine is purchased for £25,000 and it is expected to be used within the business for five years, it may seem reasonable to spread the cost of this depreciation by charging £5,000 to the income statement for each of the five years of the asset's life.

To calculate the depreciation charge to be included in the income statement, a business will need to consider four pieces of information:

- the cost of the asset;
- the expected useful life of the asset;
- any expected residual value – ie what value will the asset have at the end of its useful life;
- what depreciation method is to be applied.

Cost of an asset

The cost of the asset is the purchase price of the asset. It may also include additional costs such as the following: installation cost, transport cost of the asset to the business, legal costs in acquiring the asset.

Expected useful life

The expected useful life of the asset is an estimate of the asset's working life expressed in years. This will be limited by the following:

- wear and tear;
- technical obsolescence – whereby an asset becomes out of date owing to advances in technology;
- market obsolesence – whereby an assets loses value owing to changes in market conditions;
- depletion – some assets will lose value as they are depleted. Examples would include oil and gas fields as well as mineral deposits (eg a goldmine).

Once a business has decided on the expected useful life of an asset, this should be applied to all assets held of the same class. For example, if a business decides that machinery will have a life of 10 years then it should treat all machinery in the same way – that is, with a life of 10 years.

Obviously, this expected lifespan is an estimate, but a business should be as realistic and as prudent as possible. It should not overstate the expected lifespan of an asset in order to manipulate profits. There have been a number of cases where businesses have been accused of artificially boosting the profits of the business by revising upwards the expected life of an asset. This longer expected lifespan would lead to a lower charge appearing in the income statement each year for depreciation.

Residual value

The residual value of an asset is very likely to be an estimate. It is often assumed to be zero in order to be prudent. However, businesses may have experience of assets having a certain value after a period of time. There may also be an arrangement with the supplier of the asset to buy it back after an agreed number of years.

Method of depreciation

There are several methods available to allocate depreciation for a non-current asset to the income statement. The method chosen should reflect how the business expects to benefit from the use of the asset. For some assets the main benefits will accrue in the early years of the asset's life, therefore the method chosen should reflect this. For assets that are based on the exploitation of a particular natural resource (eg oil and mineral reserves), the benefits are clearly linked to the rate of exploitation of the asset – the more extraction from the asset, the greater the benefit. A method based on the rate of depletion of the resource would seem appropriate in this case. For other assets, linking the benefits gained to particular periods of time may prove difficult. The two main methods of depreciation are straight-line and reducing balance.

Straight-line

This is the easiest method in terms of its calculations. It makes the assumption that the business will benefit from an asset equally over each year of the asset's life. This means that the depreciation charged each year will be the same amount. The straight-line depreciation will be calculated using the following formula:

$$\text{Depreciation per year} = \frac{\text{Cost} - \text{Residual value}}{\text{Expected useful life}}$$

Example 4.4

A vehicle costs £24,000 and is expected to have a useful life of five years. If the residual value at the end of this life is expected to be £3,000, then the annual depreciation charge would be calculated as follows:

$$\text{Depreciation per year} = \frac{£24,000 - £3,000}{5} = £4,200$$

This £4,200 should appear in the income statement as a charge for each year the asset is held. If, using the same data, we had estimated that there was unlikely to be any residual value, then the annual depreciation charge would become £24,000/5 = £4,800 per year.

Reducing balance

This method calculates the depreciation as a percentage of the asset's **net book value**. The net book value of an asset is the cost of the asset less all accumulated depreciation charged to that asset. Over time the depreciation charged to the asset will accumulate, meaning that its net book value will be reduced gradually. The percentage charged for calculating depreciation will remain the same. This means that the annual depreciation charge will get progressively smaller over the asset's life.

Net book value = Cost of asset – Accumulated depreciation

Example 4.5

A vehicle costs £15,000 and is to be depreciated using the reducing balance method with a percentage rate of 20 per cent. Depreciation to be charged on this vehicle will be as follows:

	£
Cost of vehicle	15,000
Depreciation in year 1 (20% of £15,000)	3,000
Net book value at end of year 1	12,000
Depreciation in year 2 (20% of £12,000)	2,400
Net book value at end of year 2	9,600
Depreciation in year 3 (20% of £9,600)	1,920
Net book value at end of year 3	7,680
Depreciation in year 4 (20% of £7,680)	1,536
Net book value at end of year 5	6,144
Depreciation in year 5 (20% of £5,144)	1,229
	4,915

(Amounts are rounded to nearest full £)

The percentage used in reducing balance calculations is based on the following, admittedly complicated, formula:

$$r = 100 - \sqrt[n]{\left(\frac{\text{Residual value}}{\text{Original cost}}\right)} \times 100$$

where r is the percentage rate to be used expressed as a decimal and n is the expected number of years for the asset's lifespan.

Depreciation and the balance sheet

On the balance sheet of a business the non-current assets are initially valued at **historical cost** – the original cost of acquiring the assets. However, this is modified as the assets age. Non-current assets should be shown at their net book value. As we know, the net book value (also known as the **carrying amount**) is the historical cost of the asset less all depreciation charged on the asset (up to the present date). This means that as the asset ages, the accumulated depreciation will increase and therefore the net book value of the asset will be reduced.

Example 4.6

A business purchases machinery at a cost of £30,000. It is expected to have a life of six years, after which it will have no residual value. It is to be depreciated using the straight-line method.

The annual depreciation for the machinery will be £5,000. This would appear as a charge in the income statement for each of the six years. The relevant section of the balance sheet showing machinery would appear at the end of each year as follows:

Balance sheet extract at year-end date	Year 1	Year 2	Year 3	Year 4	Year 5	Year 6
Non-current assets	£	£	£	£	£	£
Machinery at cost	30,000	30,000	30,000	30,000	30,000	30,000
Less depreciation	5,000	10,000	15,000	20,000	25,000	30,000
Net book value/carrying amount	25,000	20,000	15,000	10,000	5,000	0

Disposal of non-current assets

Asset disposal refers to the sale or scrapping of a non-current asset before the end of its useful life. In the same way that we treat the purchase of non-current assets as capital expenditure, the sale of a non-current asset is treated as a capital receipt. This means that revenue generated from the sale of a non-current asset cannot be included as income on the income statement. However, an adjustment will be made in the income statement when this occurs.

When a non-current asset is disposed of (for whatever reason), it is the profit or loss on the asset disposal which will appear in the income statement as either revenue income (in the case of a profit on disposal) or as a revenue expense (in the case of a loss on disposal).

It is highly unlikely (with the exception of sales of property or freehold land) that the business would be able to sell a non-current asset for more than the purchase price of the asset. However, the profit or loss on disposal is based on the difference between the selling price (if the asset generates any revenue on its disposal) and the net book value of the asset.

Example 4.7

A delivery van originally cost £18,000 and was to be depreciated at 25 per cent using the reducing balance method. The van was held by the business for two years before it was sold for £8,500. The profit or loss on the disposal would be calculated as follows: we need to ascertain the net book value of the asset. Therefore we need to calculate the depreciation for each of the two years:

- In year 1, the depreciation on the van would have been 25% × £18,000 = £4,500.

- In year 2, the depreciation would have been 25% × £13,500 (net book value at end of year 1) = £3,375.

- This means the net book value of the van at the moment of sale would have been £10,125.

- Therefore, the business made a loss on the disposal of this van of £1,625 (£8,500 − £10,125).

This loss would appear as revenue expenditure in the income statement.

It may seem strange that the income statement records this as an expense, given the business has seen its cash balance increase. This is because profit and cash, though related, are not the same. This issue is one reason why analysts also wish to look at a firm's statement of cash flow (see Chapter 16) when analysing a business.

Bad debts

A business that allows sales to be made on credit always runs the risk of incurring debts which are never paid. Bad debts are the debts owing to the firm which are never collected – usually because of a debtor of the business being unable to honour its debts (often due to business failure). Bad debts are 'written off' (ie cancelled) and are treated as revenue expenditure in the income statement in the period in which the business decides that it no longer realistically expects to collect the amount owing (an application of the accruals concept).

Bad debts are an unfortunate consequence of allowing credit sales. An obvious solution to avoiding bad debts may appear to be not allowing sales on credit terms. However, businesses that allow credit sales will also benefit from being able to make purchases on credit. Not allowing credit sales may well mean that overall sales levels fall as customers buy from other firms that do allow credit. Action to minimize the incidence of bad debts is explored in Chapter 11.

If any debts that were previously written off are subsequently collected at a later date then these would be classified as **bad debts recovered**. Any bad debts recovered are treated as revenue income in the income statement in the period in which the amount is recovered – not the period in which the debt was originally written off.

Provision for doubtful debts

The balance sheet should always present a true and fair view of the business. Given that bad debts are a frequent and unfortunate occurrence, the value of the trade receivables (the total of all the debtors of the business) on the balance sheet is likely to overstate the actual amount that will eventually be collected. The business will not know which of the debts is likely to turn into a bad debt – if it did, then it would not allow credit to that customer in the first place. However, given that bad debts are likely to occur, it is fairly common practice for a business to reflect this anticipated loss by the creation of a provision for doubtful debts.

The provision for doubtful debts is based on the firm's past experience of the size of past bad debts and an estimate of how large these bad debts are likely to be in the future. Often, the provision will be based on a percentage of the outstanding year-end balance of trade receivables. This percentage rate can be maintained and will mean that its overall size will be adjusted in proportion to the size of outstanding trade receivables. In addition, the firm can alter this percentage if it thinks bad debts are more or less likely, say, owing to worsening of the business climate.

The adjustment in the provision (ie the change in the size of the provision only) will appear in the income statement. A rise in this provision will appear as an expense in the income statement, whereas a fall in the provision will be reflected as income added on the income statement. The full size of the provision will appear on the balance sheet and will be deducted from the amount of outstanding trade receivables – that is, showing the firm's estimate of a more realistic figure for trade receivables.

Discounts

One way of encouraging debtors to settle their accounts quickly is the offering of cash discounts by the firm. These are usually based on a small percentage, say 1–2 per cent of the outstanding invoice. Although the firm will lose revenue by offering these discounts, it also should benefit from being the beneficiary of discounts offered by the firm's creditors. The discounts offered and received will appear in the income statement as an expense and income respectively. These are summarized in Figure 4.2.

FIGURE 4.2 Treatment of discounts in the income statement

Type of discount	Given by:	Treated as:
Discounts allowed	Firm to its credit customers	Revenue expense
Discounts received	Firm's credit suppliers	Revenue income

Example 4.8

The following trial balance and additional information covers all the new adjustments featured in this chapter. The income statement and balance sheet constructed from this trial balance are accompanied by explanatory notes which should be viewed carefully.

Ian Yates
Trial balance as at 31 December 2018

	£	£
Opening inventory	12,560	
Sales		328,000
Purchases	185,000	
General expenses	15,755	
Salaries and wages	51,010	
Electrical and power expenses	7,590	
Insurance	2,310	
Rent	6,745	
Bad debts	690	
Plant	110,000	
Equipment	32,000	
Provision for depreciation: Plant		22,000
Provision for depreciation: Equipment		8,000
Provision for bad debts		220
Trade receivables	8,760	
Trade payables		11,120
Bank	5,420	
Capital		88,000
Drawings	19,500	
	457,340	457,340

Additional information:

1 Inventory in trade at year end was valued at £15,105.

2 The following expenses were accrued as at the year end:

   a Wages and salaries: £2,780 outstanding

   b Electrical and power expenses: £310 outstanding.

3 Insurance prepaid at the year end amounted to £160.

4 The allowance for doubtful debts is to be maintained at 5% of outstanding receivables at the year end.

5 Depreciation is to be provided for as follows:

   a Plant: 20% straight-line method

   b Equipment: 20% reducing balance method.

Answer

Ian Yates
Income statement for year ended 31 December 2018

Notes		£	£
	Sales		328,000
	Less Cost of goods sold		
	Opening inventory	12,560	
	Add Purchases	185,000	
		197,560	
	Less Closing inventory	15,105	182,455
	Gross profit		145,545
	Less: Expenses		
	General expenses	15,755	
1	Salaries and wages (£51,010 + £2,780)	53,790	
2	Electrical and power expenses	7,900	
	(£7,590 + £310)		
3	Insurance (£2,310 − £160)	2,150	
4	Provision for doubtful debts	218	
	Rent	6,745	
5	Bad debts	690	
6	Depreciation of plant	22,000	
7	Depreciation of equipment	4,800	114,048
	Net profit		31,497

Explanations for some of the entries in the income statement are as follows:

1 Salaries and wages are adjusted upwards by the amount owing (£2,780 added on to the amount paid).

2 Electrical and power expenses are adjusted upwards by the amount owing (£310 added on to the amount paid).

3 Insurance prepaid of £160 will be subtracted from the amount paid in respect of insurance.

4 The provision for doubtful debts is to be maintained at 5% of trade receivables. Given that these amount to £8,760, the provision should be 5% of this, which is £438. However, there already exists a provision for £220 which means we only include the change (an increase of £218) in the income statement.

5 Bad debts amounting to £690 are written off – this will have already been subtracted from the debtors figure, so no further adjustment is needed to the debtor's total.

6 Depreciation on plant will be 10% of the cost value of plant (£220,000), ie £22,000.

7 Depreciation on equipment will be 20% of the net book value of the asset. This will be calculated as 20% of £24,000 (£32,000 – £8,000), ie £4,800.

The balance sheet will appear as follows:

Ian Yates
Balance sheet as at 31 December 2018

Notes

		Costs	Depreciation	Net book value
1	Non-current assets	£	£	£
	Plant	110,000	44,000	66,000
	Equipment	32,000	12,800	19,200
		142,000	56,800	85,200
	Current assets			
	Inventory		15,105	
2	Debtors	8,760		
	Less Provision for doubtful debts	438	8,322	

3	Prepayments		160	
	Bank		5,420	
			29,007	
	Less Current liabilities			
	Accounts payable	11,120		
4	Accruals	3,090	14,210	14,797
				99,997
	Capital			88,000
	Add Net profit			31,497
				119,497
	Less Drawings			19,500
				99,997

Explanations for some of the entries on the balance sheet are as follows:

1 Non-current assets are shown with the relevant subtraction for depreciation. The depreciation is the accumulated depreciation which includes both this year's depreciation and also the previous year's depreciation which was found in the trial balance. The figure on this year's balance sheet for depreciation will be carried forward to future years.

2 The trade receivables are shown with the full provision subtracted from the total. This is meant to represent a more realistic value for the likely amount to be collected. Notice that it is the full provision that is deducted from the trade receivables figures.

3 Prepayments are included with current assets. It would be normal, if there were more than one entry, to add them all together and include them under the entry 'prepayments' rather than list them separately.

4 Accruals are listed as current liabilities and are grouped together rather than shown individually.

Review questions

1 From the following trial balance and additional information construct an income statement for the year ended 31 March 2016 and a balance sheet as at that date.

K Emery
Trial balance as at 31 March 2016

	Dr £	Cr £
Sales		92,300
Purchases	65,620	
Opening inventory	4,232	
Premises	85,000	
Vehicles	11,200	
Debtors	3,453	
Creditors		5,981
Returns inwards	328	
Returns outwards		209
General expenses	1,897	
Office expenses	2,310	
Wages	14,600	
Insurance	880	
Provision for depreciation on premises		12,000
Provision for depreciation on vehicles		4,500
Capital		85,000
Drawings	13,200	
Bank		2,730
	202,720	202,720

Additional information:

(a) Inventory as at 31 March was valued at £6,790.

(b) As at 31 March 2016 the following balances were prepaid:

   i   Office expenses £450

   ii Insurance £260.

(c) Depreciation is to be provided for as follows:

   i   Premises: 2% on cost

   ii Vehicles: 20% on reducing balance.

Solution

K Emery
Income statement for year ended 31 March 2016

	£	£
Sales		92,300
Less Returns inwards		328
		91,972
Less Cost of goods sold		
Opening inventory	4,232	
Add Purchases	65,620	
	69,852	
Less Returns outwards	209	
	69,643	
Less Closing inventory	6,790	62,853
Gross profit		29,119
Less Expenses:		
General expenses	1,897	
Office expenses	1,860	
Wages	14,600	
Depreciation: Premises	1,700	
Depreciation: Vehicles	1,340	
Insurance	620	22,017
Net profit		7,102

K Emery
Balance sheet as at 31 March 2016

	£	£	£
Non-current assets	Cost	Depreciation	Net book value
Premises	85,000	13,700	71,300
Vehicle	11,200	5,840	5,360
	96,200	19,540	76,660
Current assets			
Inventory		6,790	
Trade receivables		3,453	
Prepayments		710	
		10,953	
Less Current liabilities			
Trade payables	5,981		
Bank overdraft	2,730	8,711	2,242
			78,902
Capital			
Balance as at 1 April 2015			85,000
Add Net profit			7,102
			92,102
Less Drawings			13,200
			78,902

2 From the following trial balance and additional information construct an income statement for the year ended 31 July 2017 and a balance sheet as at that date.

K Atkinson
Trial balance as at 31 July 2017

	Dr £	Cr £
Sales		168,000
Purchases	75,000	
Opening inventory	11,000	
Property	200,000	
Machinery	28,000	
Debtors	7,850	
Creditors		5,670
General expenses	5,400	
Maintenance expenses	8,900	
Wages	35,000	
Office expenses	5,470	
Provision for depreciation on property		5,500
Provision for depreciation on machinery		11,000
Provision for doubtful debts		250
Capital		148,000
Drawings	17,500	
Bank	4,300	
Loan		60,000
	398,420	398,420

Additional information:

1 Inventory as at 31 July 2017 is valued at £19,800.

2 Depreciation is to be provided on cost at the following rates:
   a Property   2%
   b Machinery   20%.

3 Wages still owing as at 31 July 2017 were £2,400.

4 Maintenance prepaid as at 31 July 2017 was £450.

5 The provision for doubtful debts is to be maintained at 4% of debtors.

Solution

K Atkinson
Income statement for year ended 31 July 2017

	£	£
Sales		168,000
Less Cost of goods sold		
Opening inventory	11,000	
Add Purchases	75,000	
	86,000	
Less Closing inventory	19,800	66,200
Gross profit		101,800
Less Expenses:		
General expenses	5,400	
Maintenance expenses	8,450	
Wages	37,400	
Depreciation on property	4,000	
Depreciation on machinery	5,600	
Provision for doubtful debts	64	
Office expenses	5,470	66,384
		35,416

K Atkinson
Balance sheet as at 31 July 2017

	£	£	£
Non-current assets	Cost	Depreciation	Net book value
Property	200,000	9,500	190,500
Machinery	28,000	16,600	11,400
	228,000	26,100	201,900
Current assets			
Inventory		19,800	
Trade receivables	7,850		
Less Provision for	314	7,536	
doubtful debtors			
Prepayments		450	
Bank		4,300	
		32,086	
Less Current liabilities			
Trade payables	5,670		
Accruals	2,400	8,070	24,016
			225,916
Less Non-current liabilities			
Loan			60,000
			165,916
Capital			
Balance as at 1 August 2016			148,000
Add Net profit			35,416
			183,416
Less Drawings			17,500
			165,916

3 A firm purchases a piece of equipment for £56,000. It is to be depreciated using the reducing balance method at a rate of 25 per cent.

(a) What would be the net book value of this asset on the balance sheet at the end of the equipment's third year in use in the business?

(b) What would the net book value have been if the straight-line method of depreciation had been used instead?

Solution

(a) £23,625

(b) £14,000.

4 Construct the ledger account for Rent and Rates based on the following information (it is to be presented in one ledger account rather than as separate accounts).

- Rent owing as at 1 January £980.
- Rates prepaid as at 1 January £250.
- Rent owing as at 31 December £560.
- Rent paid during year £8,900.
- Rates paid during the year £6,520.

Solution

Rent and rates

	£		£
1 Jan Balance b/d	250	1 Jan Balance b/d	980
31 Dec Bank	8,900	31 Dec Income statement	15,250
31 Dec Bank	6,520		
31 Dec Balance c/d	560		
	16,230		16,230
		1 Jan Balance b/d	560

5 The following data are available about the firm's trade receivables:

- The balance of trade receivables as at 31 December is £48,000. However, this total includes an amount of £1,200 which is to be written off as a bad debt.
- In addition, the firm has an existing balance on its provision for doubtful debtors of £1,100 and it wishes to maintain the value of this provision at 2% of outstanding debtors at the year-end.

What would be the balance of trade receivables on the balance sheet?

How much would appear in respect of these entries in the income statement?

Solution

Provision for doubtful debts = (£48,000 − £1,200) × 4% = £1,872.

Balance on balance sheet would be £48,000 − £1,200 − £1,872 = £44,928.

Entries in income statement: £1,200 for bad debts and £772 as the increase in the provision for doubtful debts − both appear as expenses.

Accounting concepts

05

Introduction

Accounting concepts are the rules, guidelines and principles that are applied to the construction and maintenance of accounting records. Although it may seem that producing accounts is mechanistic and rigid in its approach, there are plenty of occasions when decisions will have to be made on how best to produce accounting statements. In these cases the set of accounting concepts should provide guidance on which direction to follow in producing accounting statements. There are many accounting concepts (also known as accounting conventions) which are used within the accounting profession.

These concepts are referred to throughout this book. Some of them have been formalized and are contained within the formal accounting industry guidance in the shape of Accounting Standards. These standards are set both nationally and internationally. For instance, the IASB (International Accounting Standards Board) has produced a 'Conceptual Framework' which basically sets out the accounting principles (including explicit references to a number of concepts) which are to underlie the presentation of all financial statements. This conceptual framework is covered later in the book.

Accounting concepts

The accounting concepts should be followed by those responsible for maintaining the financial records of the business. When presenting the financial statements of the business – mainly the income statement and the balance sheet – these concepts should be followed. Occasionally, these concepts may contradict each other and a decision will have to be made as to which one should be followed. This will often depend on the situation – the type and size of the business for which the accounting records are to be constructed.

The main accounting concepts are as follows.

Prudence

The accountant should be cautious when presenting financial statements. This does not mean being unduly pessimistic but it would certainly mean that optimism should be avoided when items of a discretionary nature are to be included.

What this means is that neither revenues nor profits should be anticipated too early. They should only be recognized once they are earned with reasonable certainty. For example, the income from sales should only be included once the sale has been made with reasonable confidence that it is a real sale; this would be when delivery of the goods is made. Sales made that can be returned by the customer with no conditions attached should not be called sales until money has been received, as this sort of sale cannot realistically be called a true sale.

By being cautious, expenses and likely losses should always be anticipated wherever possible. This doesn't mean that the worst should always be assumed, but that if any expense is likely to be due or a loss in the value of assets is likely to be incurred – for example, a reasonably certain bad debt – then this should be recognized in the income statement.

Linking in with prudence, inventory should generally be valued at its original cost. However, this is modified if the estimated selling price of the inventory is lower than the cost. Inventory should be valued at the lower of cost or net realizable value (estimated selling price less any costs involved in getting the inventory into saleable condition).

Going concern

It is assumed that each business operates as a going concern. This is where we assume that the business will continue trading into the future and it is not expected to be wound down or sold any time soon. The implication of this is that the valuation of assets can be based on their original (historic) cost and not the current saleable value of the asset. This may well mean that assets have out-of-date valuations but this is preferable to making the assumption that the business will not be continuing to trade into the future.

Consistency

One should aim to be consistent when constructing the accounts of the business. This will mean that policies chosen by the business – for example, its depreciation policy – should remain unchanged as far as possible over time. By following the principle of consistency, comparisons can be made with prior accounting periods when using the financial performance data of the business. If there has been a change in accounting policies, this would be likely to make comparisons with previous periods less valid.

A common focus of this concept is on the policies used with regard to depreciation of non-current assets. A firm can select different approaches for depreciation and, given that depreciation is charged against the firm's profits, a change in the depreciation policy will affect the firm's profits. As a result, once chosen, a firm should stick with the same depreciation policy. This will make comparisons with previous periods easier. For example, if the firm changes its depreciation policy and the profits of the business increase, we may find it hard to analyse the accounts to see the reason for the profit increase – is it an improvement in business performance or is it that the new depreciation policy charges a lower amount to the income statement?

Changes in accounting policies are allowable, but should be avoided unless necessary. In fact, it is a requirement of the international accounting standards that if a business changes its accounting policies between one period and the next, it should provide a restatement of the previous period's income statement based on what the results would have been if the change had already been enacted in the earlier period.

Accruals (or matching)

We have already referred to the principle of the accruals concept in Chapter 2 on income statements. However, it is worth repeating here just to reinforce its importance.

When accounting for the income, the expenses and, ultimately, the profit or losses of the business, we apply the accruals concept. Obviously a business will spend and receive money over the accounting period. However, we will only count the incomes or the expenses towards the profit of a particular accounting period if that income or expense was generated in that accounting period. This means that the monies paid or received belonging to other periods will not be accounted for in the current accounting period. For example, if a bill remains unpaid by the end of the period, we would still include this as an expense in the current period because it was generated as an expense in the current accounting period – regardless of the fact that it has yet to be paid. Likewise, if we sell goods on credit towards the end of the accounting period, the income would still count towards this period's profits even if the receipt for the sale is received in the next period.

A further extension of the accruals concept is that the costs associated with selling goods – that is, the purchase of stocks to be sold – should be matched to the income that is generated from selling those goods. This can be seen in the cost of goods calculation where we only charge for stock once it has been sold – literally, 'the cost of goods sold'. This is why we always subtract any stock left over at the end of the period, because it has not been sold and, presumably, will be matched against sales sometime in the next period.

Separate entity

The business is assumed to be a separate entity from the owner(s) of the business even if the distinction is not made in the eyes of the law. Business affairs and personal affairs (of a financial nature!) are kept separate. This is particularly important for, say, a sole trader who uses assets and resources for both business and private (ie personal) usage. A car may be used by the owner of a business for personal and business use but it is important that the costs are kept separate. Any expenses incurred by the business which are in reality those of the owner as a private individual should be charged to drawings.

Materiality

We have already covered the topic of capital and revenue expenditure (see Chapter 2). We know that items of capital expenditure (such as the purchase of and improvement to any non-current assets) should be 'capitalized' on the balance sheet and should not be placed as an expense in that period's income statement. However, there are limits to this arrangement. This is where the concept of materiality can be applied.

Imagine a business which purchases a new chair or desk for the office; the amount spent on this asset might represent a trivial amount of expenditure. In this case the amount spent may be considered immaterial and will be treated as an item of revenue expenditure. However, for a smaller business this amount will be more significant and the amount spent may well be treated as capital expenditure and will therefore appear on the balance sheet; that is, the purchase of furniture is of a material amount for the smaller firm.

This concept can also be applied to items which may appear as current assets. For example, imagine that a firm has small items of office supplies on stock at the end of the period – amounting to no more than a few pounds in value. These could be included as a current asset as they will be used up over the next accounting period as part of the firm's working capital cycle. However, if the amount is really so small then it may well be considered immaterial and office supplies may well be treated as revenue expenditure (ie the full amount for supplies purchased – including the amount of supplies remaining – is included on the income statement for that period).

Money measurement

Accounting records should adhere to the concept of money measurement. This means that items which cannot be reliably measured in money terms – that is, do not have a monetary value that can be measured with reasonable certainty – should not be included within the accouting records.

This issue has become especially important for a business whose success is partly or substantially determined by the performance of intangible assets such as brand names, customer loyalty and the image of the products that provide the firm's profits. Intangible assets of the firm may well be important in generating the firm's revenues and profits. For example, a successful brand name will enable a firm to charge a premium price for the product (if you want convincing of this, visit any supermarket and look at the prices of the leading brands compared with the supermarket own label prices). However, these brand names and other intangibles cannot easily be valued. As result, an accountant would not include the value of those items which cannot be measured in monetary terms.

The money measurement concept would also apply to intangible assets that are externally acquired. For example, if a brand name is purchased from another firm, its value can be measured in monetary terms and therefore this can be recorded and can appear in the accounts of the firm.

Realization/recognition

This concept deals with the issue of when to recognize income. For a cash-only business, this issue will probably not occur as any sale will generate an immediate transaction which can be recorded as it occurs. However, for a business which allows sales on credit, this concept will deal with the intricacies of deciding when to recognize the income from the sale in the income statements.

The moment of sale will not be the same for every business. However, for a sale to occur it must involve more than simply the production of goods (however successful the business is). A repeat customer might always purchase the same amount of goods at the same period each year. However, any future sale cannot be included in the accounts until the actual sale is made. For most businesses the sale will be recognized on delivery of the goods to the customer. This is because at this point the legal title will pass to the customer. It may be that the firm allows the goods to be returned if they are faulty or the wrong order, but at this stage the firm can be reasonably certain that a sale has been made.

Some firms allow sales to customers on a 'sale or return' basis. This means that the customer can return the goods without any issue. In this case, it is highly likely that an accountant would not want to count these as sales as the legal title of the goods really remains with the original firm rather than the customer.

Objectivity

This may seem rather obvious, but it is important that accounting transactions and accounting records are based on objective, verifiable information (ie information that can be checked as actually occurring) rather than subjective interpretation. Any subjective value provided by managers or anyone else connected to the business may well be biased and not provide an accurate account of the transaction. Sometimes estimates may well be needed (such as estimating the number of years of an asset's life for the purpose of calculating the annual depreciation). However, where objective values exist, these should be used.

A contradiction does occur between the concepts of objectivity and that of materiality. In deciding whether or not an amount is material, a subjective decision has to be made. There are no formal guidelines as to what is and is not material and therefore this will always be based on a personal decision.

Historical cost

This concept is similar to that of objectivity. Assets should normally be valued using the historic cost concept. The historic cost of assets represents the price that the business paid to acquire the assets and any additional costs (such as installation costs) in getting the asset in working condition. This value is objective and can be verified.

However, the historic cost of a long-lasting asset may well prove out of date later into the asset's life. Therefore businesses often use **fair values** for the assets on the balance sheet. Fair values are estimates of what the asset could be sold for at current market prices.

Even if the historic cost concept is applied to a firm, the firm will modify this concept by providing for depreciation on the non-current assets. This means that the historic cost concept is modified by the accruals concept of matching the cost of the asset to the period in which the firm will benefit from the use of the asset.

From accounting concepts to accounting standards

As companies began to look for external sources of finance it was recognized that some general guidelines for maintaining accounts would be useful in order to convince potential investors that they were not being misled by the accounting statements produced by a company. Eventually these rules and guidelines would be adopted on a national scale. These accounting concepts and other rules and regulations were gradually adopted by each country as part of their own **GAAP – Generally Accepted Accounting Principles**. Each country's own accounting authorities would produce their own version of GAAP relevant to that country only. This would set out rules, laws, guidelines and procedures to be followed by countries under its jurisdiction. Accounting Standards were gradually drawn up which were meant to provide guidance on a variety of different areas within accounting. In the UK these were initially known as **SSAPs (Statements of Standards Accounting Practice)** and eventually they were updated, phased out and replaced with **FRSs (Financial Reporting Standards)**.

Over the past century, companies looked increasingly to operate on a multinational level and investment has become more globally mobile. Governments recognized that it was becoming increasingly impractical to limit the movement of financial capital across borders. Given this situation, it was realized that some form of coordination and integration was needed between the different systems of each country's own GAAP. The IASB, over the past 20 years, has developed a system of accounting standards which are to be used on an international level. These consist of **IASs (International Accounting Standards)** and **IFRSs (International Financial Reporting Standards)**. Governments in many countries are placing more importance on companies in their own countries following these international standards and are, by implication, downgrading the importance of their own national GAAP. EU listed companies have been following the international accounting standards now for almost 10 years. In addition, a major change is currently set to take place in the UK accounting framework from 2015, when current UK GAAP accounting standards are set to be replaced with one overall accounting standard (and one for smaller firms).

In Chapters 14 and 15 we will consider how companies are affected by the changes being proposed and how accounting statements are to be produced when following this IFRS framework.

Review questions

1 Wheatcroft owns and runs a computer supplies and repair shop. He has operated for a number of years and has generally been successful. He has never worried about expansion, particularly as he would rather avoid having to manage a larger business and prefers to avoid the administration that this may bring. He is preparing financial statements for the year ended 31 December 2017 and wants your advice on a number of issues:

   (a) He sells blank recordable discs which he purchases from a wholesaler in bulk. At the end of the year he has a very small number left in stock. Should these be included within current assets as inventory?

   (b) He performs an annual service every November on a local school's computer network. However, the school has delayed the service and it will now be undertaken in January 2018. Should this still be included in the 2017 income statement?

(c)   His has worked out that he could boost his profits if he extended the lifespan of his non-current assets as it would lead to a lower depreciation charge each year. Should he do this?

Using knowledge of accounting concepts, advise Wheatcroft on the three points he has raised.

Solution

(a)   The relevant concept here would be materiality. In this case, the decision would be based on the significance of the value of the remaining blank discs. If this is a significant amount, he should include them within current assets. However, if the items would total only a few pounds, the amount may be considered immaterial. In this case, Wheatcroft would be best advised to include them as a cost within the income statement – part of the purchases for the year.

(b)   A number of concepts would apply here. The accruals concept of matching income to the time period in which it is generated would count – the sale is not to be made until 2018, so it should not appear in the statements relating to 2017. The realization concept would also be relevant here. A 'sale' has not yet been recognized – even if the school is likely to go ahead with the annual service, the income should only be recorded once the sale is reasonably certain – in this case not until January 2018. The prudence concept would also apply here as we should not anticipate income and profits before they have occurred.

(c)   Depreciation charges should represent the amount that the firm has benefited from the asset over the relevant trading period. Depreciation policy should not be changed just to boost profits. The accruals concept would be relevant here in that the firm should charge an appropriate amount relating to how much of the asset has been consumed during this period and no more. It certainly would not be prudent to attempt to boost profits by reducing depreciation charges. This would also violate the consistency concept, which states that accounting policies should, where they are found to be appropriate, remain constant over time.

2 Simper is doing a stocktake in order to ascertain the value of her closing inventory. It has been discovered that there are four items that are damaged. These items had cost £18 each. Given that the damaged items can be sold for only £12 each and the estimated repaid costs of the inventory would be £20 in total, how much would these four items be valued at on Simper's balance sheet?

Solution

Cost of items = £72 (4 × £18).

Net realizable value = 4 × £12 = £48 – £20 = £28.

In this case, the net realizable value of £28 is lower than the cost of £78, so £28 would be the value on the balance sheet.

3 Chase runs a sandwich shop. She is compiling her end-of-year financial statements and wants your advice on a number of items:

(a) She has a high degree of customer loyalty and wants to include this within the value of the business overall. She proposes including a value for goodwill on her balance sheet – in order to represent the estimated selling price of the business, which would be higher than the original cost of the business.

(b) She thinks she can boost her profits if she delays some of her payments.

(c) She uses her own car to make some deliveries to business customers. At present she includes none of these costs as business expenditure as it is her private car.

Advise Chase on whether her accounting treatment is correct. Refer to any relevant accounting concepts as part of your recommendations.

Solution

(a) Given that the sandwich shop is, presumably, a going concern, we would not expect a business to be valued at selling price. Historic cost should be used for non-current asset valuations (less any depreciation). In addition, it would not be prudent to overstate the value of her non-current assets with this 'goodwill'. Objectivity and money measurement concepts would also apply here.

(b) Applying the accruals concept means that incomes and expenses should be charged to the period in which they are incurred, not when they are paid or received. Therefore, delaying payment of bills may improve cash flow but would not lead to any improvement in the profits as the expense will still appear whether or not it has been paid.

(c) The separate entity concept states that business costs and private costs should always be treated separately. Only business expenses should be charged to the income statement and private costs should not be included. In this case, she is using private resources within the business – in effect, she is contributing more capital to the business.

4 'Applying the consistency concept means sticking with the same method of depreciation even if it results in the net book value of a non-current asset being unrealistic.'

To what extent do you agree with the above statement?

Solution

The consistency concept means that we should stick with the same accounting policy over time. This makes comparisons with earlier financial statements more meaningful. The point of depreciation is not to show realistic values of non-current assets anyway. Depreciation is meant to reflect the consumption of the asset over a period of time. The depreciation policy chosen should reflect how the business benefits from the asset's use. Depreciation policy can be changed if it is not appropriate but should not be changed just because it does not show realistic values for non-current assts.

5 Goods sold on a sale or return basis are not normally included within the sales figures. Explain why this is the case and what relevant concepts are applied.

Solution

According to the realization concept, sales will occur once the legal title of the goods has passed to the receiver of the goods with reasonable certainty. In the case of goods sold on a sale or return basis, customers can send the goods back to the original supplier without any question. This indicates that the potential customer has not reasonably taken on the legal title and the risks of ownership of the goods. Therefore this should not be counted as a sale.

Accounting for other business organizations

06

Introduction

So far we have looked at the accounting records of a very simple type of business organization – that of a sole trader. The sole trader, as the name suggests, is owned and run by one person. This owner will contribute their own capital and this will probably be supplemented with forms of borrowing. The sole trader will be the sole beneficiary of any profits that are earned. However, if this business makes a loss, they would have to cover this out of business resources (with capital falling) and might have to use personal resources to cover any unpaid debts, owing to their lack of limited liability.

In addition, we have dealt with a particular type of sole trader so far – that of a trader. The main activities of the trader will be to generate profits through the buying and selling of goods. This has kept the accounting statements of the businesses we have looked at so far simple. In this chapter will consider the business which manufactures its own output by looking at manufacturing accounts. We will also briefly examine two further types of business organization – the partnership and the not-for-profit organization.

Although the areas we are covering will become more complex, we are still applying the basic rules of accounting that were explained and followed in the earlier chapters. The accruals concept will still underpin the income statement (or its equivalent) for a business organization.

Manufacturing organizations

Most businesses that sell a physical product will not simply buy and sell these goods. It is likely that even if the firm does not manufacture them from basic raw materials, it will buy in components or part-finished goods which are then added to and sold to the final consumer. There are good reasons why a firm may wish to manufacture (or part-manufacture) its own products rather than purchase them in from an outside supplier:

- The product may not be available to purchase from elsewhere.
- The firm may be able to produce a superior version compared to others available.
- It may result in cost savings owing to efficiency in manufacturing.

Whatever the reason, a firm that does manufacture its own goods will need to replace the purchases figure in the trading account section of the overall income statement. The purchases figure will need replacing with the cost of manufacturing the products and this cost will be arrived at in a manufacturing account.

Manufacturing accounts

The manufacturing account will show the costs incurred in the production of goods during the relevant period of time. The account is split into two sections: **prime cost** and **factory overheads**. The total of these two sections will represent the cost incurred in manufacturing those goods completed in the most recent period.

Prime cost

This section of the manufacturing account will contain all the **direct costs** incurred by the firm in the production of goods. As covered in later chapters on costing, a direct cost is one which is directly connected with the production of a unit of output. This means that the direct costs will be proportionate to the level of output. This prime cost is likely to consist of the following:

- direct materials costs;
- direct labour costs;
- any other direct expenses (such as manufacturing royalties).

Applying the accruals concept will mean that even if a firm has spent money on purchasing materials or components, these are only included as a cost of manufacturing if the goods are completed during the period. In the same way that we deduct closing inventory from purchases in the cost of goods sold calculation, we will adjust the cost of raw materials for any raw materials inventory at the start and at the close of the period.

Factory overheads

When manufacturing goods, a business will incur other production-related costs which cannot be directly linked to the each individual unit of output. These costs are likely to be indirect in nature. They are often termed 'factory' or 'indirect' expenses to indicate that they are still connected to the production of goods but not in a direct manner. Examples of these expenses will include the wages of supervisory labour and the power costs incurred within the production facility part of the business as well as the depreciation of assets used in the production process.

In some cases, an expense of the business cannot be accurately divided into the costs relating to the production activities of the firm (which would belong in the manufacturing account) and those which are related to the non-production activities of the firm (which would belong in the income statement). It is therefore common to find that some expenses are divided up and a proportion of the expense will appear in the manufacturing account and also in the income statement. If this appears in an assessment question, the portion to be included in the manufacturing account will normally be clearly stated in the additional information provided. If the expense has an adjustment to be made for either an accrual or a prepaid amount, this should be adjusted for first, before the expense is apportioned between the different financial statements.

Cost of manufacturing completed goods

Once the two sections of the manufacturing account are completed, the total will be adjusted for any opening and closing balances of work-in-progress. The work-in-progress will represent the value of materials which are still in the production stage – goods which are partly, but not fully, completed.

Once the cost of manufacturing goods for the period has been completed, this figure will be used in the calculation of gross profit for the organization. For a manufacturing organization, the cost of manufacturing goods will replace the purchases figure within the trading account section. This figure will still need adjusting for opening and closing inventory of finished goods.

Example 6.1

The following data relate to the financial records of Bellwood Ltd, a manufacturer, for the year ended 30 June 2019.

	£
Inventory of raw materials as at 1 July 2018	15,665
Inventory of work-in-progress as at 1 July 2018	24,411
Purchases of raw materials	298,080
Direct power	11,180
Direct labour	301,500
Royalties	5,560
Supervisory wages	56,110
Factory rent	17,891
Machinery depreciation	6,600
Factory maintenance	4,513
Inventory as at 30 June 2019 was valued as follows:	
Work-in-progress:	31,241
Raw materials:	14,186

The manufacturing account based on this data for the appropriate time period would appear as follows:

Bellwood Ltd
Manufacturing account for year ended 30 June 2019

	£	£
Opening inventory of raw materials		15,665
Add Purchases of raw materials		298,080
		313,745
Less Closing inventory of raw materials		14,186
Cost of raw materials consumed		299,559
Direct labour		301,500
Direct power		11,180
Royalties		5,560
Prime cost		617,799
Add Indirect factory overheads:		
Supervisory wages	56,110	
Factory rent	17,891	
Machinery depreciation	6,600	
Factory maintenance	4,513	85,114
		702,913
Add Opening work-in-progress		24,411
		727,324
Less Closing work-in-progress		31,241
Production cost of goods completed		696,083

Points to note:

- The cost of raw materials consumed is the term used to describe the cost of materials that were used in the production process during this period. Applying the accruals concept means that we have to adjust for both opening and closing inventory.

- The production cost of goods completed would then be used in the trading account to replace the purchases figure which is not applicable when a business manufactures rather than purchases goods.

Partnerships

As was the case with a sole trader, the partnership is another unincorporated business organization. This means that the partnership is not a separate legal entity from the owners of the business in the eyes of the law. The separate entity concept still applies, but the partners do not benefit from limited liability. The partnership will be owned and controlled by at least 2 partners (the previous upper limit – of 20 partners – on the maximum number of partners was abolished in 2002).

Reasons for setting up as a partnership would include the potential access to a much larger pool of financial resources, assuming that each partner will contribute capital to the business. Each partner may bring particular specialist areas of expertise which would not be present in the sole trader organization. Obviously this allows more flexibility for partners in terms of covering for each other's absence and of the ability to utilize a wider range of inputs into the decision-making process. However, the downside of this form of organization is the fact that profits have to be allocated between the partners and disagreements may arise.

Accounting for partnerships

In terms of accounting records, the income statement of the partnership will appear almost identical to that of a sole trader. However, given that there are multiple owners of the business, the profits of the business will need to be shared between the partners. The account in which the residual profits of the business are shared out between the partners is known as an **appropriation account**. The content of the appropriation account will be guided by the contents of the **partnership agreement** which may have been constructed by the partnership. This agreement (sometimes known as a **deed of partnership**) will set out various rules for how the partnership is to be run. In terms of financial considerations, it will normally contain some or all of the following.

Features of a partnership agreement

Interest on capital

As a reward for contributing differing amounts of capital, partners may be allocated interest on capital from the profits of the partnership. This reward will be given to partners in direct proportion to the capital contributions of each partner. It will usually be calculated as a fixed interest rate on capital contributions given to partners each year. Although the current account balance represents part of each partner's overall capital balance, the interest is usually calculated on the capital account balance for each partner.

Partnership salaries

A partner may be allocated a partnership salary if they perform a particular skill or function within the business. This can be thought of as a form of guaranteed profit which will be allocated to the partner regardless of the overall level of profit. Partnership salaries are not the same as any business salaries the firm incurs. Partnership salaries are an appropriation of profits rather than an expense and must be listed separately.

Interest on drawings

Drawings are a reduction in the capital of the business. To deter a partner from taking excessive drawings it may be appropriate to charge partners for the privilege of being able to take drawings. Interest on drawings is a charge made to partners for drawings made.

Profit sharing ratio

How profits are to be shared will be important. Partners may share profits (and losses) equally, but there are various reasons why partners may be allocated a bigger or smaller share of the profits. This will also apply to losses incurred by the partnership. The shares of profits and losses will be made after the above appropriations have been made. It is perfectly possible that, although the partnership generates a net profit, the appropriations made to each partner are greater in total than the available profit. In this case, the residual loss that remains would be shared between the partners in their normal profit (and loss) sharing ratio.

If any of the above items are not present in the partnership agreement, they should not be accounted for. If there is no agreement, all profits and losses should be shared out equally between the partners.

Current and capital accounts

For a sole trader's capital account, the only adjustments will be for any further capital contributions, for any drawings taken and for the profits or losses for the year. For a partnership, each partner will need their own capital account. The partner's capital will be subject to many more adjustments than that of a sole trader in the form of the appropriations which were outlined in the previous section.

As a result, it is reasonably common for each partner to have two separate capital accounts. One would be known as the capital account and this would contain the long-term capital of the partner, with any adjustments arising out of structural changes to the partnership (such as new capital contributions and revaluations of the firm's assets). Most of the adjustments will be entered into the other capital account for the partners, which is known as the **current account**. The current account records the appropriations made to the partner's capital balance over time and can be thought of as a flexible capital account.

Example 6.2

Pratt and Meara have been in partnership for a number of years. The net profit for the year ending 31 December 2016 was £40,000. The following details were available from their accounts:

	£
Capital balances:	
Pratt	30,000
Meara	20,000
Current account:	
Pratt	5,500
Meara	4,800
Drawings:	
Pratt	10,000
Meara	8,000

The partnership agreement stated that Meara was entitled to a partnership salary amounting to £6,000, interest on capital is given to partners at a rate of 4 per cent and interest on drawings was to be charged as follows: Pratt £340 and Meara £260. Any residual profits and losses were to be shared equally.

The appropriation account of the partnership would appear as follows:

Pratt & Meara
Appropriation account for year
ended 31 December 2016

	£	£
Net profit		40,000
Add Interest on drawings:		
Pratt	340	
Meara	260	600
		40,600
Less Interest on capital:		
Pratt	1,200	
Meara	800	2,000
		38,600
Less Salary (Meara)		6,000
		32,600
Profits to be shared:		
Pratt	16,300	
Meara	16,300	
		32,600

Although there are no adjustments needed to the partners' capital accounts, the current accounts would be adjusted as follows:

Current accounts

	Pratt	Meara		Pratt	Meara
	£	£		£	£
Drawings	10,000	8,000	Balance b/d	5,500	4,800
Interest on drawings	340	260	Interest on capital	1,200	800
Balance c/d	12,660	19,640	Salaries		6,000
			Profit shares	16,300	16,300
	23,000	27,900		23,000	27,900
			Balance b/d	12,660	19,640

Balance sheets for partnerships

The balance sheet is very similar to the balance sheet of a sole trader. The capital section of the balance sheet will consist of the capital balance for each partner and the updated current account balance for each partner. In our example, the capital section of the balance sheet appears in Figure 6.1.

FIGURE 6.1 Balance sheet extract for a partnership

Pratt & Meara
Balance sheet extract as at 31 December 2016

Capital accounts:	£	£
Pratt	30,000	
Meara	20,000	50,000
Current accounts:		
Pratt	12,660	
Meara	19,640	32,300
		82,300

Partnerships as a form of business organization are becoming increasingly rare. This decline in the numbers of partnerships is partly due to the increased ease of setting up as a company, but has been accelerated by the creation of a new form of partnership, that of the limited liability partnership.

Limited liability partnerships

A **limited partnership** has been allowed in the UK since 1907. In the limited partnership a partner who does not take part in the running of the business – known as a **sleeping partner** – can be allowed to benefit from limited liability (where they are limited in what they are liable for, should the business fail, to their original investment and no more). However, in the limited partnership, the partnership as a whole will not benefit from limited liability and 'active' partners may still be forced to clear general trading debts of the partnership. The **limited liability partnership**, however, is a new form of business organization that does allow all partners to benefit from limited liability.

In the UK, the Limited Liability Partnership Act of 2000 created this new form of business organization, the limited liability partnership (LLP). This partnership has some features in common with the traditional partnership organization, but also shares some features with those of a limited company (covered in Chapter 13). For example, as with the normal partnership, the partners will pay income tax based on the income generated for each partner from the business. This is different from a company which, because it exists as a separate legal entity, will be taxed on its profits. However, the limited liability partnership is treated as a separate legal entity in the eyes of the law.

Not-for-profit organizations

A not-for-profit organization is one that does not engage in the pursuit of profits. These organizations will often include clubs, societies and charities. The organization will not have owners in the same sense as a profit-making business. Not-for-profit organizations are run by members or trustees who will often work on a voluntary basis. Accounting records will still be maintained and financial statements will be produced for the organization. However, the accounting records of a not-for-profit organization are less likely to be as detailed as those of an organization that exists to earn profits as its main objective. Often the accounting records are constructed using single-entry bookkeeping (see Chapter 1), and the legal requirements placed on these not-for-profit organizations are fewer in number. In the case of small organizations, the accounting records can often be constructed by the treasurer of the organization rather than a professional accountant.

Accounting for not-for-profit organizations

The receipts and payments account of the organization – the record of money paid into and out of the organization – is often the focal point of the accounting records. However, the organization may want to present a simple set of financial statements – showing the varying incomes and expenses incurred as well as a balance sheet showing the assets and liabilities of the organization. The incomes and expenses are still calculated on an accruals basis, which means that any outstanding expenses will still be accounted for in the period that they were incurred. However, there are differences in the make-up of these financial statements.

The equivalent of the income statement of the not-for-profit organization will be the income and expenditure account. It will list the varying incomes and expenditures of the organization. However, given that the aim of the organization is not to generate profits, any difference between income levels and expenditure levels is not termed profit (or loss) but is termed as shown in Table 6.1.

TABLE 6.1 Differences in measures of profit and loss

Profit-making organization	Not-for-profit organization
Net profit	Surplus of income over expenditure
Net loss	Deficit of income over expenditure

Income of the not-for-profit organization

The organization is likely to have income generated from a number of different sources and many clubs will run additional fundraising activities. These are often seen as a necessary contribution to the cash funds needed to keep the club running. These are likely to cover some, if not all, of the following:

- member subscriptions;
- bar trading profits (clubs often run a bar within their clubhouse and profits made on the bar would be contributed towards the income of the organization);
- donations;
- profits on ancillary activities, such as fundraising events.

Member subscriptions
Especially for clubs and societies, a significant source of income will come from member subscriptions. These are usually levied on an annual basis. It is possible that there will be several outstanding balances relating to those subscriptions paid in advance and those yet to be collected. This will mean that adjustments will need to be made to the amounts received for subscriptions in respect of overall subscriptions income.

Example 6.3

The Lexden Football Club charges its members subscription fees. The following data relate to the year ended 31 December 2014:

	£
Subscriptions owing to the club as at 1 January 2014	64
Subscriptions received in advance as at 1 January 2014	31
Subscriptions owing to the club as at 31 December 2014	95
Subscriptions received in advance as at 31 December 2014	42
Money received during 2014 in respect of subscriptions	397

The amount that would be credited to the income and expenditure account as income for the year ended 31 December 2014 can be calculated by constructing a ledger account for subscriptions. This would appear as follows:

Subscriptions

2014		£	2014		£
1 Jan	Balance b/d	64	1 Jan	Balance b/d	31
31 Dec	*Income &*	*417*	31 Dec	Money received	397
	Expenditure				
31 Dec	Balance c/d	42	31 Dec	Balance c/d	95
		523			523
2015			2015		
1 Jan	Balance b/d	95	1 Jan	Balance b/d	42

In this case, the £417 would appear as income in the income and expenditure account for that period.

Life membership subscriptions

Some clubs and societies will offer life membership subscriptions. In return for a larger payment a member will be able to remain a member of the organization for the rest of their natural life. The life membership would normally be arranged so that it was financially advantageous in the long run for a member to purchase. However, there is the issue of how to account for the life membership.

Life membership incomes do not belong to one particular period of time. In this case, the organization should aim to spread the income of a life membership subscription over an estimated lifespan. For example, if a life membership rate is available at £500, and the average length of a life membership is 10 years, then we would credit the income and expenditure account with £50 (£500/10) for each year. This method may not always produce accurate results, but it does provide a useful approximation. Of course, it will depend on the treasurer of the organization providing a reasonable estimate of the average length of time for the life membership.

Bar trading account

One common activity is that of running a bar which will sell refreshments to members and their guests. Although the club may not be a profit-making organization, the activities run to generate funds for the organization may produce a profit. A bar trading account will show the profits (or losses) made during the period on running the bar and will appear very similar to the standard trading account of a profit-making organization.

Example 6.4

The activities relating to the bar of the Meadowhead Football Club are as follows:

	Balances as at 31 Dec 2018	Balances as at 31 Dec 2019
	£	£
Bar inventory	434	721
Bar creditors	667	398

Further details for the year ending 31 December 2019 are as follows:

	£
Bar sales	6,455
Payments to bar suppliers	3,876
Bar staff wages	1,045

The bar trading account of the football club will be calculated as the difference between the incomes received by the bar compared with the costs incurred in running the bar. The costs of the bar will consist of the cost of sales incurred by the organization but also any other related expenditure, such as the bar wages.

Given that there are outstanding balances relating to amounts owing both at the start and at the end of the year, we must still apply the accruals concept.

The cost of bar purchases is as follows:

Bar purchases for the year
= Cash paid for bar supplies (£3,876)
 – Amounts owing at the end of the year (£667)
 + Amounts owing at the start of the year (£398)
= £3,607

The full bar trading account would appear as follows:

Meadowhead Football Club
Bar trading account for year
ended 31 December 2009

	£	£
Bar sales		6,455
Less Cost of bar		
Opening inventory	434	
Add Purchases	3,607	
	4,041	
Less Closing inventory	721	3,320
Gross profit on bar		3,135
Less Bar wages		1,045
Bar profit		2,090

This bar profit would appear as an income in the income and expenditure account.

Income and expenditure account

The income and expenditure account will draw together all the varying forms of income received by the organization and the expenses incurred. As stated earlier, the accruals concept will still apply. Capital expenditure will only appear in the income and expenditure account in the form of depreciation.

A fully worked example now follows.

Example 6.5

The Norton Boys' Tennis Club is a small, local club. The club is run for young people aged between 11 and 18. Although the club has been successful in the regional junior leagues, it is facing financial problems. The rent charged on the clubhouse and on the ground is set to rise by 20 per cent next year and it is felt that increasing subscription charges would only lead to a decline in the number of people playing.

The financial details for the 2015/16 season are as follows:

	1 August 2015	31 July 2016
	£	£
Subscriptions owing	400	650
Subscriptions paid in advance	125	240
Cash at bank	700	(1,200)
Rent of clubhouse/courts accrued	360	540
Equipment	5,000	5,200
Snack bar inventory	130	80
Creditors for snack bar purchases	60	45

Over the 2015/16 season the following payments were recorded:

	£
Snack bar purchases	460
Rent of clubhouse and courts	2,300
New equipment	500
Heating and lighting	250
Telephone	115
Transport costs	250
Hire of disco equipment	189
Costs of running disco	111
Stationery	75

The following revenues were also received over the same period.

	£
Subscriptions	650
Income from discos	1,230
Snack bar sales	470

In order to produce the income and expenditure account we will first of all have to calculate the varying incomes for the period, as well as any profits or losses on any ancillary activities. The subscriptions income for the period will be calculated as follows:

Subscriptions account

	£		£
Balance b/d	400	Balance b/d	125
Income & expenditure	785	Bank	650
Balance c/d	240	Balance c/d	650
	1,425		1,425

The snack bar trading account would appear as follows:

Norton Boys' Tennis Club
Snack bar trading account for year ended 31 July 2016

	£	£
Snack bar sales		470
Less Cost of snack bar		
Opening inventory	130	
Add Purchases (*)	445	
	575	
Less Closing inventory	80	495
Loss on snack bar		25

(* Snack bar purchases = £460 + £45 – £60 = £445)

The disco run by the club generated both income and expenses; therefore it makes sense to combine these figures to produce an overall profit or loss on the activity:

Calculation of profit from discos

	£	£
Income from discos		1,230
Less Expenses:		
Hire of disco	189	
Other expenses	111	300
Profit on disco		930

We can now produce the overall income and expenditure account. The expenses will also include the depreciation on the club's equipment. Although this is not stated explicitly, it can be taken to be the difference in the values given for equipment at the start and the end of the year.

Norton Boys' Tennis Club
income & expenditure account
for year ended 31 July 2016

Income	£	£
Subscriptions	785	
Profit on discos	930	1,715
Expenditure		
Rent of club house (£2,300 + £540 − £360)	2,480	
Telephone	115	
Transport costs	250	
Stationery	75	
Heating and lighting	250	
Depreciation on equipment	300	
Loss on snack bar	25	3,495
Deficit of income over expenditure		1,780

Balance sheets of not-for-profit organization

The balance sheet of a not-for-profit organization will appear very similar to that of a profit-making organization. One major difference is that as a club is not owned by anyone, there will be no capital figure for the organization. Instead of capital, we refer to the **accumulated fund** of an organization.

The accumulated fund represents the difference between the assets and liabilities of the organization. The calculation of the accumulated fund is sometimes presented as a **statement of affairs** – which lists the assets and liabilities of the organization. Continuing with the previous example, the calculation of this is shown in Figure 6.2.

FIGURE 6.2 Statement of affairs

Norton Boys' Tennis Club Statement of affairs as at 1 August 2015		
	£	£
Equipment	5,000	
Subscriptions owing	400	
Cash at bank	700	
Snack bar inventory	130	6,230
Subscriptions paid in advance	125	
Creditors for snack bar purchases	60	
Rent of clubhouse/pitch accrued	360	545
Accumulated fund as at 1/8/2000		5,685

If the organization makes a surplus of income over expenditure, this would be added to the accumulated fund on the balance sheet. The balance sheet for our example would appear as in Figure 6.3.

FIGURE 6.3 Balance sheet of a not-for-profit organization

Norton Boys' Tennis Club Balance sheet as at 31 July 2016			
	£	£	£
Non-current assets			
Equipment			5,200
Current assets			
Inventory		80	
Subscriptions owing		650	
		730	
Current liabilities			
Snack bar creditors	45		
Subscriptions in advance	240		
Rent owing	540		
Overdraft	1,200	2,025	(1,295)
			3,905
Accumulated fund			
Balance as at 1/8/2015			5,685
Less deficit			1,780
Balance as at 31/7/2016			3,905

Review questions

1 From the following data construct a manufacturing account for the year ended 31 December 2015.

	£
Purchases of raw materials	89,500
Opening inventory:	
Raw materials	12,450
Work-in-progress	43,100
Carriage inwards	875
Returns outwards	2,190
Labour costs:	
Factory supervisors	29,000
Manufacturing wages	87,500
Depreciation of factory equipment	5,600
Rent	18,000

Additional information:

1 Rent is to be apportioned between factory overheads and office expenses in a 3:1 ratio.

2 Inventory as at 31 December 2015 was as follows:

a Raw materials £15,650

b Work-in-progress £38,700.

Solution

Manufacturing account for year ended 31 December 2015		
	£	£
Opening inventory of raw materials		12,450
Add Purchases of raw materials	89,500	
Add Carriage inwards	875	
	90,375	
Less Returns outwards	2,190	88,185
		100,635
Less Closing inventory of raw materials		15,650
Cost of raw materials consumed		84,985
Direct labour		87,500
Prime cost		172,485
Add Factory overheads		
Depreciation of equipment	5,600	
Factory supervisors	29,000	
Rent (3/4)	13,500	48,100
		220,585
Add Work-in-progress as at 1 Jan 2015	43,100	
Less Work-in-progress as at 31 Dec 2015	38,700	4,400
Factory cost of goods completed		224,985

2   Sheridan, Wilson and Palmer are partners. They share profits and losses in the ratio of 3:2:1. In the first year of trading, ending 31 December 2016, the partnership earned a net profit of £26,000. They have agreed on the following:

- Interest should be allowed on fixed capital balances at 10% per annum.

- Wilson should receive a partnership salary of £7,000 per annum.

Capital account balances are as follows:

Sheridan	£10,000
Wilson	£8,000
Palmer	£5,500

You are required to draw up the appropriation account of the partnership for the year ended 31 December 2016.

Solution

Sheridan, Wilson & Palmer Appropriation account for year ended 31 December 2016			
	£	£	£
Net profit			26,000
Less Interest on capitals			
Sheridan	1,000		
Wilson	800		
Palmer	550		
		2,350	
Salary: Wilson		7,000	
			9,350
			16,650
Balance of profits shared:			
Sheridan		8,325	
Wilson		5,550	
Palmer		2,775	
			16,650

3   Mahoney and Sutton are in partnership, sharing profits in the ratio of 3:2 respectively. Their capital account balances are as follows:

Capitals:	£
Mahoney	25,000
Sutton	16,000.

They allow themselves interest on capital at the rate of 8 per cent. Mahoney receives a salary of £5,000 and Sutton receives as salary of £7,000. Both partners have taken drawings as follows:

Drawings	£
Mahoney	6,900
Sutton	4,800

They charge 5 per cent interest on drawings. The net profit for the year ending 30 April 2015 was £45,000.

Produce an appropriation account for the financial year for the partnership.

Solution

Mahoney & Sutton
Appropriation account for year ended 30 April 2015

	£	£	£
Net profit			45,000
Add Interest on drawings			
Mahoney		345	
Sutton		240	585
			45,585
Less Interest on capitals			
Mahoney	2,000		
Sutton	1,280	3,280	
Less Salaries			
Mahoney	5,000		
Sutton	7,000	12,000	15,280
			30,305
Balance of profits shared			
Mahoney		18,183	
Sutton		12,122	30,305

4 The Blay Darts Club charges its members an annual subscription of £60.
   It currently has 35 members. The following balances are available for the year
   ended 31 December 2014:

	Balances as at 1 Jan 2014 £	Balances as at 31 Dec 2014 £
Subscriptions in arrears	90	113
Subscriptions paid in advance	18	27

From the above information, calculate how much money was actually received
in respect of subscriptions during the year of 2014.

Solution

Subscriptions account for Blay Darts Club

2014		£	2014		£
1 Jan	Balance b/d	90	1 Jan	Balance b/d	18
31 Dec	Income & expenditure	2,100	31 Dec	Receipts & payments	2,086
31 Dec	Balance c/d	27	31 Dec	Balance c/d	113
		2,217			2,217

5 The following receipts and payments account for the year ended 31 December 2017 has been prepared for the St Mary's Sports Club:

Receipts	£	Payments	£
Balance b/d	765	Sports day prizes	545
Membership subscriptions	2,343	Bar staff wages	260
Sports day incomes	756	Insurance	345
Bar sales	1,890	Advertising	154
Dinner dance income	230	Payments to bar creditors	1,010
		Dinner dance expenses	190
		New equipment	1,600
		Balance c/d	1,880
	5,984		5,984

The assets and liabilities of the club other than the bank balance were:

	1 Jan 2017 £	31 Dec 17 £
Premises	60,000	60,000
Equipment	8,900	8,600
Subscriptions in advance	56	87
Subscriptions owing	111	67
Creditors for bar inventory	324	256
Insurance owing	88	47
Bar inventory	213	451
Dinner dance expenses accrued	0	67

Required:

(i)   Prepare a bar trading account for the St Mary's Sports Club for the year ended 31 December 2017.

(ii) Prepare an income and expenditure account for the St Mary's Sports Club for the year ended 31 December 2017.

(iii) Prepare a balance sheet for the St Mary's Sports Club as at 31 December 2017.

Solution

St Mary's Sports Club
Bar trading account for the year ended 31 December 2017

	£	£
Bar sales		1,890
Less Cost of bar		
Opening inventory	213	
Add Purchases (£1010 + £256 – £324)	942	
	1,155	
Less Closing inventory	451	704
Gross bar profit		1,186
Less Bar staff wages		260
Bar profit		926

A ledger account for the subscriptions will show us how much to include within the income and expenditure account for the year:

Subscriptions

Balance b/d	111	Balance b/d	56
Income & expenditure	2,268	Receipts	2,343
Balance c/d	87	Balance c/d	67
	2,466		2,466

St Mary's Sports Club Income and expenditure
account for the year ended 31 December 2017

	£	£
Income		
Annual subscriptions	2,268	
Profit on sports day	211	
Bar profit	926	3,405
Expenditure		
Insurance (£345 + £47 – £88)	304	
Equipment depreciation	1,900	
Advertising	154	
Loss on dinner dance	27	2,385
Surplus of income over expenditure		1,020

St Mary's Sports Club
Balance sheet as at 31 December 2017

	£	£
Non-current assets		
Premises		60,000
Equipment		8,600
		68,600
Current assets		
Inventory	451	
Subs owing	67	
Bank	1,880	
	2,398	
Current liabilities		
Bar creditors	256	
Subs in advance	87	
Insurance accrued	47	
Dinner dance expenses accrued	67	
	457	
		1,941
		70,541
Accumulated fund as at 1 Jan 2017		69,521
Add Surplus		1,020
Accumulated fund as at 31 Dec 2017		70,541

A few points to note here:

1   The depreciation of the club's equipment was not stated explicitly but can be calculated as the difference in the book value of equipment at the start and at the end of the year (after allowing for the new purchase of the equipment).

2   The opening balance of the accumulated fund would be the same as the value of the net assets (assets less liabilities) of the club at the start of the year.

An introduction to business costing

07

Introduction

A business will only earn a profit if its revenue earned exceeds the costs and expenses that the firm incurs in generating sales. Profits can be increased if either sales can be increased or costs can be reduced. Therefore knowledge of the costs that are generated through business activity is particularly important for the profitability of the business.

Costing as a distinct accounting topic for study is concerned with the analysis of costs incurred by the business – not only past and present costs but also expected future costs. Costing is normally concerned with the generation of information internal to the business – that is, not for publication. The costing information generated will be useful for managers making decisions about the present and future activities of the business. Some of the main aims of costing as a branch of accounting would include the following:

- to monitor the location (by branch, by department, by person etc) of where costs are generated;
- to attempt to control the level of expenditure on costs;
- to compare the various costs of products and services produced by the business;
- to analyse the trends that emerge from past and current cost patterns.

Costing information for managers of the business will arise from many different sources. In the same way that daybooks and ledger accounts were constructed from the information contained in source documents (see Chapter 1), costing information will be obtained from a variety of sources. These sources of costing information will include the following:

- cost data sheets;
- material purchase invoices;
- budgetary data;
- timesheets, clocking-in cards (for labour).

Cost centres and cost units

In order to manage, monitor and control the costs incurred by the business a **cost centre** will often be used to monitor where within the business the costs are being incurred. A cost centre is a location of the business designated for the collection of costs. This cost centre can be a production or service location – it could be an item of machinery or a piece of equipment, a department of the business, a branch of a business or even a designated person within the organization. The managers of the business will make the decision as to how many cost centres a business will have, and how they will be designated.

A further distinction which will be important later is made for classifying cost centres which are designated service cost centres and those which are designated as production cost centres. Service cost centres are those which will provide services to other cost centres. A production cost centre is one in which production will occur in some form. More of this later.

Cost units are either units of output or units of service and are measured by the firm. For example, a firm which manufactures goods will normally classify each good produced as a cost unit. It is possible that if these are small in terms of the amount of expenditure, the cost unit will be a batch of goods produced.

If a firm produces continuous output – for example, a soft drinks manufacturer that sells the drinks in terms of quantity rather than by bottle or can – it may consider a cost unit to be measured in terms of a particular quantity of output, that is, per litre, per 10 litres etc.

Cost behaviour

It is useful to know how costs are affected by certain variables, for example how a cost relates to the production of output. Some of the costs that go into the production of output and those generally incurred by the business are as follows.

Direct costs

These costs can be linked to the output of a particular cost unit and are directly related to the production of a particular unit of output. When costing a unit of output the direct costs can be directly allocated to the unit of production. The total of the direct costs is often referred to as the prime cost of production. Direct costs are often divided into three different types:

- Direct materials are the cost of raw materials that would be included within the cost of direct materials as well as any other materials used in the actual production of a cost unit.

- Direct labour refers to the cost incurred by workers in the production of output. Rationally, these would be the production-line workers directly involved in the production of output. For a service provider, direct labour would be the wages of those directly providing the service. For example, a hairdresser's wages may be considered a direct labour cost.

- Direct expenses refer to any other costs that can be directly linked to the output of the business – to a cost unit. Given that most direct costs are covered by materials and labour, these will not always be present in the costing data. An example which appears in the data of manufacturing companies is that of manufacturing royalties which are paid to the copyright holder and are paid on a cost per unit basis.

Indirect costs

These costs are incurred by a firm but cannot be easily traced back to the production of a unit of output. These are indirectly related to production. The total of the indirect costs is often referred to as the overheads of the organization.

Indirect materials are those costs of materials that are not directly related to the production of a cost unit. These could be components that are used within production but not used for each unit output.

Fixed costs

A fixed cost is a cost which remains unaltered as output levels change. This cost will be incurred irrespective of the output level of the firm. Common examples of fixed costs will be rent of premises, insurance of machinery and equipment. These costs can be connected with the production of output, but the crucial element is that they are not affected in total by changes in the level of output. For example, the payment made to a factory supervisor may be connected to production, but if the supervisor is paid an amount unconnected with output levels, this would be classified as a fixed cost.

The graphical representation of fixed costs is shown in Figure 7.1. When plotted against output, fixed costs will appear as a horizontal line, indicating that they remain constant as output increases. It is important to realize that fixed costs can change, but the nature of the term 'fixed' is that it is fixed in relation to changes in the level of output.

Although fixed costs will remain at the same level as output increases, this cannot continue indefinitely. If output continues to increase then sooner or later an element of the fixed costs of the firm is also likely to rise. For example, if a firm expands production then with higher output levels new machinery is likely to be needed and this will require extra expenditure on insurance. Even if the firm concentrates on selling services it is unlikely to

FIGURE 7.1 Fixed costs

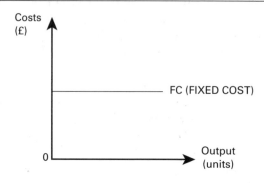

incur the same level of fixed costs as output continues to rise. For example, with rising sales, the firm is likely to need extra administration support, or higher office expenses, which will mean higher fixed costs.

Therefore, fixed costs can be also considered to be stepped fixed costs. This is shown in Figure 7.2. Fixed costs will remain constant up until a critical output level is reached. At that point the firm cannot expand output without incurring a rise in fixed costs – that is, we 'move up' to the next level on the stepped fixed costs curve. Given that the rise in fixed costs at this stage may be significant, a firm will have to decide whether the rise in output is worthwhile, as the extra revenue may not compensate for the rise in fixed costs. It may require the firm's managers to decide either to reduce selling prices in order to make extra sales more certain, or actually increasing selling prices so as to reduce the demand so that the firm does not have to incur the extra fixed costs that come with higher output.

FIGURE 7.2 Stepped fixed costs

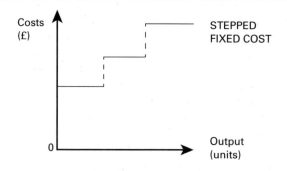

Variable costs

A variable cost will increase in direct proportion to the level of output produced. For example, the materials and labour costs that are incurred in the
production of a unit of output would be considered to be variable costs
because the costs in total for materials and labour would rise as output
increases. The unit cost of production is assumed to be constant – that is, the
cost incurred in labour and materials will be the same for each additional
unit of output, but the total of these will rise in a linear fashion as output
levels increase. As shown in Figure 7.3, the variable cost curve will appear
as an upward-sloping straight line beginning at the origin. It begins at the
origin because with no output there should be no variable costs. The variable
cost curve is a straight line because we assume a constant unit cost.

FIGURE 7.3 Variable costs

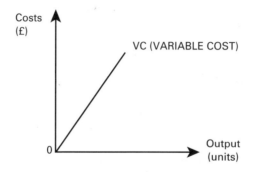

In reality, the constant unit cost assumption is unlikely to hold exactly.
Bulk-buying discounts may be available which will lead to a lower unit cost
for materials. In addition, increases in productivity that arise out of larger-
scale production may lead to a falling unit cost in terms of labour costs. For
example, economies of scale exploited by firms operating on a larger scale
will allow a falling unit cost of production. At very large production runs it
is possible that a firm may even experience diseconomies of scale and see
unit costs begin to rise.

Principles and methods of costing

An area of confusion might arise from the inclusion of many apparent
methods of costing. The terms costing method, costing system and costing
principle are often used interchangeably. Unlike financial accounting, which
is governed by reasonably rigid terminology, the terms used within costing

are more fluid and we should be careful in exactly which type of system is being employed. Flexibility in how the costing information is used is important. However, at this stage some clarification is necessary to establish the difference between **costing principles** and **costing methods**.

Costing principles

The principles of costing are often divided into two categories:

- absorption costing – which looks at how a firm accounts for its overhead expenditure;
- marginal costing – when a firm uses only information on variable costs and contributions to make a decision.

'Absorption costing' is considered in the next section and 'marginal costing' in Chapter 8. The principles of or approach to costing should not be confused with the costing methods used within business, which are considered towards the end of this chapter.

Absorption costing

When attempting to cost a product or a cost unit we are faced with the decision of what to include in this cost. Obviously we would include the direct costs incurred with the production of any output. This is likely to include the cost of the materials that were used to make the product. We would also include the labour costs incurred in the production of the output. There may be other expenses that we would want to include as part of the cost of the unit because they are directly connected with the production of output, such as the packing costs incurred for each unit, or the manufacturing royalties incurred for each unit produced. We have seen this category of cost classification before when we looked at the categorization of direct and indirect costs in the manufacturing account of an organization that produces rather than purchases finished goods. However, we would want to know how far we go in the inclusion of the other costs – those costs that are indirectly related to the output of the business, commonly known as the overheads of the business.

Imagine a firm that sets its selling price on the basis of the direct costs incurred in the production of each unit of output. If the selling price is not sufficiently high, the firm is likely to make a loss, even though each unit is being sold for more than it 'costs'. This is obviously because the firm is failing to recover all the costs incurred that are only indirectly related to the production of output. A firm would need to ensure its selling price is sufficiently high that it covers not only direct, but also the indirect costs of production (as well as all the costs incurred which are not related to production at all).

The principle of **absorption costing** is that, when applied to costing a unit of output, we will include both the direct costs of production and also the indirect costs – the overheads – in the unit cost of a business.

The principle of absorption costing may initially seem odd – how can a business include, within the cost of a unit of output, costs which may be far removed from the actual production of this unit? However, the costs incurred by the business that are indirect in nature – that is, part of the firm's overheads – are still important for a business. These overheads cannot be simply ignored. To some extent they need to be accounted for in some way and the principle of absorption costing allows this to happen.

Absorption costing and full costing

Absorption costing is based on the principle that both direct and indirect costs are contained within the cost unit of the business. Under absorption costing, the cost per unit would consist of the following components:

	£
Direct materials	XX
Direct expenses	XX
Overheads (fixed and/or variable)	XX
Absorption cost per unit	XX

The absorption cost will only include the costs incurred which are related to the production activities of a firm – both direct costs and indirect costs. A similar approach to cost would be the 'full cost' similar which would include non-production overheads as well – such as selling and distribution overheads.

The decision has to be made as to how to include the 'right' proportion of overheads as part of the cost of a unit of output. Costing a product will be easy if it contains only direct costs. However, the method used for including elements of the overheads (the indirect costs) into the cost of each unit is less clear. Absorption costing as a topic considers the various ways in which overheads can be included within the cost.

Example 7.1

Yarrow Ltd makes water tanks for collecting rainwater. In an average week, it produces 500 tanks. A summary of the costs incurred in a typical week is follows:

	£
Direct materials	4,500
Direct labour	3,200
Direct expenses	800
Overheads	2,500
Total cost	11,000

The unit cost of each water tank can be found by dividing each of the above figures by 500. This gives us a total cost of £22 per water tank (£11,000/500).

Here, the treatment of the overheads is easy to deal with. The firm is making one uniform product and therefore the overheads can be shared out equally between each water tank produced. The total of overheads is simply divided by the number produced to give the 'overheads per unit' figure (£2,500/500 = £5 per unit).

Recovery of overheads

In Example 7.1 as long as the firm sets the selling price of each water tank above the 'full' cost of £22 per tank, we would expect the firm to make an overall profit. However, this profit will only be earned if the firm manages to sell all the water tanks it has produced. If sales fall below 500 per week, the firm will not sell enough tanks to 'cover' the overheads incurred. A smaller output level would mean that the overheads have to be 'absorbed' into a smaller number of units.

In our example, if the weekly output had fallen to 200 units, the overheads to be included within the full cost of each unit would be £2,500/200 = £12.50. This would have the implication that the cost per unit (including the overheads) would have to rise to cover these increased overheads per unit.

The firm's ability to pay in full the overheads incurred is referred to as overhead recovery. How this is achieved is discussed in this chapter.

Global overhead recovery rates

Example 7.1 illustrated a simple business producing only one type of product. Most businesses will produce a range of products or services. In this case, the task of sharing out the overheads among the output of the firm will not be as straightforward. A method should be selected for the basis of recovering the overheads which is seen to be as fair as possible.

If a firm's products make use of common labour but take varying times to manufacture, it may be appropriate to apportion overheads on the basis of the time taken – with those products taking longer to produce incurring a greater share of the overheads of the firm. Similarly, the firm's products might make use of different quantities of materials. The proportion of materials used by each product might serve as the basis for the apportionment of the overheads.

For a firm that produces a limited range of products or services, the firm may choose to utilize a global overhead recovery rate. This would use one basis for the apportionment of overheads to each unit of output.

Example 7.2

A kitchen fitter works a 45-week year and for 36 hours per week. He estimates that his overheads for the year will be £9,000.

When billing customers, the fitter may wish to include a fraction of his overall overheads into the cost of each 'job' he performs for customers and he does this on the basis of the time of each job completed. This means that jobs that take longer will incur a higher proportion of overheads. For example, for a job that takes 25 hours he would want to include the following amount of overheads into the cost of the job:

$$\text{Hours worked in one year} = 45 \times 36 = 1{,}620$$

Given that the job takes 18 hours, he would apportion $(18/1{,}620) \times £9{,}000 = £100$ of overheads for this job on top of the direct materials and his direct labour. The selling price charged for this job would be based on both the direct costs of the job and this £100 share of the overheads.

A problem with using the global overhead recovery for apportioning overheads is that a particular job might incur higher indirect costs which are unrelated to the time taken for each job. In this case, the charging of overheads on the basis of the time taken for each job would not reflect the true amount of overheads expenditure incurred by this job.

Another problem with the global overhead recovery rate is that it will be based on an estimate. In Example 7.2, the overheads were apportioned on the basis of the time taken by each job in relation to the time worked in a full year. If, for some reason, our kitchen fitter didn't work all the hours expected, the charging of overheads in this manner would not receive all the overheads incurred. As with Example 7.1, the forecast variable, whether it be output or time, is only an estimate and if it is incorrect it can mean that either the overheads charged per unit or per job are not high enough to recover the overheads, or too high. In the case of the overheads being charged at too high a rate, this may not seem a problem, but if this means a higher selling price and a lower sales volume then the overall effect might be to reduce the overall profits.

Larger organizations are less likely to use a global overhead recovery rate. They are more likely to face competition from other firms and therefore will not want to risk deriving inappropriate selling prices for their output from an inappropriate basis for charging overheads to units of output. In this case, a more complex method of charging overheads to cost units is through the basis of a multi-departmental approach.

Multi-department overhead recovery rates

This is a more sophisticated method of charging overheads to unit of output. It is still trying to achieve the same result as before, that of charging an appropriate amount of overheads to each unit of output or each job undertaken by a firm, but involves more detailed calculation and will involve the consideration of each type of overhead.

'Overheads' is a blanket term for the indirect production costs of the business. However, the overheads incurred will be varied and will be generated by a variety of different activities. As a result, each overhead will be apportioned to cost centres by using a basis specific to each type of overhead incurred. Initially the firm will have to decide on what cost centres are to be utilized. These, as mentioned earlier, are a part of the business which can have costs designated to the centre. In effect, these cost centres are taking 'responsibility' for the costs incurred – without the inclusion of cost centres, the costs may become much more difficult to monitor and control. The use of cost centres for collecting costs allows a business to begin to see where costs arise and how they are generated. For manufacturing organizations, these cost centres will be either production cost centres or service cost centres designed to support the production activities of the business.

How are costs allocated to cost centres?

Some of the costs incurred will be easy to link and charge to particular cost centres and cost units. Direct costs will be easily linked to the particular cost units. Indirect costs can be easily linked if they arise from only one cost centre or cost unit. However, by their very nature, indirect costs are often hard to link to the activities of a particular cost centre or the production of one particular cost unit. As a result, there is a four-stage process to be completed for absorption costing:

1 allocation of direct costs;

2 apportionment of overheads;

3 reapportionment of overheads;

4 absorption of overheads into cost units.

These stages will now be considered in turn.

Allocation of direct costs

As stated above, direct costs should be relatively easy to allocate. These should be linked to either the cost centre or the cost unit where they are generated. For direct materials and direct labour these costs can be easily linked with the output of the business. Some overheads may also be allocated to a particular cost centre. For example, the supervisory wage within a factory may belong to a particular department exclusively and therefore may be allocated to that department – assuming that the business has designated departments as cost centres in that organization. However, it is more than likely that overheads will not be allocated, and this brings us on to the next stage in the absorption costing process – the apportionment of overheads.

Apportionment of overheads

It is highly likely that overheads, which by their very nature are indirect costs, cannot be allocated to either a particular cost unit or one cost centre alone. In this case, we will need to apportion the overheads to the cost centres of the business by some other method.

Cost apportionment will occur where a cost is shared among at least two cost centres. The method of how the cost is apportioned between the various cost centres will be determined by some logical and appropriate basis. However, we must be fully aware that, by definition, no method of apportionment is going to be completely fair and realistic – if it were, we would be allocating the cost rather than apportioning the cost. The basis of apportionment for the overhead is meant to reflect the benefits gained by the cost centres for that overhead incurred.

Basis of apportionment

Allocation of costs to cost centres would be ideal in trying to link costs closest to where they are generated. However, in the case of overheads which cannot be allocated, we need a basis of apportionment that most closely reflects where the costs are generated. In this case, it is important to arrive at methods of apportionment which are seen as a fair reflection of how the cost was generated. Given that there are a number of different types of overhead, it is possible that we may wish to use a number of different methods of apportionment for overheads. Common methods used to apportion overheads are shown in Table 7.1.

TABLE 7.1 Typical bases of apportionment

Basis of apportionment	Example of relevant overheads
Floor area of cost centre	Heating of factory, rent of factory
Value of non-current assets	Insurance of assets, depreciation of assets
Number of machine hours worked	Power costs, repair costs
Numbers of employees	Staffing costs

In each case we would compare the size of the cost centre by whatever basis of apportionment had been selected to the overall size of the cost centres in total. For example, if factory rent was £100,000 for the business and one cost centre accounted for approximately 25 per cent of the floor space in total, then if using floor area as the basis of apportionment, we would apportion £25,000 (25 per cent of £100,000) of the factory rent overhead costs to that cost centre.

Reapportionment of overheads

Before we can absorb the overheads into the cost units of the business we will need to engage in further apportionment of overheads. The overheads which were apportioned to the service cost centres will need reapportioning to the production cost centres. The service departments of the business exist to support the production departments, so logically it is appropriate to transfer the overheads apportioned to the service cost centres to the production cost centres. This process of reapportionment is also known as secondary apportionment.

How service cost centre overheads are reapportioned will depend on the nature of the service cost centres – that is, what function the cost centre performs. It is possible that each service cost centre performs work for the other service cost centres – a situation known as reciprocal servicing. However, it is also possible that the service cost centre performs work for another service cost centre which is not reciprocated. In an assessment question, the relevant situation will be made clear. It now makes sense to look at an example of how overheads are apportioned and reapportioned.

Example 7.3

Rand Ltd produces steel pipes for industrial use. There are three stages to the production of a steel pipe:

1 cutting;

2 moulding;

3 assembly.

There are also two departments providing services: storage and maintenance. Each of these five departments (the three production stages and two service departments) represents a cost centre of the business.

Overhead expenditures for the year ended 31 December 2014 are as follows:

	£
Rent and rates	90,000
Lighting and heating	36,000
Asset depreciation	54,000
Asset maintenance	18,000
Total	198,000

The following information is available for the different departments.

	Value of non-current assets (£)	Floor area (m²)	Machine hours	Direct labour hours
Cutting	60,000	5,000	200,000	10,000
Moulding	72,000	8,000	50,000	25,000
Assembly	100,000	10,000		25,000
Storage	50,000	4,000		
Maintenance	18,000	3,000		
Total	300,000	30,000	250,000	60,000

The overheads will be apportioned on the basis which appears most relevant to the nature of the overhead. For example, using floor area as the basis for apportioning rent would mean that for the cutting department we would be apportioning as follows:

$$\frac{\text{Cutting dept floor area}}{\text{Total floor area}} = \frac{5,000 \text{ m}^2}{30,000 \text{ m}^2} \times \text{£90,000} = \text{£15,000}$$

We would repeat this process for each of the cost centres and for each of the overheads. The overheads would therefore be apportioned as follows:

Overhead	Basis of apportionment	Total £	Cutting £	Moulding £	Assembly £	Storage £	Maintenance £
Rent and rates	Floor area	90,000	15,000	24,000	30,000	12,000	9,000
Lighting and heating	Floor area	36,000	6,000	9,600	12,000	4,800	3,600
Asset depreciation	Machine hours	54,000	10,800	12,960	18,000	9,000	3,240
Asset maintenance	Value of asset	18,000	3,600	4,320	6,000	3,000	1,080
		198,000	35,400	50,880	66,000	28,800	16,920

As mentioned earlier, we need to know how to deal with the overheads from the service departments. In this example, the service cost centres do not provide work for each other and therefore are to be reapportioned to the production cost centres as follows:

- Storage department – on the basis of labour hours;

- Maintenance department – on the basis of machine hours.

The reapportionment of these overheads would therefore appear as follows:

Overhead	Basis of apportionment	Cutting £	Moulding £	Assembly £	Storage £	Maintenance £
Total overheads after first stage of apportionment		35,400	50,880	66,000	28,800	16,920
Storage overheads	Labour hours	4,800	12,000	12,000	(28,800)	
Maintenance overheads	Machine hours	13,536	3,384			(16,920)
Total overheads after reapportionment		53,736	66,264	78,000	0	0

Overheads have now been apportioned to the production cost centres. It is now time to absorb these overheads into the cost units of the business.

Absorption of overheads into cost units

The principle of absorption costing, you may remember, is to include the direct costs of production and the indirect costs of production as well. Now that the cost centres have had overheads allocated and apportioned into them, we can begin to transfer these overheads into the individual cost units.

The absorption of the production cost centre overheads into each cost in it is achieved by deciding on a basis on which an overhead absorption rate (OAR) will be calculated. This basis will depend on the nature of the firm's production methods. It is usually based on either machine hours or labour hours, but there are other bases that could be used to calculate this OAR. Once the basis has been decided, the overhead absorption rate can be calculated and then the cost unit can have the 'correct' amount of overheads charged to it – a process known as overhead recovery.

To calculate the OAR we will therefore need the following information:

● overheads to be absorbed for the total period;

● the basis used for the calculation of the OAR;

● the total number used for the period from the basis decided upon (eg total machine or labour hours for the period).

The basis chosen is usually the one that seems most appropriate for the department concerned. If the production cost centre covers the work of a department which incorporates a large proportion of machine work, the machine hours' basis may be appropriate for the OAR. Alternatively, if the department in question is largely performing work of a labour-intensive nature, the direct labour hours completed in that department would probably be the most appropriate basis of the calculation of the OAR.

In our example we can see that the cutting cost centre is largely machine intensive (200,000 hours out of 250,000 hours in total), which makes the machine hours' basis the most appropriate. The assembly department uses no machine hours, which means that the labour hours' basis is the most appropriate. For the moulding department, either machine hours or labour hours could have formed the basis. For the purpose of this example we will use the machine hours as the basis for the OAR calculation.

Calculation of overhead absorption rates

$$\text{Cutting dept} = \frac{\text{Cutting overheads}}{\text{Machine hours}}$$

$$= \frac{£53,736}{200,000} = £0.27 \text{ per machine hour}$$

$$\text{Moulding dept} = \frac{\text{Moulding overheads}}{\text{Machine hours}}$$

$$= \frac{£66,264}{50,000} = £1.33 \text{ per machine hour}$$

$$\text{Assembly dept} = \frac{\text{Assembly overheads}}{\text{Direct labour hours}}$$

$$= \frac{£78,000}{25,000} = £3.12 \text{ per direct labour hour}$$

The relevant overheads can then be added on to the cost unit depending on how many hours are taken in each department.

Example 7.4

Using the OAR data calculated for Rand Ltd we can calculate the following job. An order was received for 500 steel pipes. The costing data for this order is as follows:

	£
Direct costs per steel pipe	
Direct materials	4.50
Direct labour	6.00

The job passes through each of the production departments as follows:

	Machine hours	Direct labour hours
Cutting	200	70
Moulding	350	90
Assembly		110

The cost of this particular job would then be calculated as follows:

		£
Direct costs:		
Materials	500 × £4.50	2,250.00
Labour	500 × £6.00	3,000.00
Indirect costs:		
Cutting overheads	200 hours × £0.27	54.00
Moulding overheads	350 hours × £1.33	465.50
Assembly overheads	110 hours × £3.12	343.20
Total cost	500 steel pipes	6112.70

Underabsorption and overabsorption of overheads

The calculation of the OARs will almost always be based on budgeted information. The budgeted overheads for a business will probably form the basis of these calculations. This, of course, is a necessity – how can a firm know exactly how much the overheads will amount to in advance of them actually occurring? Both the total for overheads and the basis used for the OAR are likely to be estimates (ask yourself, can one accurately predict how many hours a machine will be used in each department, or how many labour hours will be spent?). Data on overheads and timings will only really be known by the end of the period and therefore it will be too late to calculate the rate at which overheads are to be recovered within the cost units (how overheads are to be absorbed).

Smaller businesses, especially those not facing intense competition, may set their selling prices charged to consumers on the basis of a cost-plus approach. This is where the selling price will be based on the total cost of a particular order plus a certain pre-set percentage as the 'profit' on that order. This allows a firm to ensure that it is always covering its costs and that each order does generate a profit. However, if we are using budgeted data for the absorbed overheads, it is possible that a business will either charge too many overheads, or not charge enough.

It is highly unlikely that a firm will be able to absorb exactly the correct amount of overheads over the entire period. This means that a firm is likely to either underabsorb or overabsorb its overheads (ie either not recover the full amount, or charge more than those actually incurred). It is probably more important for a firm, especially a smaller firm, that overheads are fully recovered:

- Underabsorption means that the amount of overheads charged is less than those actually incurred.
- Overabsorption means that the amount of overheads charged is more than those actually incurred.

In the case of overabsorption, the excess charged would be corrected for by an addition to the net profit of the firm in the end of period's accounts (think about it – more has been charged over the period than was actually incurred). Likewise, the amount by which overheads are underabsorbed will appear as an expense in the year's profit and loss account owing to the shortfall between those charged for and those incurred.

Costing methods

As well as the decision on how to account for the overheads, a business will also select a method of costing which will depend on the scale of its operations and the nature of its business. The costing methods which are variable for a business are broadly split into two categories:

1 specific order costing;
2 continuous operation costing.

These categories of costing are further divided as shown in Figure 7.4.

FIGURE 7.4 Costing methods

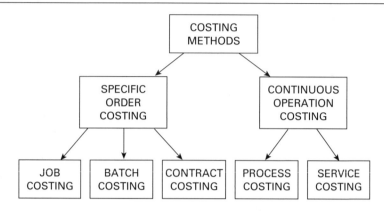

Specific order costing is appropriate when the work completed by the business consists of separate jobs, batches or contracts which are undertaken by the firm. Each piece of work being completed as a separate order will allow a business to calculate the cost of each job, to set a selling price and to calculate the overall profit to be earned.

Continuous operation costing applies to types of work which are produced in continuous operations or processes.

As the diagram shows, both specific order costing and continuous operation costing are subdivided. The sub-categories are as follows.

Job costing

This method of costing applies to a business which produces specific jobs at the request of customers. Each job is costed separately and will contain all the direct costs specific to that job. Overheads would be apportioned to each job as described in this chapter. Often the business will provide a quote for the customer in advance of the work being commenced. This will consist of the selling price of the job to be completed.

Batch costing

Some businesses will produce a number of identical products which form a batch of products. In effect, the batch is equivalent to one job and would be costed in exactly the same way as in job costing. The cost per batch can be subdivided so that the cost of a particular unit of output or product can be ascertained.

Job costing and batch costing are very similar and, in effect, batch costing is simply a specific type of job costing – one where the job consists of a number of identical products.

Example 7.5

Nutt Ltd produces clothing for the retail trade. A small retail store, 'Fashion Craze', has approached Nutt Ltd for a quotation to supply them with a bulk order for 50 pairs of leather trousers.

The following information is estimated:

Materials	£10 per pair
Direct labour:	
Cutting	£6 per hour
Sewing	£8 per hour
Processing	£5 per hour

Each pair of trousers will require 1 hour of cutting, 2 hours of sewing and 30 minutes of processing.

Overheads are apportioned on the basis of £10 per pair of trousers completed.

A mark-up of 40% is added for profits.

A batch of 50 pairs of trousers would be priced as follows:

Batch cost: 50 pairs of leather trousers

		£
Materials	50 × £10	500
Direct labour:		
Cutting	50 × £6 × 1 hour	300
Sewing	50 × £8 × 2 hours	800
Processing	50 × £5 × 0.5 hour	125
Overheads	50 × £10	500
		2,225
Mark-up (40%)		890
Price to be quoted		3,115

Contract costing

This method will differ from job and batch costing in the following respects:

- It is likely to be of long duration – potentially spanning more than one reporting period.
- It is likely to be of high value – necessitating a formal contract between the business supplying the order and the customer.

This method is favoured by the construction industry and firms engaging in other large-scale projects, such as civil engineering projects.

When accounting for contracts, it is not appropriate to wait until the contract is completed if this is likely to be in the next accounting period. Attributable profit from a long-term contact should be included in the income statement for the year, if appropriate. This will be the profit on the work completed so far certified by the customer (eg on the approval of an architect) once a significant proportion (usually at least 35 per cent) of the contract has been completed. The customer is likely to pay in instalments based on completion of certain stages of the contract. If the contract is between 35 and 85 per cent complete, it is common practice to include a fraction ($^2/_3$ or $^3/_4$) of the profit calculated as the value of work certified so far less the cost of the work certified. This would be modified further if the customer has not yet paid in full for the value of work competed so far.

Example 7.6

Lamb Ltd is constructing a new college building for a local authority. The contact begins in 2014 and the price agreed for the college is £6 million. However, the college in unlikely to be completed until 2016 owing to extensive remedial work being necessary, and Lamb Ltd will incur the following costs:

2014	£1.8 million
2015	£2.2 million
2016	£0.8 million

The profit on the contract is estimated to be £1.2 million. This notional profit can be included as income if we make adjustments for the ongoing progress on the contract.

Imagine that, in our example, by 2015 the value of the work certified had been £4 million and the cost of the work certified so far was £3.8 million. If the amount Lamb Ltd has received so far for work certified totalled £3.6 million, attributable profit would be calculated as follows:

$$\text{Notional profit} \times \frac{2}{3} \times \frac{\text{Cash received on account}}{\text{Value of work certified}}$$

$$£200,000 \times \frac{2}{3} \times \frac{£3,600,000}{£4,000,000} = £120,000$$

Contract costing is favoured by the construction industry but will also apply to any large job undertaken. Given the size of the job it is usually outlined in a more legally binding contract, although each contract is likely to be different.

Process costing

Process costing involves the production of goods or services on a continuous, often mass-produced, level. The process rarely or never stops and as a result it is not appropriate to talk about the costs of a particular job. In process costing it is the costs involved in running the process that are costed. The total costs incurred in the running of the process are divided by the volume of output in order to give the cost per unit of measurement.

Example 7.7

A soft drinks manufacturer produces a cola-type drink which is sold to other retailers who sell the product under their own label. The costs incurred in running the process for one week total £60,000. Output during the average week totals 800,000 litres.
The cost per litre is £60,000/800,000 litres = £0.075 per litre (or 7.5p per litre).

If there are multiple steps involved in the process, the costs incurred in each step of the process would be carried forward and included within the costs of the next process.

Work in progress and process costing

It is not always the case that all goods costed under process costing are completed at the end of the period. Any products which are partially completed are referred to as work-in-progress. In this case, the costs for the period cannot be divided by the total number of finished products to give unit costs. Any products which are work-in-progress must be accounted for.

The method used to account for work-in-progress is to include them as equivalent finished goods based on how far proportionately along the production process these actually are and then adjusting for this. For example, if the work-in-progress goods were exactly halfway through the production process, they would be valued at the equivalent of 50 per cent of a finished article.

Example 7.8

Flower Ltd produces computer desks. The cost of making one desk has been calculated as follows:

	£
Wood	10
Labour	15
Overheads	5
	30

As at 31 December 2017, the business has 30 finished desks in stock, but also 20 desks which are estimated to be 75 per cent complete and 10 desks estimated to be 50 per cent complete.

The cost value of these desks would be as follows:

	£
Completed desks (30)	900
Desks 75% complete (20)	450
Desks 50% complete (10)	150
	1,500

Service costing

Costing for a service is similar to process costing. For a service provider there are no worries about valuing inventory and work-in-progress. However, service costing can be difficult if multiple services are provided by the same people or the same department.

In the case of a service provider, the business will need to decide how to measure the unit of service being provided. For example, a haulage company may judge the unit of service as the mile (or kilometre) provided. For example, a haulage company has annual costs of £2 million and annual mileage of one million. The cost per mile would be £2. However, this would be complicated if the firm was attempting to charge customers if there were specific costs incurred by some orders. For example, a common measurement used by haulage companies is tonne-miles (a modification of the distance travelled to incorporate the weight of any freight as well).

Activity-based costing (ABC)

Activity-based costing (ABC) is a fairly new approach to costing which emerged from the absorption costing principle of costing. The conventional approach to costing is to cost a product based on the combin... the direct costs and apportioned overheads which have been added on ... an overhead absorption rate. The OAR will usually be based on either dire... labour hours or machine hours. However, there are limitations of this approach.

Most modern manufacturing is largely conducted through automated production. The fixed overheads of the business are likely to be high in relation to the direct costs incurred. Apportioning overheads on a time basis does not take into account how these overheads actually arise.

Cost drivers

Costs incurred in modern manufacturing do not predominantly arise from labour or from time. A cost driver is an activity within the business which will cause an overhead to be generated. For example, a cost driver may arise out of a need to set up machinery for a new batch of products. If products are not homogeneous, appropriate machinery may need to be hired and existing machinery set up differently in order to produce this new batch. Similarly, the need to transport goods from one part of the production facility to another will generate costs. For example, the internal transport of materials from one warehouse to the factory may incur the charges associated with this transport. These cost drivers are driven by the activity of the business. It is these costs that would be included within the cost of each product. For example, a specialist product which requires the use of specialist machinery may be more expensive and the cost of the product should reflect this increased cost. This has nothing to do with time taken or labour costs, but is purely driven by the costs actually incurred.

Cost pools

Although each separate overhead cost could, in theory, be a cost driver, this is unlikely to be the case. There are overheads which arise from similar circumstances. For example, the setting up of new machinery may generate costs connected with a skilled engineering team as well as a safety inspection cost. In this case it would make sense to group these costs together into a cost pool. Likewise, costs associated with the purchase of materials, such as the ordering costs, the transport costs and so on, could be grouped together in the same cost pool.

Once overhead costs have been sorted into the respective cost pools, they can then be analysed in terms of what influences these costs, that is, what activity is the cost driver. Once the cost drivers have been established, they can be included within the cost of the activity. This is summarized in Figure 7.5.

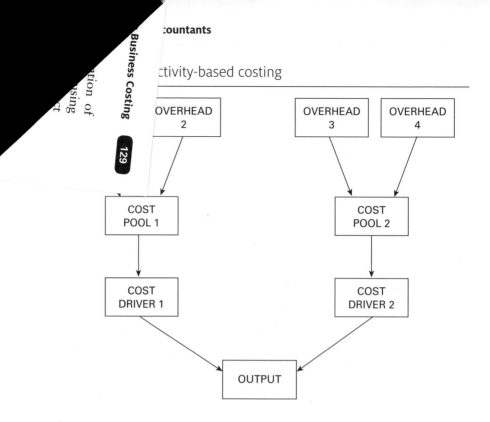

ABC evaluated

ABC is useful in that it will allow managers to see what activity is generating each cost. This can serve as a stimulus to reduce the costs that are incurred. For example, waste can be identified if costs arise that are not necessary for an activity to take place. Although ABC received plenty of positive publicity and attention in the 1990s, it has not grown especially in usage since this time. Reasons for the low take-up of ABC would include: ABC requires a lot of time and investment to set up as a costing system. This will not be cheap. In addition, there will be the time taken to educate people in implementing and running the new system as well as the time taken to transfer from the existing costing system. Students of accounting will have been brought up on the traditional approach to costing which they should know well. ABC will require these people largely to forget what they have learnt and study a new system.

There are overheads which are not specially driven by particular activities within the organization. For example, the rent of the factory facilities represents an indirect overhead of the business. However, this will be paid regardless of the level of activity. The time basis probably provides the best method of apportioning the overheads charged.

Target costing

This is not a costing method as such but an approach to costing which attempts to incorporate a marketing perspective into how a firm costs its products. The costing principle of absorption costing is very much based on the idea that the firm can dictate the price that it charges to its customers. The selling price will be determined only after we have arrived at the cost for a product. This is believed to be unwise and, in a competitive environment, is likely to lead to a business losing customers to a more price-conscious business which is perhaps more market than product orientated.

Target costing starts from the selling price of a product and works backwards to the cost of the product. For example, if the ruling 'market' price of a product is £100 and the firm wants to achieve a profit of £20 on each unit it sells, then the cost of the product cannot exceed £80 without either the price being higher than the current market conditions will allow, or the firm having to accept a lower profit margin.

By working backwards to the cost, this should lead to a more disciplined approach to controlling costs. Emphasis should be placed on the planning and design stage of a product to ensure that it can be produced within the cost constraints the firm imposes if it follows a target costing approach.

Life-cycle costing

This approach to costing looks at the costs and revenues of the product over the life of the product. A product will be profitable if, over its lifetime, it generates more in revenue than it incurs in costs. This does not mean that the product is always going to be profitable. There may be times when the product is priced at a loss – especially in the early years of a product's life. The costs incurred in the design and planning stages of a product are likely to be high. However, it is hoped that the product will be successful and will eventually bring in greater revenue than it incurs in costs.

Similarly, a business should consider life-cycle costing when the product is not a one-time purchase. In the case of men's razors or mobile phones, there is an initial purchase followed by extra costs in the form of replacement blades for the razor, or the contract costs of a mobile phone. In both cases, the costs of the product may exceed the initial selling price and therefore the firm incurs an initial loss on the sale. However, over time, the revenue that both products generate means that the original costs are exceeded by inflows of revenue.

Review questions

1 The following information relates to the production departments of Gadd Ltd:

	Welding Department	Processing Department
Direct machine hours	3,000	100,000
Direct labour hours	15,000	8,000
Cost of equipment	£20,000	£100,000
Floor area m²	4,000	12,000

The factory overheads for the year ended 31 December 2003 were:

	£
Business rates	50,000
Insurance of machinery	18,000
Machinery maintenance	6,000
Heating and lighting	10,000

(a) Prepare an overhead apportionment schedule apportioning the factory overheads to the appropriate departments. Use the headings shown:

Factory overheads	Basis of apportionment	Welding dept (£)	Processing dept (£)

(b) Calculate the overhead absorption rates for each production department. State the bases used and give one reason for your choice.

Solution

(a) Although we could use machine hours as a basis for allocating machinery maintenance costs, the answer provided has used cost of equipment – an equally valid approach:

Factory overheads	Basis of apportionment	Welding £	Processing £
Business rates	Floor area	12,500	37,500
Insurance of machinery	Cost of equipment	3,000	15,000
Machinery maintenance	Cost of equipment (*)	1,000	5,000
Heating and lighting	Floor area	2,500	7,500
		19,000	65,000

(*) You may have chosen the 'machine hours' for the basis of apportioning overheads from machinery maintenance. This would also be seen as an appropriate basis for appointment.

(b) Welding dept is labour intensive, therefore use direct labour rate for basis of OAR:

$$\frac{£19,000}{15,000} = £1.27 \text{ per direct labour hour}$$

Processing dept is machine intensive, therefore use machine hours for basis of OAR.

$$\frac{£65,000}{100,000} = £0.65 \text{ per machine hour}$$

2 The following information relates to the departments of Scaife plc for the year ending 31 December 2013.

	Production Dept		Service Dept
	Cutting	**Tooling**	**Administration**
Overheads	£28,800	£42,500	£18,600
Direct machine hours	4,750	8,240	
Direct labour hours	12,750	2,490	

The overheads of the service departments are allocated to the production departments on the following basis:

- cutting   75%;
- tooling   25%.

Calculate the overhead absorption rates for the Cutting and the Tooling departments. State the bases used and why.

Solution

	Cutting	Tooling	Administration
	£	**£**	**£**
Overheads	28,800	42,500	18,600
Service overheads	13,950	4,650	(18,600)
Total overheads	42,750	47,150	0

Absorption rates:

Cutting dept is labour intensive, therefore use direct labour hours.

Tooling dept is machine intensive, therefore use machine hours.

Cutting

$$\frac{£42,750}{12,750 \text{ hours}} = £3.35 \text{ per labour hour}$$

Tooling

$$\frac{£47,150}{8,240 \text{ hours}} = £5.72 \text{ per machine hour}$$

3 Jukes Ltd bases its job estimates on the following formulae:

Total cost = Prime cost plus 50% for overheads

Selling price = Total cost plus 30% for profit.

Estimates for job PW1 and for job JC2 are as follows:

	Job PW1	Job JC2
Direct materials (£5 per kg)	£400	£200
Direct labour (£8 per hour)	£160	£240

Calculate the selling price for each job.

Solution

Selling price:

	Job PW1	Job JC2
	£	£
Direct materials	400	200
Direct labour	160	240
Prime cost	560	440
Overhead	280	220
Total cost	840	660
Profit	252	198
Selling price	1,092	858

4 Parker Ltd bases its job estimates on the following formulae:

Total cost = prime cost plus 20% for overheads

Selling price = total cost plus 25% for profit.

Estimates for jobs SN18 and TY12 are as follows:

	Job SN18	Job TY12
Direct materials (£2 per metre)	£100	£150
Direct labour (£6 per hour)	£200	£250

Calculate the selling price for each job.

Solution

	Job SN18 £	Job TY12 £
Direct materials	100	150
Direct labour	200	250
Prime cost	300	400
Overhead	60	80
Total cost	360	480
Profit	90	120
Selling price	450	600

Marginal costing and decision making

08

Introduction

In the previous chapter on absorption costing we saw that the cost of a unit of output would be assumed to include not only the physical costs associated with the production of the unit – the direct or variable costs of production – but also the costs that were either only indirectly connected with the unit or which are fixed in relation to the level of output produced. The principle of absorption costing can be useful in that it attempts to ensure that all costs are covered so that the firm can hopefully generate an overall profit. However, there are problems in using this approach to costing.

We know that the methods chosen to apportion and absorb fixed and indirect costs into cost centres and cost units are arbitrary in nature and that there is never a completely satisfactory method of linking the indirect costs to cost units and cost centres. Even without this limitation, there are still times when a manager may find that the absorption costing approach provides misleading information.

An alternative approach to costing is the principle of marginal costing. **Marginal cost** is a term used to describe the overall change in the costs that result from the production of one additional unit of output. This approach is particularly useful for decision-making by managers of the business. Marginal costing as an approach to costing will be based on the idea that we only charge to cost units those costs that can be directly linked to the activities and costs generated by this extra cost unit, that is, only the direct and the variable costs of production. Therefore, the only costs relevant are those costs which are directly affected by changes in the level of output.

Obviously, the fixed costs and the indirect costs of the business are still incurred and will still be paid. However, if we use the marginal costing approach, these fixed costs will not influence the decision-making process of the business in respect of costing and management decisions.

Contribution

Central to the usefulness of marginal costing for making decisions is the concept of contribution. Contribution is the difference between the selling price of output and the variable cost of that output. It can be calculated either on a unit basis or as a total amount:

Contribution per unit = Selling price – Variable cost of production per unit

Total contribution = Sales revenue – Total variable costs

In terms of what it means, it will help to think of contribution as the amount that each additional sale of a unit of output 'contributes' towards paying the firm's fixed overheads and, once these have been covered, how much each additional sale 'contributes' towards the profits. Contribution is not the same as profit, as it includes only the variable costs of production. However, once a firm has covered its fixed costs, each additional sale will contribute an amount to the overall profits of the firm exactly equal to the contribution per unit.

Note that we are now talking about variable cost of production. In effect, this is the same as the direct costs of production – those which vary directly with the level of production. Direct costs can be thought of as those which are related to a particular product or cost unit. Variable costs are, more generally, those costs relating to overall level of output. Within the marginal costing approach, the distinction between variable cost and direct cost is not critical and often these terms will be used interchangeably.

Uses of marginal costing

Marginal costing is often used for making decisions that cover the short-term time period. In the long term, all costs are, in effect, variable as the firm can always deicide to close down and therefore would not incur any costs at all – fixed or variable. However, although the fixed costs will still have to be paid in the short term, the firm will have control over the variable costs and can either increase or decrease these by making decisions about production levels.

There are a number of situations where the marginal costing approach will provide more useful information for decision making than the absorption costing approach. Situations where marginal costing proves useful would include the following:

- break-even analysis;
- devising an optimum production plan where resources are limited;
- deciding whether to make a product or to buy in the product instead;
- accepting an order at lower than the normal selling price;
- closing down either a branch or a segment of the business.

Break-even analysis

A firm will break even if it exactly covers its total revenue with its total costs. If revenue exceeds the total level of costs, a profit will be generated, and if revenue is lower than total costs, a loss will be generated. However, breaking even is often seen as an important stepping stone for businesses, especially in their early years when struggling to survive might be more important than earning substantial profits. As long as a firm can avoid making losses, breaking even is often seen as a bare-minimum target to be aimed for. In this case, the level of sales or output needed in order to achieve this break-even level will be useful knowledge.

Knowing how many units of output have to be produced and sold will give managers something to plan for in terms of organizing purchases of materials, knowing how much labour may be required, and whether or not the assets (eg machinery) of the business are adequate to reach this level of production. In order to calculate the break-even level of production, we need to introduce the concept of total revenue.

Revenue in the break-even model

In this simplified model, total revenue is the only income for the firm and arises out of the sale of output (goods or services). We assume a constant selling price and that the firm can sell all its output at this selling price. This gives us a total revenue curve which is presented in Figure 8.1.

FIGURE 8.1 Total revenue

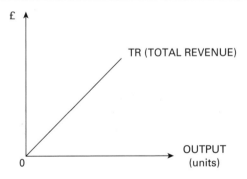

It is a simplifying assumption that the firm has a constant selling price. Most firms will actually change selling prices according to the circumstances. For example, a firm wanting to sell more output may have to consider reducing its selling price in order to attract more customers. However, in a competitive market it is more likely that a firm may be more constrained in setting its selling price.

Costs in the break-even model

In the break-even model, the costs of the business are considered to be either fixed costs or variable costs. Therefore the total costs of the firm in our simplified model will consist of both the fixed costs and the variable costs (which were defined in Chapter 7). A representation of total costs for a business is shown in Figure 8.2.

FIGURE 8.2 Total costs

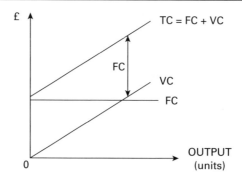

The total cost curve will not start at the origin. This is because at zero output the firm still has to account for the fixed costs incurred. Therefore the total cost curve will start where output is zero and the only costs incurred are those which are fixed by nature. As output increases, the total cost curve rises and this is due to the rise in the variable cost of production. Fixed costs are constant but as output rises the cost of that output leads to the upward-sloping nature of the total cost curve.

Break-even chart

The break-even level of output is shown in Figure 8.3. If we superimpose the cost curves and revenue curves on the same chart, we can see where the firm would reach its break-even output level. We can see that the total cost and total revenue curves eventually intersect. This intersection is known as the break-even point. This can be measured in two ways:

- break-even in terms of the output level – measured along the horizontal axis (shown as BEP);
- break-even in terms of revenue earned – measured along the vertical axis (shown as £*).

At the break-even point the total revenue is exactly equal to the total costs and the firm makes neither a profit nor a loss.

FIGURE 8.3 The break-even chart

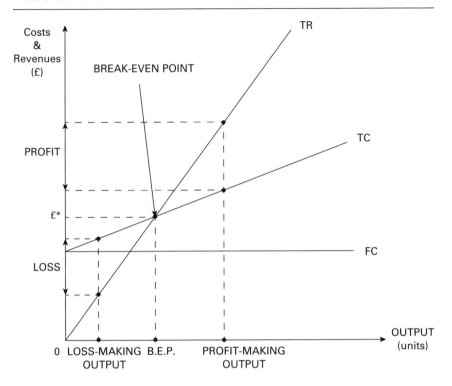

Using the break-even chart

As shown in Figure 8.3, the profit or loss earned by the firm at a given level of output can be measured by the 'distance' between the total cost and total revenue curve at any particular level of output. We can see that at low levels of output, the total cost curve is higher than the total revenue curve. This can be measured in financial terms on the vertical axis and the gap between the two curves would measure the loss at that output level.

Similarly, if we consider output levels in excess of the break-even point, the total revenue curve is higher than the total cost curve and, by measuring the distance between the two curves on the vertical axis, we can measure the profit earned by the firm. Obviously at the break-even point there is no gap between the curves as the total costs and total revenue are identical in size.

We can also factor in changes to the cost and revenue data to the chart. The effect of a change to the selling price will either steepen or flatten the slope of the revenue curve and will lead to a change in the break-even point. Similarly, a change in either the fixed cost or the unit variable cost will lead to changes in the cost curves. These can all be redrawn on the break-even chart.

Calculating the break-even output level

The break-even level of output will occur where the revenue earned covers both the variable cost for that level of production and the fixed costs. As long as the selling price is higher than the unit variable cost (ie there is a positive unit contribution per each unit sold), eventually the firm will always reach the break-even point as long as output is sufficiently high. At low levels of output, the contribution generated by the sales is unlikely to cover the fixed costs of the business. However, as output and sales rise, eventually this contribution will accumulate and eventually cover the fixed costs of the business. As sales rise above the break-even level, the firm will begin to generate a profit which will rise continually as output rises. This can be seen in a schedule of costs and revenues.

Example 8.1

Simper Ltd produces a single product which sells for £20. The product itself costs £12 to produce and fixed costs for the business are £50,000 per year. The following is a schedule of the costs and revenue of the business for varying levels of output.

Output (units)	Fixed costs (£)	Variable costs (£)	Total costs (£)	Total revenue (£)	Profit (£)
0	50,000	0	50,000	0	(50,000)
1,000	50,000	12,000	62,000	20,000	(42,000)
2,000	50,000	24,000	74,000	40,000	(34,000)
3,000	50,000	36,000	86,000	60,000	(26,000)
4,000	50,000	48,000	98,000	80,000	(18,000)
5,000	50,000	60,000	110,000	100,000	(10,000)
6,000	50,000	72,000	122,000	120,000	(2,000)
7,000	50,000	84,000	134,000	140,000	6,000
8,000	50,000	96,000	146,000	160,000	14,000
9,000	50,000	108,000	158,000	180,000	22,000
10,000	50,000	120,000	170,000	200,000	30,000

At low levels of output, the firm incurs a loss as the revenue is not high enough to generate sufficient contribution to cover the fixed costs of the business. However, we see that as output rises from 6,000 units to 7,000, the firm moves from making losses to generating profits, which rise as output increases. We can infer, therefore, that the break-even level of output is somewhere between 6,000 and 7,000 units.

The break-even level of output can therefore be ascertained by constructing a schedule of costs and revenues as above, or we can construct a break-even chart to ascertain the break-even level by graphical means. However, there is a more convenient method of calculating the break-even level of output by using the following formula.

If we assume that the break-even point is where Total cost (TC) = Total revenue (TR), we can substitute both terms as follows:

$$TR = \text{Selling price (SP)} \times \text{Quantity sold (Q)}$$

and

$$TC = \text{Fixed costs (FC)} + \text{Variable costs (VC)}$$

We can simply fit the TC further as TC = FC + VC × Q (where VC is the variable unit costs).

In this case, the break-even point will be where SP × Q = FC + VC × Q. Rearranging this equation, we find that FC = SP × Q – VC × Q. Dividing both sides by Q, we arrive at the following: Q = FC / (SP – VC).

In other words, the break-even point (BEP) is found as follows:

$$BEP = \frac{\text{Fixed costs}}{\text{(Selling price} - \text{Variable cost per unit)}}$$

As mentioned earlier, we know that the denominator of the break-even formula includes the calculation for the contribution per unit sold. It might help to think that each extra sale will contribute towards paying the fixed overheads and therefore, eventually, the number of contributions generated by the sales will reach the level of the fixed costs and therefore the firm will break even.

The break-even point in output can also be expressed in terms of the revenue generated. This is found simply by multiplying the break-even level of output by the selling price:

$$\text{Break-even in money terms} = \text{Break-even in output} \times \text{Selling price}$$

Example 8.2

A business produces high-quality wooden dining tables. These are sold for £300 each and are made to order. Each table costs £140 to produce in terms of materials, labour and other variable costs. The fixed costs of this firm are estimated to be £60,000 for the first year.

We can see that each table sold contributes a total of £160 (£300 less £140) towards the fixed costs of the business. However, in order to see exactly how many tables it will need to sell we can use the break-even formula. The calculation is as follows:

$$BEP = \frac{£60,000}{(£300 - £140)} = \frac{£60,000}{£160} = 375 \text{ tables per year}$$

If the firm sells less than 375 tables a loss will be incurred for the year. If sales are higher than 375 tables, a profit will be earned. In terms of revenue, at the breakeven level of output, the firm will earn:

$$BEP = \frac{£60,000}{(£300 - £140)} \times £300 = £112,500$$

Margin of safety

A useful concept for business is that of the margin of safety. This measures the amount by which sales can safely fall without the firm incurring a loss. The margin of safety is measured as follows:

$$\text{Margin of safety (in units of output)} = \text{Current output level} - \text{Break-even output level}$$

This can also be expressed in percentage terms. The margin of safety expressed as a percentage of the current output level allows a firm to see how far sales can fall in percentage terms before losses occur.

Example 8.3

A newly opened milkshake bar sells shakes for an average price of £3.50 and they cost on average £1.90. If the fixed costs of this business are £3,000 per month, the break-even number of milkshakes to be sold will be:

$$BEP = \frac{£3,000}{(£3.50 - £1.90)} = 1,875 \text{ milkshakes per month}$$

If the shop is currently selling 2,000 milkshakes, the margin of safety would be 125 milkshakes. In percentage terms, this would be calculated as follows:

$$\text{Margin of safety (\%)} = \frac{125}{2,000} \times 100 = 6.25\%$$

In other words, sales can fall by up to 6.25 per cent each month before the firm makes losses.

Limitations of break-even analysis

Break-even analysis has a number of uses but is limited in several ways. Some of the limitations are as follows:

1 We have already mentioned that it is unlikely that the variable unit cost will be constant. This does not stop us calculating the break-even output level, but will make it more difficult than one simple calculation. Costs which are variable in nature – such as materials used in the production of output and the direct labour costs used in producing output – may not be constant per unit of output produced. For example, changes in labour productivity will mean that the output takes varying times to produce and, given that most workers are paid either a fixed salary or a time-related wage, the labour cost per unit will not be constant.

2 Again, as mentioned earlier, the assumption that the selling price will be constant is also unrealistic. Many firms will alter their selling price as a result of changing market and economic factors. New entrants to the market will often force the price down and may affect the expected sales levels. Even in a market without intense competition a firm will not be able to sell everything it produces. Some form of price discounting might be required to achieve a higher sales volume.

3 The assumption that all output produced is sold can often be highly unrealistic. This is possibly true for a firm operating in a market where the firm is small in relation to the size of the overall market.

However, the effect of competition is unlikely to mean that a firm can simply assume that all that is produced is sold.

4 The distinction between fixed and variable costs is not as easy as this chapter may have implied. Many costs will have both fixed and variable elements. For example, heating and lighting costs will incorporate some variable elements in terms of the costs of powering equipment, but will also include some fixed elements in terms of the costs of heating office space.

5 A fixed cost will only be fixed over a particular range of output. For example, rent of production facilities may be seen as a fixed cost. However, as output increases, the firm will eventually reach full capacity where no more output can be produced unless capacity is expanded – which may mean a higher rental charge.

6 If a firm is producing more than one type of product, it becomes very difficult to separate out the fixed costs individually. The fixed costs are related to the firm and not the product, therefore this makes it hard to include the fixed costs per product type.

Optimum production plans

It is possible that a firm will be unable to produce all the output it has planned to produce because there is a shortage of a particular input into the production process. Resources that are limited would include:

- specific raw materials;
- skilled labour;
- machine hours;
- lack of storage space.

The factor which is in short supply is known as a **limiting factor** or a **key factor**. The impact of this shortage is that the firm will have to reassess its production plans. For a firm which produces only one type of product, the shortage may simply lead to lower output levels. However, if the firm produces a range of products, it will need deicide on the new output levels for its products within its full product range. The marginal costing approach will assist in devising the **optimal production plan** – the level of output which maximizes the firm's profits.

The basis on which the production plan is devised is to consider which of the firm's products maximizes contribution per unit of the scarce resource used. The scarce resource should be allocated to that product until the demand for it is satisfied. At that point, the scarce resource should be allocated to the product with the second-highest contribution per unit of the scarce resource, and so on. This may result in the firm having to discontinue (temporarily if the shortage is not expected to continue indefinitely) a product in its range, or it may just mean that one or more products have to experience cuts in planned production levels.

Example 8.4

Emery Ltd manufactures three models of garden greenhouse:

● standard model;

● economy model;

● deluxe model.

All three types include the same type of aluminium. The aluminium costs £5 per square metre.

The following is a unit cost statement for each type:

	Standard £	Economy £	Deluxe £
Selling price	80	55	120
Direct materials:			
Glass	11	7	15
Aluminium	12	10	25
Direct labour	15	8	20

Sales for May 2015 are expected to be:

● standard model: 1,000 greenhouses;

● economy model: 1,200 greenhouses;

● deluxe model: 1,000 greenhouses.

Owing to a shortage of aluminium, the suppliers have stated that they can only deliver 6,000 m² to cover production during May 2015. This means that the management will have to alter their production plans, which will influence the level of sales of the various types of greenhouse. All greenhouses produced in each month are sold.

We can use marginal costing to calculate the most profitable production pattern based on this shortage:

1 Contribution per greenhouse is calculated as follows:

	Standard £	Economy £	Deluxe £
Glass	11	7	15
Aluminium	12	10	25
Direct labour	15	8	20
Total direct costs	38	25	60
Selling price	80	55	120
Contribution per unit	42	30	60

2 The amount of the scarce resource (aluminium that each unit of output requires):

	Standard £	Economy £	Deluxe £
Aluminium cost per unit	12	10	25
Aluminium usage per unit (cost/£5)	$2.4\,m^2$	$2\,m^2$	$5\,m^2$

3 Calculate the contribution per square metre of aluminium. This is the contribution per greenhouse sold, divided by the amount of aluminium used in each greenhouse:

	Standard £	Economy £	Deluxe £
Contribution per unit	42	30	60
Usage of aluminium per unit	$2.4\,m^2$	$2\,m^2$	$5\,m^2$
Contribution per m^2 of aluminium	17.50	15	12

4 Therefore the ranking in order of priority should be:

Standard	Economy	Deluxe
1	2	3

To produce the planned output for May we would need the following quantity of aluminium:

	Planned level of output	Amount of aluminium per greenhouse	Total aluminium needed
Standard	1,000	$2.4\,m^2$	$2,400\,m^2$
Economy	1,200	$2\,m^2$	$2,400\,m^2$
Deluxe	1,000	$5\,m^2$	$4,000\,m^2$

As we have only 6,000 m^2, available, we should aim to produce the following:

Standard: 1,000 greenhouses – this leaves 3,600 m^2 available.

Economy: 1,200 greenhouses – this leaves 800 m^2 available.

There is not enough aluminium to produce 1,000 Deluxe greenhouses, and we will only produce:

$$800\,m^2/5\,m^2 = 160 \text{ Deluxe greenhouses}$$

Although marginal costing proves useful in providing the most profitable production pattern, the results it gives should always be treated with caution. It is possible that it is in a firm's interest to ignore the most profitable production pattern and concentrate on producing a full range of its products.

Consider the example of a firm producing high-prestige crockery; in this case, customers are less likely to buy individual bowls, individual plates and so on, and are more likely to want to buy these only in a matching set. Therefore, it would not make much sense if, owing to a scarce resource, the firm discontinued one of its product range in order to maximize profits. Doing so might lead to further losses of sales as customers can no longer buy a complete set of crockery. Producing a full range of its products might still be the best way of maximizing profits despite marginal costing telling us otherwise.

Make-or-buy decisions

A firm may be faced with the choice of whether to make a product itself or to buy in the product from an outside supplier. The product may be the finished good, which is then sold on by the firm, or may be an intermediate good which the firm will use in the production of a final product. In these decisions, the firm can usually produce the good for a lower cost than the cost of buying in the product. However, there will be fixed costs associated with the 'in house' production of the goods, which may represent a major investment if the production of the goods is going to go ahead. Once a firm is engaged in the production of a product, it would have to consider carefully any decision to cease production and to buy in the product from an outside supplier.

Marginal costing can help in this type of decision as it is the marginal cost of each unit of production which will be compared to the price offered by the outside supplier. If the price quoted by the supplier is lower than the marginal cost of production, the firm may wish to consider whether or not it is worthwhile ceasing production in its own facilities and purchasing the output from the outside supplier. In addition, the impact of closing down at least part of the production facilities may also result in the saving in those costs not directly related to production. For example, if production ceases, the rent of factory space or insurance of production machinery may no longer be necessary expenditure.

Of course, a decision to cease production should not be taken lightly. A supplier may be willing to offer a product for a price slightly lower than the current marginal cost but the decision to close down production may end up backfiring. The trust placed in this supplier that any goods supplied would be of a sufficient quality, could be reliably delivered on time and would be available at the same price for at least the medium term would have to be very high to make such a decision.

Example 8.5

Lucas runs a small firm that makes dining room tables. The tables are largely handmade and in a year the following costs are expected to be incurred in the production of 500 tables:

	£
Direct materials	50,000
Direct labour	30,000
Factory overheads: Fixed	6,000
Factory overheads: Variable	4,000
Selling and distribution costs	8,000
Administration costs	8,000
Total	106,000

Each table is sold for £300. All of the administration costs are fixed, whereas it is estimated that 50 per cent of the selling and distribution costs are fixed.

A supplier has offered Lucas the chance to buy in tables which would be made to Lucas's specification but could be supplied to him for £200 each. This would give Lucas the chance to close down his production facilities and allow him to concentrate on the selling and marketing of the tables. Would you advise Lucas to accept the offer to buy in the tables or to continue production?

Initially, the purchase of tables from the outside supplier might be look like a good idea. The average cost of a table is £212 (£106,000/500 tables). However, this decision requires us not to use the average total (or full) cost, but the marginal cost of each table.

If the decision is to be made on financial grounds alone, we should be comparing the marginal cost of each table with the price offered by the outside supplier.

Based on the information we are given (which was based on the total of 500 tables), the marginal cost of each table would consist of the following:

	£
Direct materials	100
Direct labour	60
Factory overheads: Variable	8
Selling and distribution costs	8
Total	176

In most cases, the cost per table is taken as the total cost divided by 500. However, only half of the selling and distribution costs would be included as half of this type of expenditure is not connected with the production of tables (ie it is fixed). The administration costs are fixed in nature and therefore do not count towards the marginal cost.

As we can see, the marginal cost of producing each table is £176. This means that the price quoted by the outside supplier is actually higher than the 'cost' of making each table. Therefore, on financial grounds alone we would recommend that Lucas rejects the offer. However, there may be other issues to consider.

By ceasing production, Lucas may be able to claw back some of the other indirect costs incurred by his firm. In this case, the decision of whether to make or buy in the tables would depend more on how many tables Lucas expects to sell.

For example, if, by buying in the tables, all the fixed factory overheads and half of the administration overheads can be saved, we can calculate the profit under each scenario. Based on the sale of 500 tables, the profits would be as follows:

	Continuing production £	Buying in from supplier £
Sales revenue	150,000	150,000
Buy-in costs		100,000
Administration costs		4,000
Selling and distribution costs		4,000
Total costs	106,000	108,000
Profit	44,000	42,000

As we can see, the profit of the firm is £2,000 lower if Lucas continues to produce the tables for himself. Therefore he should turn the offer down.

There are wider issues that should be considered as well when deciding whether to make or buy, such as:

- if the outsider supplier can match the quality of output that Lucas expects;
- whether the outside supplier can deliver the tables on time and to order;
- whether customers would be just as happy buying the tables that are now made by another firm;
- if there are any additional costs connected with this order;
- if the supplies will be guaranteed at this price in the long term.

Special order decisions

Marginal costing can also be used in the case of deciding whether or not to accept a special order. The special order is normally a one-off order for the firm's output but at below the normal selling price. Although it may appear to be not a good idea for a firm to be willing to sell output at a lower than normal price, it is often financially profitable if this special order is accepted.

The decision of whether to accept this special order can be decided by a combination of both financial (quantitative) and non-financial (qualitative) factors. It is normal to establish the case for making a decision on the special order in financial terms first, and then the wider issues would be considered before arriving at the final decision.

In terms of financial assessment, the key variable to consider is the amount of contribution that the special order would generate. This means that if a firm has costed its products using full or absorption costing, we may need to disaggregate the data so as to find out the marginal cost of production.

As mentioned earlier, financial considerations will provide the justification for accepting or rejecting the special order. However, there are wider issues which may outweigh the financial considerations which should be taken into account when making such a decision:

- If regular customers find out that the firm has accepted an order at lower than the normal selling price, they may respond by demanding a similar price discount, and threaten to withdraw their custom if they are not offered this discount. Although these extra orders may generate positive contribution towards the profits of the firm, the assumption was made that the fixed costs have already been covered by regular customers paying the full price. If all sales were made at this lower price, the firm could find itself making a loss or having to sell many more products in order to cover the fixed overheads.

- Spare capacity may be able to be utilized for the special order. However, if normal 'full price' sales have to be turned down because of lack of spare capacity, the firm will be worse off financially. Firms will need to ensure that there is sufficient capacity to make this special order and also that by moving closer to full capacity output the firm doesn't start utilizing factors which are less productive than those currently being utilized. For example, as the firm gets closer to operating at full capacity it may notice that the costs begin to rise as it uses less productive machinery, or less productive staff. Obviously, we can only base the financial aspect of the decision on the data we are presented with, but this factor should be monitored.

- Accepting this special order may lead to this new customer becoming a repeat customer. As long as the firm can avoid the continuation of the discount offered for the first sale, accepting the order may provide a long-term boost to future profits.

- Unforeseen costs may be incurred by the accepting of this special order.

- These additional costs may lead to the special order not being as profitable as initially anticipated.

Example 8.6

Alec Powell runs a small firm that produces ornate wine racks for customers. These are high-quality products and Powell has gradually built up a reputation for high-quality output. Each wine rack sells for £50.

A Spanish buyer, Ramadal, wants to import the wine racks for sale in her domestic market. She believes that market conditions would dictate a lower selling price and has offered to buy 500 wine racks from Powell at a price of £35 each.

Powell is unsure whether or not to accept this order as it is for a price significantly lower than his normal selling price. His data below are based on the planned production level of 10,000 wine racks per year:

	£
Direct materials	12.00
Direct labour	8.50
Variable overheads	2.50
Fixed overheads	6.00
Selling and distribution costs: Variable	4.00
Selling and distribution costs: Fixed	5.00
Total cost	38.00

Initially, the order looks, on financial grounds, an unwise one to accept. Each wine rack has a unit cost of £38, which implies that Powell would lose £3 on each wine rack sold to Ramadal. However, the £38 cost includes those costs that are not part of the marginal cost of producing a wine rack. Hence, we should look at the marginal cost of producing each wine rack. This would be as follows:

	£
Direct materials	12.00
Direct labour	8.50
Variable overheads	2.50
Selling and distribution costs: Variable	4.00
Marginal cost of each wine rack	27.00

Here we can see that each wine rack sold would help to generate additional contribution to Powell's profits. This order would generate an extra £8 × 500 = £4,000 contribution towards the overall profits of the firm. Therefore, based on the financial information given, the order should be accepted.

However, Powell should consider other issues, such as:

- Could he have sold these 500 wine racks in his domestic market at the normal selling price of £50? If he could, he will be losing out on the contribution that could have been earned from these sales. The 'lost' contribution that could have contributed to profits if the wine racks had been sold domestically would total £7,500 (the difference in contribution of £50 – £35 multiplied by the 500 units).

- The special order may generate additional fixed costs such as extra administration or extra transport costs which would eat into the contribution earned. Changes in the exchange rate may lead to a lower amount of revenue collected, depending on whether he asks for the price in the domestic currency or the foreign currency.

- Regular customers may not be happy if they hear about the apparent price reduction being offered by Powell, though it would be difficult for others to find it, given that these are sold in another country. Powell may find that this order could lead to future sales in the Spanish market or perhaps even further afield.

Closing down an unprofitable business segment

Marginal costing can be used to compare the profitability of a particular business segment. The segment referred to could be a particular product sold by a firm, or a department of a firm or even a branch of the overall business.

Analysing the business profits by segment is not an unusual concept to grasp. Analysis of each distinct segment within the business will allow managers to take action if part of the business does not seem to be performing as well as other parts of the business. For example, a producer of confectionery would probably analyse profits earned by each separate item of confectionery offered. Any items which are not performing as well as others would be monitored and action could be taken either to improve the item's profitability if possible, or to discontinue the product if it was felt that the decline in (or lack of) profits was unlikely to be arrested.

The analysis of each segment could be done in terms of the profits of each segment. However, given that profits will include deductions for both direct and indirect costs, we should be careful when using the profits of a particular segment in order to make recommendations on whether or not to close down a segment which is loss-making.

Example 8.7

Clayton runs a small chain of greengrocers. There are three branches open in the same town. The overall business is profitable but Clayton is concerned with the performance of the Batemoor branch which is run by his least experienced store manager. He is considering whether or not to close down this branch if it continues to be loss-making. Analysis of the profits of each branch is provided below:

	Appleby £	Batemoor £	Compton £	Total £
Sales	130,000	80,000	90,000	300,000
Direct materials	40,000	30,000	35,000	105,000
Direct labour	35,000	28,000	27,000	90,000
Rent	7,000	6,000	5,000	18,000
Selling and distribution costs	11,700	7,200	8,100	27,000
Administration costs	14,000	11,200	10,800	36,000
Total expenses	107,700	82,400	85,900	276,000
Profits (Losses)	22,300	(2,400)	4,100	24,000

The materials, labour and rental expenses are all directly connected with the activities of each individual branch. However, both selling and distribution costs and administration costs are indirect in nature and have been apportioned to each branch on the following basis:

Selling and distribution costs – apportioned on the basis of the sales earned by each branch;

administration costs – apportioned on the basis of the labour costs of each branch.

Clayton wants your advice on whether or not to close down the Batemoor branch.

The advice given to Clayton can be analysed in terms of what would happen to the profits of the business if the Batemoor branch was closed down. If the selling and distribution and administration costs are indirect in nature, these will be unaffected by the closure of one branch and would still be incurred in the full amount.

If we analyse the performance of each branch by contribution made, we can see what would happen:

	Appleby £	Compton £	Total £
Sales	130,000	90,000	220,000
Direct materials	40,000	35,000	75,000
Direct labour	35,000	27,000	62,000
Rent	7,000	5,000	12,000
Total direct costs	82,000	67,000	149,000
Contribution	48,000	23,000	71,000

Once we subtract the indirect costs, we can see the overall impact on the profits of the business:

	£
Total contribution	71,000
Total indirect costs	63,000
Profit	8,000

We can see that the projected profits of the business with the closure of the Batemoor branch would fall from £24,000 to £8,000. This would suggest that the closure of the Batemoor branch is not a good idea.

The confusion could have been avoided if we had analysed each branch in terms of the contribution each makes towards the indirect costs and to the overall profits of the business. The original table of data is now presented again with only direct costs deducted from the sales revenue:

	Appleby £	Batemoor £	Compton £	Total £
Sales	130,000	80,000	90,000	300,000
Direct materials	40,000	30,000	35,000	105,000
Direct labour	35,000	28,000	27,000	90,000
Rent	7,000	6,000	5,000	18,000
Direct costs	82,000	64,000	67,000	213,000
Contribution	48,000	16,000	23,000	87,000

We can see that the Batemoor branch makes a positive contribution of £16,000 towards the overall profits of the business. If this branch is closed, this contribution would no longer be generated and profits would fall by this £16,000.

What has confused the issue is the focus by Clayton on the profits earned by each branch, which are partly determined by an arbitrary apportionment of indirect costs which would be paid regardless of whether the branch closed or remained open. No doubt, we could find another method of apportioning these indirect costs that would give data which suggest that the Batemoor branch should remain open but makes one of the other two branches 'loss-making' and an apparent drain on business resources.

In general, as long as a business segment is making a positive contribution it should not be closed. In our example, we would want to know whether or not any savings would be made in the indirect costs of the firm if the Batemoor branch was closed. It is likely that these would be reduced to some extent. For example, the administration costs of the firm are likely to be reduced if the firm operates with two rather than three branches. However, in order to improve the overall profits of the business, the savings in indirect costs would have to outweigh the lost contribution before such a move could be justified.

Clayton would, of course, be unwise to make any snap judgement on the basis of one year's profit data. It is perfectly possible that one branch may periodically perform poorly. Even if the branch had made a negative contribution it may still be worthwhile keeping open. The objectives of the business may be more concerned with maximizing market share in the local community, or the low profits achieved by one segment may be expected to recover in the next year or two.

Marginal and absorption costing compared

Both costing principles, absorption and marginal, are concerned with determining the cost of a unit, or number of units, of output. They will give different results though, owing to the inclusion of overhead expenditure in absorption costing and the exclusion of these overheads in marginal costing. The uses of these two distinct approaches to costing are as follows.

Absorption costing

This approach to costing will attempt to ensure that all costs incurred in production are included within the costs of output. Setting prices based on absorption costing will help to ensure that all costs are covered and that a profit is made. For example, a restaurant that prices its meals by only looking at the cost of waiting staff, the ingredients and the cooking costs would probably make a loss unless the price was set significantly above these direct costs.

Using an absorption costing approach is appropriate for the valuation of inventories. IAS 2 stipulates that the cost of inventory should include the direct costs and a fair portion of overhead expenditure incurred by the firm in the production of output.

Disadvantages of absorption costing

As discovered, there are no completely accurate ways of apportioning overheads. Even the 'best' methods of apportioning overheads will not produce a completely accurate result in costing a product. Conversely, a firm which does not pick appropriate methods of apportioning overheads can find it has misleading information relating to the costs of its products. If selling prices are based on this misleading cost, the firm may find it cannot sell its output or that the price is too low to generate a profit. Absorption costing is ill-suited for making one-off decisions such as those covered earlier in this chapter.

Marginal costing

This approach includes only the direct and variable costs of production when costing a product, which means that all indirect overheads connected with production are kept separate and are not included in the cost of a particular unit of output. This means that this approach is less time consuming and easier to complete. There are no arbitrary decisions as to which costs to include.

Marginal costing is useful for decision making, such as the decision on whether to accept a special order and, in general, for one-off decisions that are likely to be unique to particular situations.

Disadvantages of marginal costing

If marginal costing is used for price setting, there is a danger that the price will be set too low and all costs will not be covered. Contribution and profit are not the same, even though they will move in the same quantities. In addition, not attempting to include overhead expenditure into the unit cost of production may lead to these costs drifting and becoming harder to control owing to them being lumped together and not factored into decisions in the same way as direct costs. IAS 2 does not permit marginal costing to be used for valuation of inventory.

For profit statements drawn up under marginal and absorption costing, there will be some minor differences. Although the overall profit will be the same under each system, how the costs are stated will be different. Under absorption costing, the closing inventory will be higher, which would mean that the 'gross profit' will be different under each system (unless operating and closing inventories are identical). In a marginal costing statement, the direct and indirect costs would be separated out so as to give both a gross profit and a net profit on production. For absorption costing, all costs would be grouped together.

Review questions

1   A product costs £3 to produce and sells for £8. If fixed costs are £2,500, produce a schedule of costs, revenue and profits for an output range of 0–600 units.

Solution

Output (units)	Fixed costs (£)	Variable costs (£)	Total costs (£)	Total revenue (£)	Profit (£)
0	2,500	0	2,500	0	−2,500
100	2,500	300	2,800	800	−2,000
200	2,500	600	3,100	1,600	−1,500
300	2,500	900	3,400	2,400	−1,000
400	2,500	1,200	3,700	3,200	−500
500	2,500	1,500	4,000	4,000	0
600	2,500	1,800	4,300	4,800	500

2   Oliver Saunders manages a sandwich stall in town. He estimates that his costs in producing the sandwiches are as follows:

	£
Bread	0.20
Sandwich fillings	0.80
Packaging	0.10

His fixed costs per week are as follows:

	£
Rent of stall	100
Advertising	30
Wages	200

The average selling price of a sandwich is £2.60. Calculate how many sandwiches need to be sold each week in order for Oliver to break even.

Solution

$$\text{BEP} = \frac{(£100 + £30 + £200)}{(£2.60 - £1.10)} = 220 \text{ sandwiches}$$

3   Will Pierce sells organic vegetable boxes, which cost on average £4.80, for an average price of £8. The fixed costs of his business are £26,800 per year. He is currently selling 10,000 boxes per year. Based on this data, calculate the following:

(i)   break-even level in number of boxes;

(ii)   margin of safety in output;

(iii) margin of safety as a percentage of current sales.

Answer

(i)   8,375 boxes (from the break-even formula);

(ii)   1,625 boxes;

(iii) 16.25%.

4 Fowler Ltd manufactures a range of products. One type of product is interactive whiteboards for schools and colleges. Data relating to the costs for October 2014 are as follows:

		£
Direct materials		30,000
Direct labour		15,000
Manufacturing overheads:	Fixed	5,000
	Variable	7,000
Selling and distribution costs	Fixed	15,000
	Variable	12,000

The fixed costs are factory specific and are not specially related to the output of whiteboards. Planned output for October is 500 whiteboards. Each whiteboard is sold for £300.

A foreign supplier has offered to supply Fowler Ltd with the whiteboards for £150.

(a) Produce financial data which assess the case for discontinuing production and buying in the whiteboards from the foreign supplier.

(b) Outline three factors which would suggest that Fowler Ltd should continue to produce whiteboards regardless of any cost savings that could be made in the short term.

Solution

(a) Marginal cost of each whiteboard is as follows:

	£
Direct materials	30,000
Direct labour	15,000
Variable manufacturing overheads	7,000
Variable selling and distribution costs	12,000
	64,000
Cost per whiteboard (= £64,000/500)	128

Based on this data Fowler should buy whiteboards instead of producing them.

(b) Possible factors to be considered would include:

- extra fixed costs associated with the buying in of whiteboards;
- guarantee that the current price offered by suppliers is to remain fixed beyond the short term;
- loss of employment and negative publicity;
- spare capacity generated could be utilized for other productive means.

5 Hinds Ltd, as part of its product range, produces the 'SILVTO'. This product normally sells for £160. The following costs are associated with its production:

	Cost per unit £
Direct materials	34
Direct labour	75
Variable overheads	12
Fixed costs	25

The directors have recently received a request from a Latvian company offering to purchase 2,000 SILVTOs at a price of £140 each. Advise them as to whether they should accept or reject the Latvian offer.

Solution

The marginal cost of each SILVTO is as follows:

	Marginal cost per unit £
Direct materials	34
Direct labour	75
Variable overheads	12
	121

Each SILVTO sold to the Latvian company would generate £19 of extra contribution (£140 – £121). Overall profits would be increased by £19 × 2,000 = £38,000.

On financial grounds the order should be accepted. However, the following must also be considered:

● Are there any extra fixed costs associated with the order?

● Would the Latvian firm re-export the SILVTOs to the UK?

● Is there any chance of upsetting the firm's regular customers who pay £160?

● Could it lead to future sales in Latvia or the Baltic (perhaps at the normal selling price)?

6 Hawkins Ltd manufactures three types of wheelbarrow. These wheelbarrows are designated as A1, A2 and A3. All three types of wheelbarrow use the same grade of skilled labour and the wage rate of this labour is currently £6.50 per hour.
The following is a unit cost statement for each type:

	A1	A2	A3
	£	£	£
Direct materials	5	6	8
Direct labour	9	12	11
Other direct costs	3	2	5
Selling price per unit	25	32	28

The company plans to produce 5,000 of each wheelbarrow in March 2014. However, owing to a shortage of skilled labour, there are only 15,000 hours of skilled labour available.

(a) Calculate the most profitable production pattern to follow, given to the shortage of skilled labour.

(b) Show the number of each type of wheelbarrow that should be manufactured.

Solution

	A1	A2	A3
	£	£	£
Selling price per unit	25	32	28
Direct materials	5	6	8
Direct labour	9	12	11
Other direct costs	3	2	5
Total direct costs per wheelbarrow	17	20	24
Contribution per wheelbarrow	8	12	4
Hours used per wheelbarrow	1.38	1.85	1.69
Contribution per hour of labour	5.78	6.49	2.37

Ranking of wheelbarrows is as follows:

1 A2

2 A1

3 A3

To produce 5,000 A2, we need 5,000 × 1.85 hours = 9,250 hours.

This leaves (15,000 – 9,250) 5,750 hours.

To produce 5,000 A1, we need 5,000 × 1.38 hours = 6,900 hours (not enough hours left).

Therefore, we can only produce 5,750/1.38 = 4,166 A1 wheelbarrows.

No A3 wheelbarrows can be produced.

Standard costing

09

Introduction

In order to control costs incurred for labour, materials and overheads a firm should have some basis for comparing the actual costs with some established yardstick. With a basis of comparison established, the expected level of expenditure can be determined in advance of a production period. Without any frame of reference it would be difficult to ascertain whether or not expenditure was too high, lower than expected or just about at the right level. Standard costing is the technique used by firms in order to facilitate the comparison of actual expenditure with standard costs.

Standard costs

In order to compare the efficiency of a firm in controlling its own level of expenditure we use the technique known as **standard costing**. This will involve comparing the actual results of expenditure for a period with the standard cost, which represents a level of expenditure that would be expected for the same period.

In order to use standard costing to help control expenditure and prevent inefficiencies developing, it would make sense not simply to focus on the overall level of expenditure. Standard costs will be set for categories of expenditure within an organization and for each of these categories a standard cost will be set. This standard will be determined by what costs would be expected to be incurred in the production of output. This will include:

- the costs of materials measured by the price per unit of materials multiplied by the quantity of materials used in each unit of output;
- the cost of labour included in each unit measured by the time taken in direct labour hours multiplied by the hourly wage rate;

- an amount of overheads to be apportioned to each unit of output using a suitable overhead absorption rate.

In arriving at the standard cost to be used as the basis of comparison with actual costs it may be useful to consider that we don't always have agreed standards which are universally accepted. The following standards may be used for the basis of comparison.

Basic standard

This standard would be seen as an overall standard cost which remains the same over a period of time. However, given that this is often a charging standard, it is seen as not a good basis for comparison as the basic standard cost may provide out-of-date information.

Current standard

This is likely to be a more up-to-date standard used for comparison. It may be the result of utilizing the most recent prices quoted for the purchases of materials and the current wage rates. This will mean that this is commonly used as the basis for comparison with actual costs incurred.

Ideal standard

This represents the lowest cost possible in producing output. The ideal standard would imply no wastage at all of materials, workers completing their work in the shortest time possible, with perfect efficiency in all aspects of production. As expected, this standard is not realistic in terms of the likelihood of it being achieved.

Attainable standard

This standard is achievable and realistic. The attainable standard should represent what is currently achievable but at the same time be based on a high level of efficiency. Attainable standards should provide a challenge for workers in that they should not be set too low, such that they impose no incentive to work productively, but should not be too high, such that they demotivate workers, with the standard being seen as closer to an ideal standard. Most firms using standard costing will use a standard which is both current and attainable.

Standards used should be updated based on comparison with actual results. Obviously, if actual costs incurred in the production of output are repeatedly higher than the standard cost for the same level of output, action will need to be taken. This overshoot of expenditure could be the result of inefficiencies in production but could also be the result of inappropriate standards being set. To prevent standards being ignored and being seen as demotivating, they should be reviewed in the light of actual results. This is summarized in Figure 9.1.

FIGURE 9.1 Reviews of standards by comparison with actual data

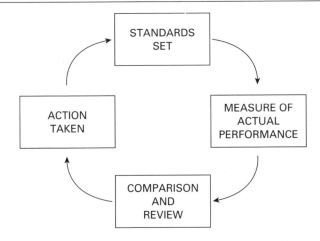

Variance analysis

Once the standards for costs have been set, it is possible for the firm to use these data by comparing the standard cost that would be expected to be incurred with the actual costs incurred by the firm in the provision of the product or job. This comparison is known as **variance analysis**, the variance in this case being the difference between the standard costs and the actual costs incurred.

The calculation of the difference will provide data which managers may choose to act upon. For example, if the firm notices that it continually incurs higher costs in production than the expected standard cost, managers may focus on whether the standard cost has been set at too low a level or whether there is inefficiency within the production process that needs to be acted on.

When calculating variances it is common to refer to any variance that arises as one of the following:

- **adverse** – where the firm is financially in a worse position than was to be expected;
- **favourable** – where a firm is financially better off than was to be expected.

We prefer to use the terms adverse (often abbreviated as simply 'A') and favourable (abbreviated as 'F') rather than a positive or negative number as this clarifies whether the variance would be a particular cause of concern. This use of adverse and favourable is more useful when we consider that we are dealing not just with cost variances but also with revenue variances.

Types of variance

It would not be particularly helpful for managers attempting to investigate the potential reasons for adverse cost variances if the only data available were the standard total cost and actual total cost. It is normal, when conducting a variance analysis, to break down the costs of production into the various components that make up the cost. The common areas for variance analysis will therefore include:

- materials cost;
- labour cost;
- variable overhead;
- fixed overhead.

In addition, it is possible that a manager might want to investigate the reasons why profits for the business or for a part of the firm's operations differ from those expected. In this case, the variances for sales revenue could also be calculated to see if this could explain a variance in the profits of the business.

Sub-variances

It is also possible to subdivide the variances mentioned above into sub-variances. These are a further calculation which attempts to give more detailed data on why a variance has arisen. These sub-variances are divided into:

- price variances – the unit price paid for a particular resource;
- volume variances – the quantity of resources used for a particular activity level.

The analysis of the sub-variance will provide information which may then be acted on as it begins to isolate the reason why the budgeted and actual amounts differ.

Materials variances

Materials variances measure the difference between the standard cost for materials and the actual cost incurred by the business. The following variance calculations are relevant here:

- total materials cost variance – the overall difference in materials cost;
- materials price variance – the variance arising from a difference in the unit price paid;
- materials usage variance – the variance arising from a difference in the quantity of materials used.

We can see how these variances would be calculated with the following example.

Example 9.1

In producing one unit of product A21, the following standard cost for materials has been set:

$$20 \text{ metres} \times £7.00 \text{ per metre} = £140.00$$

However, recent production data show that the firm is using 24 metres @ £5.50 per metre in the production of one unit:

Total materials variance = Actual materials cost – Standard materials cost

Actual materials cost	Standard materials cost	Materials cost variance
20 × £7 = £140	24 × £5.50 = £132	= £8 (Adverse)

The materials sub-variances are calculated as follows:

Materials price variance
= (Actual unit price – Standard unit price) × Actual quantity used
= (£7 – £5.50) × 24
= £36 (Adverse)

We should have expected an adverse sub-variance as the actual unit price paid for materials was higher than the standard unit price for materials.

Materials usage variance
= (Actual quantity used – Standard quantity) × Standard unit price
= (20 – 24) × £7
= £28 (Favourable)

Given that a lower volume of materials was used in the production of the A21 unit than the standard quantity, we would expect the materials usage variance to be favourable.

A useful way of verifying your calculations is to total the two sub-variances. This requires us to go against the earlier advice and treat the adverse variances as negative numbers and the favourable variances as positive numbers. In our example, this would give us £28 – £36 = –£8. This figure should match the one calculated for the overall total variance – which it does.

Labour variances

These variances measure the difference between the standard cost for labour and the actual costs incurred for labour. The three relevant variances are as follows:

- **total labour cost variance** – the overall difference between actual and standard cost;
- **wage rate variance** – the variance arising out of differences in the actual and standard wage rates;
- **labour efficiency variance** – the variance arising out of the differences in the actual and standard amount of time taken for a particular operation.

Example 9.2

Data relating to standard labour cost of one unit of product BZ5 is as follows:

$$800 \text{ hours @ £5.00 per hour} = £4,000$$

The management have observed that the actual labour costs incurred in the production of one BZ5 are 750 hours at a wage rate of £6.00 per hour.

Total labour variance = Actual labour cost – Standard labour cost

Actual labour cost	Standard labour cost	Labour cost variance
$750 \times £6 = £4,500$	$800 \times £5 = £4,000$	$= £500 \text{ (Adverse)}$

The labour sub-variances are calculated as follows:

Wage rate variance
= (Actual wage rate – Standard wage rate) × Actual time (in hours)
= (£6 – £5) × 750
= £750 (Adverse)

We should have expected an adverse sub-variance as the actual wage rate was higher than the standard wage rate.

Labour efficiency variance
= (Actual hours – Standard hours) × Standard wage rate
= (750 – 800) × £5
= £250 (Favourable)

Given that less time was used in the production of the BZ5 unit than the standard amount of time, we would expect the labour efficiency variance to be favourable.

We can see that the total of the individual sub-variances for labour is also equal to the overall labour variance.

Flexible budgets

You may assume that a favourable variance is always to be welcomed and an adverse variance should always be seen as a worrying sign that needs to be acted on. This is not necessarily the case. An adverse cost variance indicates that the firm is spending more on a particular area of production than the standard cost for that area. However, if the higher actual cost is the result of higher output and higher sales levels, this might not be a cause for concern. The goal of higher sales and higher profits may be taken as one of the main aims of the business. The higher output necessitated by the higher sales volume will inevitably lead to higher costs incurred in the production of these extra units of output. If these sales were unexpected, the extra costs incurred in the higher production would lead to adverse variances in production costs.

This creates an issue if the adverse variance caused by higher sales is treated as a sign of failure and attempts are made to reduce expenditure. This would create the perverse incentive of trying to eliminate the adverse variance by reducing the sales level – and potentially lower profits (of course, the ideal situation may be to generate higher sales revenue through higher selling prices instead of higher sales volume, but this is a side issue we will ignore for the moment). One way of dealing with this problem is through the use of flexible budgets.

A flexible budget would adjust the data used for the calculation of the variances in line with the actual level of output. The data for the budgeted quantities used would need to be calculated so that the budgeted output was the same level as the actual output. This means we are comparing 'like with like' – the budgeted quantities used for the standard cost can be more meaningfully compared with those actual costs incurred.

Example 9.3

The manager of a business has budgeted to produce 600,000 units of output in 2017. The standard quantities for this budgeted output level are as follows:

Materials (metal)	450,000 m²
Materials (fabric)	200,000 m²
Labour	50,000 hours

If actual output fell short of budgeted levels and was 40 per cent less than expected, at 360,000 units of output, we should 'flex' these standard quantities to match the actual output level. This will mean reducing the standard quantities by 40 per cent, which gives us the following:

Materials (metal)	270,000 m²
Materials (fabric)	120,000 m²
Labour	30,000 hours

It is important to know which variances will be 'flexed' when undertaking a flexible budget. As long as budgeted output and actual output levels differ, standard quantities will need adjusting. This means that total variances will need restating in terms of the flexed quantity, and volume variances will also need adjusting. However, price variances, such as the wage rate variance, will not need flexing as these do not use standard quantities in their calculations.

Example 9.4

For the following business, the data relating to the production of one unit is as follows:

Standard materials cost = 4 kg at £3.00 per kg = £12 per unit

Standard labour cost = 2 hours at £5.00 per hour = £10 per unit

If the budgeted output level is 500 units, the standard cost would be as follows:

	£
Materials (2,000 kg)	6,000
Labour (1,000 hours)	5,000
Total	11,000

Details of actual production for the forecast period were as follows:

		£
Materials	2,050 kg at £2.80 per kg =	5,740
Labour	960 hours at £5.10 per hour =	4,896
Total		10,636

Actual output was 450 units.

Although the total cost of £10,636 is lower than the standard cost of £11,000, the actual output was lower than the budgeted output, which means we will need to redraft the budgeted quantities in the light of the actual output. These are as follows:

Materials 450 units × 4 kg = 1,800 kg × £3 = £5,400

Labour 450 units × 2 hours = 900 hours × £5 = £4,500

The variances can now be calculated as follows:

Materials (total) = £5,400 − £5,740 = £340 (A)

Materials price = (£2.80 − £3) × 2,050 = £410 (F)

Material usage = (1,800 − 2,050) × £3 = £750 (A)

Labour (total) = £4,500 − £4,896 = £396 (A)

Wage rate = (£5 − £5.10) × 960 = £96 (A)

Labour efficiency = (900 − 960) × £5 = £300 (F)

Sales variances

We can also calculate the variances on the sales revenue for the firm. This will enable managers to analyse changes in the actual sales revenue from the budgeted sales revenue. As with the materials and labour variances, the sub-variances for sales can also be calculated.

Example 9.5

Budgeted sales are expected for the next trading period to be 4,000 units of product JB12 at an expected selling price of £24 per unit. However, actual results for the period were sales of 4,600 units which generated revenue of £87,400.

Total sales variance
= Budgeted sales revenue – Actual sales revenue
= 4,000 × £24 (£96,000) – £87,400
= £8,600 (A)

Sales volume variance
= (Actual volume sold – Budgeted volume of sales) × Standard price
= (4,600 – 4,000) × £24
= £14,400 (F)

Sales price variance
= (Actual selling price – Standard selling price) × Actual sales volume
= (£19 – £24) × 4,600
= £23,000 (A)

In this example, we can see that although a higher sales volume was achieved, the overall sales revenue fell owing to these extra sales being achieved with a lower selling price. In the study of economics, the responsiveness of the sales volume to changes in the selling price is referred to as the price elasticity of demand. How 'price elastic' a product is can be used to assess how far a change in the selling price will lead to an improvement or worsening of sales revenue. In our example, we can see that the fall in price did not lead to an improvement in sales revenue (hence the total sales variance being adverse).

Overhead variances

If we are going to consider the variances arising out of labour and materials expenditure, it also makes sense to calculate and analyse any variances that arise out of overhead expenditure. We will consider variances arising for:

- variable overheads;
- fixed overheads.

To calculate an overhead variance we would need to know the appropriate overhead absorption rate. This will either already be present in an assessment question or will require calculating. This will often be based on the labour hours. Overhead variances can be split into various types of variance. These are as follows:

- expenditure variances;
- efficiency variances;
- volume variances (only where fixed overheads are present).

Variable overhead variances

The variable overhead variances are calculated as follows:

- Variable overhead expenditure variance
  = (Actual hours worked × OAR) – Actual variable overheads.
- Variable overhead efficacies variance
  = (Standard hours worked – Actual hours worked) × OAR.

Fixed overhead variances

For fixed overheads we would need to use a separate OAR calculated on the basis of fixed overheads for the period. Again, this is likely to be based on labour hours. For fixed overhead variances we have another variance, referred to as the volume variance. The volume variance will arise when there is a difference between the planned level of activity and the actual level of activity. This variance illustrates the extent to which fixed overheads are under- or over-recovered based on the actual amount of production being lower or higher than the budgeted level of output. If actual output is lower than the budgeted level of output, the fixed overheads absorbed into the level of output will have not been totally recovered and this variance will be adverse. It is calculated as follows:

- Fixed overhead expenditure variance
  = Budgeted fixed overheads – Actual fixed overheads.
- Fixed overhead volume variance
  = (Actual hours worked × OAR) – Budgeted fixed overheads.
- Fixed overhead efficiency variance
  = (Standard hours worked – Actual hours worked) × OAR.

Example 9.6

The following data are available for a firm which manufactures one type of product:

	Per unit
Variable overhead	10 hours @ £2.50 per hour
Fixed overhead	10 hours @ £4.00 per hour

The OARs for the variable and fixed overheads were calculated on the basis of labour hours. Budgeted output for the period was 2,000 units.
Actual data for the period were recorded as follows:

- Output: 1,950 units

- Variable overheads incurred: £53,000

- Fixed overheads incurred: £77,500

- Actual hours incurred: 22,000.

We can calculate the variances for the overhead as follows:

Variable overhead expenditure variance = (22,000 × £2.50) − £53,000
= £2,000 (Fav)

Variable overhead efficiency variance = (19,500 − 22,000) × £2.50
= £6,250 (Adv)

Fixed overhead expenditure variance = (10 × £4 × 2,000) − £77,500
= £2,500 (Fav)

Fixed overhead volume variance = (22,000 × £4) − £80,000
= £8,000 (Fav)

Fixed overhead efficiency variance = (19,500 − 22,000) × £4
= £10,000 (Adv)

Interpretation of variances

Once calculated, managers may want to act on the data produced from the variance analysis. In order to do so, it helps to identify potential causes of these variances. It is not particularly helpful simply to state that the cause of, say, an adverse materials variance is due to a higher price being paid for each unit of the material used, as this is what the data tell us anyway. We should be looking for reasons that would explain the variance rather than simply restating the results of the variance.

Possible causes of particular variances would include the following:

Materials price variance	Materials usage variance
Different quality of materials used	Different quality of materials used
Limited supply/new supplier used	Different spoilage rates of materials
Exchange rate change affecting unit prices	Differently skilled labour used

Wage rate variance	Labour efficiency variance
Skills shortages pushing up wages	Differently skilled labour
Overtime wage rates being applied	Motivational factors
Changes in taxes on labour	Working conditions
Trade union pressure	Management styles adopted
Economic factors (eg level of unemployment)	Different machinery/equipment

Interrelationships of variances

We have considered the causes of the variances in insolation. However, a more sophisticated investigation into possible causes of variances might involve potential connections between separate variances. A variance that has arisen in one area of the business might have an effect on another variance, often in the opposite direction.

For example, an attempt to reduce expenditure on labour costs might involve reducing wage rates (or at least moderating their growth over time). The desired result of this would be a favourable wage rate variance (or at least a reduced adverse variance on the same measure). However, the reduced wage rate might have a negative impact on worker morale, which results in lower labour productivity and may lead to an adverse labour efficiency variance as workers take longer to complete tasks.

There may even be cases where an attempt to react to one variance affects a variance of another cost. A firm which experiences an adverse materials price variance might respond by switching to cheaper raw materials. However, with cheaper raw materials it is possible that the labour efficiency variance may 'turn' adverse as workers find it increasingly difficult to complete a job in the same time as in previous periods owing to inferior materials being used.

A reconciliation statement will explain why actual results are different from the budgeted results. We can reconcile actual and budgeted figures by using the variances that we have calculated to explain away any differences.

To show how this is completed, we need to calculate the set of variances based on budgeted data and the actual results.

Example 9.7

Moorcroft Ltd manufactures one product. The production budget for June 2016 shows the following costs per unit:

	£
Materials (£8 per kg)	4
Labour (£10 per hour)	15
	19

Budgeted sales for the month were 5,000 units at £100 each.

In July 2016, the management accountants compared the actual performance for the previous month and produced the following information based on actual sales of 5,000 at £80.

	£
Materials (3,600 kg)	27,000
Labour (10,000 hours)	95,000

	Budgeted profit		Actual profit	
	£	£	£	£
Revenue for June		500,000		400,000
Materials expenditure	20,000		27,000	
Labour expenditure	75,000	95,000	95,000	122,000
Profit for June		405,000		278,000

We can calculate the following variances for June 2016:

Sale price variance = (£80 – £100) × 5,000 = £100,000 (A)
Materials price variance = (£8 – £7.50) × 3,600 = £1,800 (F)
Material usage variance = (2,500 – 3,600) × £8 = £8,800 (A)
Wage rate variance = (£10 – £9.50) × 10,000 hours = £5,000 (Γ)
Labour efficiency variances = (7,500 – 10,000) × £10 = £25,000 (A)

The actual and the budgeted profits can be reconciled as follows:

Moorcroft Ltd
Reconciliation of budgeted profits
to actual profits for June 2016

	£	£
Budgeted profit		405,000
Sales variances:		
Sales price		(100,000)
		305,000
Material variances:		
Price	1,800	
Usage	(8,800)	(7,000)
		298,000
Labour variances:		
Wage rate	5,000	
Efficiency	(25,000)	(20,000)
Actual profit		278,000

1   Calculate the labour variances from the following data. Note that there is no need to 'flex' any budgeted figures in this example; you can assume that this has been done for you.

(1) Product H17	Standard hours to produce	95
	Actual hours to produce	86
	Standard wage rate per hour	£4.50
	Actual wage rate per hour	£5.25

(2) Product 128YT	Standard hours to produce	11.5
	Actual hours to produce	15
	Standard wage rate per hour	£7.50
	Actual wage rate per hour	£6.00

Solution

(1) Product H17	£
Wage rate	64.50 Adv
Efficiency	40.50 Fav
Total	24.00 Adv

(2) Product 128YT	£
Wage rate	22.50 Fav
Efficiency	26.25 Adv
Total	3.75 Adv

2 Calculate the materials variances from the following data. Again, there is no need to flex any data.

(1) Material ZX3	Standard price per kg	£7
	Standard usage per unit	14 kg
	Actual price per kg	£8
	Actual usage per unit	12 kg

(2) Material WE32	Standard price per litre	£3.25
	Standard usage per unit	113 litres
	Actual price per kg	£3.40
	Actual usage per unit	108 litres

Solution

(1) Material ZX3	£
Materials price	12.00 Adv
Materials usage	14.00 Fav
Total variance	2.00 Fav

(2) Material WE32	£
Materials price	16.20 Adv
Materials usage	16.25 Fav
Total variance	0.05 Fav

3 Thompson plc manufactures a single product. The budgeted costs per unit for the month of April 2014 were:

	£
Direct materials (£3 per kg)	6.00
Direct labour (£8 per hour)	20.00

Anticipated production for April 2014 was 10,000 units.

The actual results for April 2014 were:

	£
Direct materials (20,000 kg)	55,000
Direct labour (25,000 hours)	240,000

The actual costs were based on production of 9,000 units.
   Calculate the labour and materials variances.

Solution

Although the original budgeted total for materials would have been 10,000 units × 2 kg (£6/£3 per kg) = 20,000 kg, we would need to flex this total to match the actual level of output. Therefore the revised (flexed) budgeted materials total would be 2 kg × 9,000 = 18,000 kg.

Likewise, each unit requires 2.5 hours of labour (£20/£8 per hour). The original budget for labour hours = 10,000 × (£20/£8) = 25,000 hrs. The flexed budgeted total will be based on 2.5 hours × 9,000 units = 22,500 hours.

Material variances

Price actually paid per kg	= 55,000/20,000 = £2.75
Price variance	= (3 – 2.75) × 20,000 = £5,000 (favourable)
Usage variance	= (18,000 – 20,000) × £3 = £6,000 (adverse)

Labour variances

Actual wage rate	= £240,000/25,000 = £9.60
Labour efficiency variance	= (22,500 – 25,000) × £8 = £20,000 (adverse)
Wage rate variance	= (8 – 9.60) × 25,000 = £40,000 (adverse)

Budgeting

10

Introduction

A budget is a form of financial plan for the organization. Although we tend to think of budgets being expressed in monetary terms, this is not always the case. The budget can focus on any aspect of business activity. For example, a budget can be stated in terms of units of output that need to be purchased for future periods of time, or it can look at the production levels and sales levels measured as a level of physical output. A budget can even look at planning ahead for staffing levels in the sense that the number of hours of productive work time can be planned. The budget will relate to a future period of time and therefore will involve some form of prediction of quantities – either in financial terms or in some other unit of measurement.

It will be very hard for a business to operate without any form of budgeting, any attempt to plan ahead; even if a manager is considering the next few days or weeks for the activities of the business, budgeting will be needed. As a result, it is worth spending time on deciding how these budgets are set in the first place. The system of setting a budget can have an impact on both the quantifiable finances of the business (ie in the form of costs and revenues) and also the harder-to-quantity aspects of the business, such as staff motivation. Once a system has been set for budgeting, we should consider why we are budgeting in the first place – what is the purpose of budgeting? In this chapter we will consider both the system used to set budgets and the purpose of budgeting. We will also look at the actual appearance of some of the most common forms of budgets in action – how they would be constructed based on particular information.

Purpose of budgets

Budgets will take time to construct. The system used to set budgets for the organization will depend on a number of factors, not least the size of the organization. For a small business, the time taken in setting either an individual budget or a set of budgets may not be long, whereas for a large organization, perhaps located in many different areas, the process of setting budgets can be very time-consuming and therefore very costly. In order to justify the time spent on the construction of the budgets for an organization, the benefits gained must justify the costs incurred. The benefits that should be gained from setting budgets would include the following.

Forecasting

A budget will be based on a set of events that are expected to occur in the future. For a business planning its level of production, we would expect that it will have needed to forecast how many units it expects to sell. This will require a sales forecast. Obviously, no forecast can be expected to be entirely accurate. However, the accuracy of the forecast will be crucial in ensuring that the correct level of budgeted activity is planned. Sales forecasts themselves will depend on a number of different factors – with many of these outside the control of the business.

Sales forecasting will also depend on some factors within the firm's control, such as the pricing policy of the firm. In most cases, the level of sales varies inversely with the selling price. A firm can attempt to forecast the effect of a price change on the quantity of sales (in economics, this is often referred as a product's 'price elasticity of demand'). However, the effect on sales of a particular change in price will depend on action taken by the competitors of the organization. Factors outside the firm's control will include the state of the economy for the period in which sales are being forecast. For example, if economic growth is expected to be lower than at present, then the level of sales will normally be expected to be affected in a downwards direction. This is more complicated than it might seem. Again, the effect of the competition's actions will be important, but also the type of goods or service being sold by the firm. The demand for most goods will vary positively with the rate of growth of national income, with rising national income leading to greater levels of spending in an economy and a greater demand for goods and services. However, there are goods that do not respond in this manner. Some goods show very little variation in their demand with change in the level of national income. Some goods actually show a negative correlation with the level of national income – in other words, the demand for those goods (which are known in economics as 'inferior' goods – not a comment on their quality but just their relationship with changes in the level of national income) will increase in periods of slow or negative economic growth. Forecasts of the economic environment will therefore be important for predicting the level of sales for future periods. Obviously, the further away into the future, the less reliable the forecast. However, even over the short term economic forecasts can be unreliable, making a sales forecast vulnerable to being less valid.

Forecasting a sales level will also involve second-guessing how consumers will respond to a particular good. Market reach can shed some light on consumer motives. However, there is a danger that any attempt to forecast sales will be futile if consumer behaviour changes unexpectedly.

Seasonal factors will also impact on any forecast. The demand for most goods and services will vary over the course of a year. For retailers, there are peak sales periods depending on the type of goods produced. For the construction industry, the winter months are likely to lead to a significant decline in output. Bad weather conditions, which are almost impossible to forecast to any degree of accuracy other than seasonal variations, are also likely to affect the level of output.

In this section, we have looked at the difficulties of forecasting events. However, this should not detract from the central point that forecasting will be important in the setting of budgets. Just because events and their implications cannot be forecast with 100 per cent accuracy should not matter. The better the forecast, the better the budget. Firms with the necessary resources can make use of professional forecasts and reports. Smaller businesses will have to rely on forecasts gleaned from the media, and on extrapolation of existing trends.

Planning

Once a forecast has been made, the planning can begin. For example, a forecast may provide details on the level of expected sales. With this information, the managers of the business can begin to plan for this expected level of sales. The good or service being provided by the firm may have a long lead time in terms of production. The forecast will enable the firm to organize the purchase of materials in advance of any production needed. Even if the firm provides a service rather than a physical product, the forecast will enable the firm to plan for the correct level of staffing in order to meet this level of expected sales.

Planning will mean that the business can look ahead to ensure it has the necessary resources for the expected level of future activity. This will give the managers of the business a chance to anticipate problems in providing for the budgeted level of activity. For example, if a firm has forecast a certain level of sales, which it intends to produce, financing may need to be arranged. If a business offers generous credit terms to its customers, it may be some time before the money generated by the sales is returned to the business. In the meantime, overdraft facilities or some other form of short-term finance may need to be arranged. Staff may need to be hired, which, depending on the level of specialist skills the staff need, could be time consuming. New facilities or new equipment may also be needed. All of these things require adequate timing. Obviously the degree of confidence in the forecast will affect how far the managers of the business want to go in terms of planning for a level of activity. For example, a forecast that predicts a high level of sales may necessitate a significant expansion of the production facilities. If the confidence in the forecast is not particularly high, the managers of the firm may decide against providing for the expected sales level. As a result, businesses may plan for a range of different forecasts based on the expectations associated with a particular forecast.

Coordination

Without a system of budgeting, a manager within an organization may act in a manner which conflicts with the other areas of the business. For example, the work of the sales department may generate a level of sales which lies beyond the current capabilities of the production department or beyond the facilities available or which necessitates a certain level of sales. A coordinated budgetary system should help to ensure that actions taken by the different departments or functions within a business can take place with a more coherent, coordinated set of decisions. The initial budget will usually be set by the higher management of the organization and they can make the decisions as to where the priorities lie. Often the sales level is decided as the key factor from which other budgets will flow. However, this is not necessarily the case; the capacity of an organization or the limit on the finance available may act as the limiting factor before other budgets can be determined.

Control

A comparison between the budgeted data and the actual data can be made by the managers of an organization. A system of variances can be created (this is covered in Chapter 9). This can help a business to achieve control over costs and expenditure. This is often termed 'variance analysis' and involves a comparison between the actual outturn and the amount originally budgeted for. A department or area of the business may be consistently overspending. The monitoring of the amount actually being spent against the amount provided for in the budget can increase the ability of the business to control these costs.

The method used by a business in setting the budgets in the first place can provide a basis for controlling resources and costs within the business. For example, in some organizations, budgets are often set by comparison with previous budgets. This system of incremental budgeting is covered later in this chapter, but can be seen as a way of controlling expenditure if the firm uses gradual reductions in budgeted total for expenditure over time.

Motivation

Budgets act as a target to be met by the department or area of the business to which the budget is assigned. For example, if the allotted amount of expenditure for future periods is set at a certain level, the workers and managers might be motivated to work harder in order to achieve the set target of expenditure. If the level of expenditure allocated by the budget is seen as unduly tight (ie the cut in expenditure would be too difficult to achieve), the budget may actually act as a demotivator on those who are constrained in their activities by the budget. Likewise, if the budgeted total for expenditure is unduly lenient, it may not provide much of a challenge for those affected and this would not particularly motivate the workers within the organization to increase their efforts.

As a result, the budgeted totals need to provide a challenge for those responsible in that they need to set a level which can be achieved but which will provide a spur for workers to try harder than before in achieving the budgeted targets.

Types of budget

As stated earlier, the budgets of an organization can be set for any resource that the business is expecting to use over future time periods. Some of the more commonly used budgets are as follows:

- cash budget – also known as a cash flow forecast;
- sales budget – showing the expected sales by volume or value;
- materials budget – showing the materials needed for production over future time periods;
- production budget – showing the units of production to take place over future time periods;
- master budget – a full set of budgets – usually summarized by a cash budget and forecast income statement and balance sheet.

Some of these are explained in the following sub-sections.

Cash budget

The cash budget is one of the most common types of budget to be constructed by a business. Whatever the size of the business, the cash budget can provide useful information in terms of the management of the firm's cash resources.

The cash budget looks at the cash inflows into the business (usually from forecast sales) and the cash outflows of the business. Each cash flow is broken down into its component parts. The net cash flow of the organization can be measured for each successive time period (usually, but not necessarily, by week or by month). This will help the business to see if it has sufficient cash flow for future periods for the needs of the organization. For example, the expectation of a shortage of cash in a future period will enable a business to plan ahead. For smaller firms, the need for adequate cash flow is a key factor in the survival of a business. However, even for larger firms, the need for efficient usage of cash flow is just as important. For example, a cash budget might show that the business is building up reserves of cash which are not being used efficiently. This could help a manager to decide to whether to use the credit period being offered by a supplier or whether to pay immediately and benefit from a potential cash discount.

As a management tool, the cash budget can be useful, but, as with all budgets, the use of the budget will depend on the quality of the information present within the budget. Forecast data should have some degree of accuracy for the budget to be meaningful; this is no different from the cash budget.

The appearance of the cash budget can vary – as a management tool it does not need to follow a particular format, but most cash budgets will appear as follows:

	January	February	March	April	May	June
	£	£	£	£	£	£
Cash inflows						
Cash sales						
Receipts for credit sales						
Cash outflows						
Purchases						
Overheads						
Capital expenditure						
Drawings						
Net cash flow						
Opening balance						
Closing balance						

A cash budget is produced on a cash basis. This makes it different from an income statement which is produced on an accruals basis. This means that items will appear in the cash budget when they are expected to be paid or received in money terms. A credit sale will only appear in the cash budget when the money is received and not when the sale is made. Other differences between a cash budget and the income statement would be that the cash budget will not include any provisions that are deducted against profit in the income statement, such as for depreciation. However, items will appear on the cash budget that should not appear in an income statement. Capital expenditure and capital receipts will appear as cash outflows and inflows respectively because they involve money changing hands. For example, loan repayments and spending on non-current assets will both appear in the cash budget. Cash drawings taken by the owner will also appear, even though these are normally adjusted for on the balance sheet. These all appear in the following example.

Example 10.1

Ian Sharp is a sole trader who buys and sells electrical goods. The following data are forecast for the six-month period between 1 January and 30 June 2017:

	Purchases (£)	Sales (£)
Jan	1,200	4,500
Feb	1,400	4,800
Mar	1,300	6,000
Apr	1,400	6,200
May	1,500	7,000
June	1,800	8,000

Other information relating to cash flow is as follows:

- Sharp employs a part-time assistant whom he pays £500 each month.

- Overhead expenses are £800 per month and are paid when they are incurred.

- Sales are all on credit and customers take one month's credit.

- Half of the purchases are cash purchases and the other half are paid for one month later.

- A replacement van is to be purchased for £8,000 in March. A customer has been found for the old van, who will pay £1,500 for it in April.

- The balance at the bank on 1 January 2017 was £1,000 overdrawn.

Based on these data, the cash budget for the six-month period would appear as follows:

	Jan	Feb	Mar	Apr	May	Jun
	£	£	£	£	£	£
Cash inflows						
Receipts from credit sales		4,500	4,800	6,000	6,200	7,000
Sale of van				1,500		
		4,500	4,800	7,500	6,200	7,000
Cash outflows						
Cash purchases	600	700	650	700	750	900
Payments for credit purchases		600	700	650	700	750
Wages	500	500	500	500	500	500
Overheads	800	800	800	800	800	800
Purchase of van			8,000			
Drawings	1,500	1,500	1,500	1,500	1,500	1,500
	3,400	4,100	12,150	4,150	4,250	4,450
Net cash flow	(3,400)	(400)	(7,350)	3,350	1,950	2,550
Opening balance	(1,000)	(4,400)	(4,000)	(11,350)	(8,000)	(6,050)
Closing balance	(4,400)	(4,000)	(11,350)	(8,000)	(6,050)	(3,500)

As we can see from the forecast, the overdrawn balance on Sharp's bank account will persist over the entire six-month period. Sharp will need to ensure that he has adequate finance for the forthcoming months. The overdrawn balance does decrease from April onwards as the cash inflows outweigh the outflows.

If any of the variables on the budget were different from those forecast, the expected cash balance may be higher or lower than the budget suggests. In this example, Sharp should take care to plan for unforeseen circumstances, such as an unexpected bad debt which would worsen his cash balance.

Production budgets

Certain budgets will not be expressed in monetary terms but will be stated in the form of some other variable. The production budget will be expressed in terms of the number of units that the business expects to manufacture over forthcoming periods. This is often set once the level of budgeted sales has been set. Once expected sales are budgeted for, the business can then make plans and budget for the necessary amount of materials needed for production as well as ensuring that it has the workforce needed for production. If production involves a lengthy process, such as in the construction industry, it is important that resources are made available when they are needed. For example, if a firm needs to hire machinery for part of the production process, the cost of hiring should be minimized so that the firm incurs only the necessary expenditure. If the timing of the production process is not accurately forecast, the cost involved may be higher than is necessary.

In addition, when deciding on the production for a period of time, not only will expected sales be considered but also the expected levels of inventory held by the firm at the start of the period.

Example 10.2

Levinson Ltd is a small company producing heaters for hot-air balloons. The production manager has collected the following information in order to produce a production budget for the four months ended 30 April 2016:

- Production is completed in the month that it commences.

- Demand is expected to be 150 heaters in January. This is expected to fall to 100 in February but should rise by 25% in the following month and by 20% (on top of the earlier increase) in the next two months.

- Inventory at the end of each month is to be held at a level of 20% of the following month's sales.

- The inventory level at the start of January is 50 heaters.

Construct a production budget for the period ending 30 April 2006. Round up, if necessary, to the nearest heater.

Levinson Ltd Production budget for four months ending 30 April 2016				
Heaters:	**Jan**	**Feb**	**Mar**	**Apr**
Sales	150	100	125	150
Closing inventory	20	25	30	36
Inventory needed	170	125	155	186
Opening inventory	50	20	25	30
Production	**120**	**105**	**130**	**156**

(The sales for May are expected to be 180 units – a 20 per cent increase on April's sales; this figure is needed so that we can calculate the closing inventory figure for April.)

To calculate the number of units to be produced, we would look at the level of inventory at the start of the period and see how much was needed in addition to satisfy the sales requirement for that month as well as the buffer inventory needed for the end of the month.

This gives rise to the following calculation:

> Production for month
> = Sales + closing inventory – opening inventory (all in units)

In some cases, a firm will produce more than is necessary and stockpile goods or work-in-progress until they are needed. A firm may also decide to hold a reserve level of inventory in case of unforeseen circumstances – this is known as a buffer level.

When a firm is trying to minimize expenditure and the production process is lengthy and/or involves multiple stages in the production process, a useful management tool which can minimize unnecessary expenditure is critical path analysis. The critical path analysis for a production project involves analysing the different stages in the production process and deciding in what order in these various tasks would need to be completed. A critical path would be the tasks in the overall production that cannot be delayed without the risk of incurring extra costs.

Master budget

A master budget is the term used to describe the combined production of a cash budget accompanied by a budgeted income statement for the same period of time as well as a budgeted balance sheet for the date at the end of the forecast period.

The data used to construct the cash budget can also be used to produce the master budget. As stated earlier, the income statement will still be constructed on the accruals basis, whereas the cash budget is produced on the cash basis and this switching from one technique to the other can cause confusion.

Example 10.3

This example is based on the financial statements and budgets for a sole trader – I Yates – for the six months to 30 June 2018. Here is the balance sheet at the end of December 2017:

I Yates
Balance sheet as at 31 December 2017

	£	£	£
Non-current assets			
Premises			50,000
Equipment		20,000	
Less Depreciation		14,000	6,000
			56,000
Current assets			
Inventory	5,500		
Trade receivables	11,000		
Cash at bank	4,750	21,250	
Current liabilities			
Trade payables		9,000	12,250
Net assets			68,250
Capital			50,000
Add Net profit			25,000
			75,000
Less Drawings			6,750
			68,250

Additional information:

1 Sales and purchases are all on credit – with one month's credit being allowed by us and by our suppliers.

2 Expected sales and purchases are as follows:

	Jan	Feb	Mar	Apr	May	Jun
Sales (£)	15,000	24,000	29,000	34,000	34,000	36,000
Purchases (£)	12,000	18,000	20,000	26,000	28,000	35,000

3 The owner takes personal cash drawings each month of £500.

4 Wages and salaries amount to £2,400 each month.

5 Insurance of £100 is paid each month.

6 Overheads are £300 per month and are paid when they are due.

7 New equipment is purchased on 1 March 2007 for £6,000. Equipment is to be depreciated at 10% on cost – one month's ownership equals one month's depreciation.

8 Rent of £400 is received each quarter on 1 January and 1 April.

9 Inventory in trade on 30 June 2018 was valued at £5,700.

I Yates
Cash budget for six months ended 30 June 2018

	Jan £	Feb £	Mar £	Apr £	May £	Jun £
Cash inflows						
Receipts from trade receivables	11,000	15,000	24,000	29,000	34,000	34,000
Rent received	400			400		
Total inflows	11,400	15,000	24,000	29,400	34,000	34,000
Cash outflows						
Payments to trade payables	9,000	12,000	18,000	20,000	26,000	28,000
Wages and salaries	2,400	2,400	2,400	2,400	2,400	2,400
Insurance	100	100	100	100	100	100
Overheads	300	300	300	300	300	300
Drawings	500	500	500	500	500	500
Equipment			6,000			
Total outflows	12,300	15,300	27,300	23,300	29,300	31,300
Net cash flow	(900)	(300)	(3,300)	6,100	4,700	2,700
Opening balance	4,750	3,850	3,550	250	6,350	11,050
Closing balance	3,850	3,550	250	6,350	11,050	13,750

Points to note:

- The opening balance of cash at the start of January is taken from the balance sheet's cash at bank figure. The closing balance will then appear on the budgeted balance sheet as at 30 June.

- The receipts from trade receivables for January will be December's sales as seen on the balance sheet as at 31 December 2017.

- Likewise, the payment for trade payables in January will be found on December's balance sheet.

- The sales and purchases figures for June will not appear in the cash budget but will appear as trade receivables and trade payables on the balance sheet as at 30 June.

- Drawings appear in the cash budget but not in a budgeted profit and loss account.

The forecast set of final accounts will appear as follows:

I Yates		
Forecast income statement for six months ended 30 June 2018		
	£	£
Sales		172,000
Less Cost of goods sold		
Opening inventory	5,500	
Add Purchases	139,000	
	144,500	
Less Closing inventory	5,700	138,800
Gross profit		33,200
Add Rent receivable		800
Less Expenses		34,000
Wages and salaries	14,400	
Insurance	600	
Overheads	1,800	
Depreciation	1,200	18,000
Net profit		16,000

The depreciation provision is based on the following:

$$£20,000 \times 10\% = £2,000 \times 6 \text{ months} = £1,000$$
$$£6,000 \times 10\% = £600 \times 4 \text{ months} = £200$$
$$\text{Total depreciation} = £1,200$$

I Yates Forecast balance sheet as at 30 June 2018	£	£	£
Non-current assets			
Premises			50,000
Equipment		26,000	
Less Depreciation		15,200	10,800
			60,800
Current assets			
Inventory	5,700		
Trade receivables	36,000		
Cash at bank	13,750	55,450	
Current liabilities			
Trade payables		35,000	20,450
Net assets			81,250
Capital			68,250
Add Net profit			16,000
			84,250
Less Drawings			3,000
			81,250

Budgeting example

Budgets are linked together and do not stand in isolation. For example, once a firm has forecast a set or level of sales, it can then prepare a set of budgets based on the assumptions made within the sales budgets. This allows a firm to coordinate the other areas of the firm's activities, such as the production levels that will be needed for each period, and the level of purchases that will be needed to satisfy the production levels. From this, further details and further budgets will follow. If sales and purchases are made on credit terms, budgets for trade receivables and trade payables can be constructed. The cash budget shows the various inflows and outflows of money that will take place. This will enable a firm to ensure that it has adequate finance available. A change in the sales level would result in the other budgets being adjusted in line with the expected sales level.

Example 10.4

MacLeanan has started a business making wooden toys. These are sold on to retailers. The cost of producing each toy is as follows:

Production costs per unit	£
Direct materials	5
Direct labour	8
Direct expenses	2
	15

Labour costs are paid for in the month they are incurred, whereas materials are purchased on credit. Suppliers allow a two-month credit period. Materials are purchased in the month of production.

MacLeanan sells each toy for £40. Retailers are allowed credit terms. Half of each month's sales are given one month's credit and the remaining sales are received two months later. MacLeanan has forecast the following sales in terms of toys sold per month for the first seven months of 2014.

Units	£
Jan	220
Feb	260
Mar	300
Apr	320
May	340
Jun	320
Jul	280

MacLeanan ensures that there is inventory on hand at the end of each month equivalent to 25 per cent of the following month's sales in units.

In addition, MacLeanan has 40 units in stock on 1 January 2014.

Additional information relating to the last two months of 2013 is as follows:

November's sales	£2,000
December's sales	£2,500
November's purchases	£1,000
December's purchases	£1,200

Fixed overheads amount to £400 each month for January to March and then £700 thereafter. These are paid in the month that they are incurred.

MacLeanan is planning to purchase a machine which will help him to expand his capacity. This will cost £5,000 and will be paid for on 1 March 2014.

The balance at the bank on 1 January 2014 was £500.

The following budgets can be produced in relation to the above scenario.

Sales budget

This can be presented in terms of the sales by volume (number of units) or sales by value (in £).

Sales budget
for six months to 30 June 2014

	Jan	Feb	Mar	Apr	May	Jun
Sales (£)	8,800	10,400	12,000	12,800	13,600	12,800
Sales (units)	220	260	300	320	340	320

Production budget

The production budget would follow from this. As seen earlier, this is presented in terms of the units needed to be produced each month to satisfy both the sales level and any requirements in terms of closing inventory levels.

Production budget
for six months to 30 June 2014

(Units)	Jan	Feb	Mar	Apr	May	Jun
Sales	220	260	300	320	340	320
Closing inventory	65	75	80	85	80	80
Inventory needed	285	335	380	405	420	400
Opening inventory	40	65	75	80	85	80
Production	**245**	**270**	**305**	**325**	**335**	**320**

Purchases budget

Once the production budget has been constructed a firm can then ascertain how much and when the firm will need to purchase any raw materials. This will be expressed in terms of the value of materials purchased.

Purchases budget
for six months to 30 June 2014

	Jan	Feb	Mar	Apr	May	Jun
Purchases of materials (£)	1,225	1,350	1,525	1,625	1,675	1,600

Budgets for trade receivables and trade payables

If a firm deals with credit purchases and credit sales, it would be useful to construct the budgets for both of these. These are determined by the amounts purchased and sold on credit terms but also the length of the credit period offered by the firm to its customers and the credit period taken by the firm from its suppliers.

Trade receivables budget
for six months to 30 June 2014

	Jan £	Feb £	Mar £	Apr £	May £	Jun £
Opening balance	2,250	8,800	13,550	15,950	17,550	18,750
Add Credit sales for month	8,800	10,400	12,000	12,800	13,600	12,800
Amount owing to firm	11,050	19,200	25,550	28,750	31,150	31,550
Less Receipts from 1 month ago	1,250	4,400	5,200	6,000	6,400	6,800
Less Receipts from 2 month sago	1,000	1,250	4,400	5,200	6,000	6,400
Amounts received during month	2,250	5,650	9,600	11,200	12,400	13,200
Closing balance	8,800	13,550	15,950	17,550	18,750	18,350

The amounts received in January and February will relate to the November and December sales figures. For example, half of December's sales will be received in January with the remaining half received in February.

Trade payables budget
for six months to 30 June 2014

	Jan £	Feb £	Mar £	Apr £	May £	Jun £
Opening balance	2,200	2,425	2,575	2,875	3,150	3,300
Add Credit purchases for month	1,225	1,350	1,525	1,625	1,675	1,600
Amount owing to suppliers	3,425	3,775	4,100	4,500	4,825	4,900
Payments made during month	1,000	1,200	1,225	1,350	1,525	1,625
Closing balance	2,425	2,575	2,875	3,150	3,300	3,275

Cash budget

Bringing information from the other budgets produced so far, we can analyse the budgeted cash position. Especially for small firms, the cash flow position will be of particular importance. The need to arrange an overdraft should be identified as early as possible as banks may be less willing to lend to a firm that does not look as if it is planning its future effectively.

MacLeanan's cash budget would appear as follows:

Cash budget
for six months to 30 June 2014

	Jan £	Feb £	Mar £	Apr £	May £	Jun £
Cash inflows						
Receipts from receivables (1 month)	1,250	4,400	5,200	6,000	6,400	6,800
Receipts from receivables (2 month)	1,000	1,250	4,400	5,200	6,000	6,400
Total	2,250	5,650	9,600	11,200	12,400	13,200
Cash outflows						
Payments to suppliers	1,000	1,200	1,225	1,350	1,525	1,625
Direct labour	1,960	2,160	2,440	2,600	2,680	2,560
Direct expenses	490	540	610	650	670	640
Fixed overheads	400	400	400	700	700	700
Machine			5,000			
Total	3,850	4,300	9,675	5,300	5,575	5,525
Net cash flow	(1,600)	1,350	(75)	5,900	6,825	7,675
Opening balance	500	(1,100)	250	250	6,150	12,975
Closing balance	(1,100)	250	175	6,150	12,975	20,650

We can see that MacLeanan will need to ensure either that the firm has an overdraft authorized by his bank or that he has some other standby finance available. However, from April onwards the cash balances are rapidly accumulating. Having a build-up of cash presents a different kind of problem – what should be done with the surplus of cash? One possibility is that MacLeanan may aim to settle with his creditors immediately in cash; he can qualify for a cash discount as the credit period does not appear to be required.

Of course, the budget is based on an estimated set of sales. If sales do not materialize to the extent that he has predicted, the budgets may look less favourable. That is why it would be useful to prepare for a more pessimistic outcome just in case.

Budgeting techniques

So far we have not considered the process of budgeting as an actual activity. In reality, there are two main forms of setting budgets: incremental budgeting and zero-based budgeting.

Incremental budgeting

This budgeting process takes past historical budgets as the basis for setting future budgets. A future budgeted amount would be based on the current budgeted amount, with adjustments based on expected changes. These incremental changes can be adapted to a variety of expected changes. For example, inflation may mean that the budgeted amounts are increased in line with price increases. Alternatively, a business looking to save money might use incremental budgeting to gradually cut back on expenditure by reducing the amount allocated for each budget by a smaller amount for each successive time period.

The merit of an incremental budgeting approach is that it is easy to prepare as it is merely updating data already calculated. This ease of completion means that time and money are saved when planning the budget. However, incremental budgeting does have drawbacks.

Problems with incremental budgeting

Basing future targets for expenditure on current and, over time, historical data doesn't really justify why the expenditure is incurred. No justification is provided for the expenditure allotted in budgeted targets. This may mean that certain items of expenditure are perpetuated without being necessary. If a future budget is based on what has already happened, the question that may arise is why we are currently spending a certain amount? The answer, if we follow an incremental approach to budgeting, is that the amount being spent is not necessarily needed but is simply based on what was, perhaps, needed in some previous budget period.

If budgeted amounts are based on historical data, the challenge that a budget can present may not exist. If the amount allotted is increased in line with inflation, there is no incentive to increase efficiency. One way around this would be to reduce the size of the amount over a period of time. However, if this is presented as a cost-cutting exercise, it may not serve to motivate staff as it may appear to be imposed on the workforce.

Zero-based budgeting

A direct opposite approach to the system of incremental budgeting is the system of zero-based budgeting. This means that the budgeting process starts from scratch each time, with no reference made at all to the previous budgeted amount. All budgets under this system, therefore, start with zero and each area that has an amount allocated to it for budgeted expenditure would have to provide justification for any expenditure that was intended. This means that the budgeted amount is justified afresh in each period rather than simply adjusting a previous budget total.

A benefit of this system is that expenditure has to be justified and that expenditure will only be allowed if it can be justified by the relevant budget holder. This should lead to cost savings as each area has to provide justification of why the expenditure is needed. This will lead to activities being questioned as to why they are necessary for the organization – giving rise to the potential benefits in cost savings in cutting unnecessary expenditure.

Problems with zero-based budgeting

The time taken by managers in formulating their 'demands' for expenditure to be included within a budget will be significantly higher. Even if managers are used to a zero-based budgeting approach, this will still take considerably longer than the approach used in incremental budgeting. With less experienced staff this may take longer still.

Managers may not have the skills needed to provide justification for their expenditure. If the skills in negotiation and formulation of budgets vary among managers, it may mean that the budgets which are approved come from the managers with the greatest skills at negotiation. This may mean expenditure that proves to be necessary does not get justified and priorities for expenditure may not be organized efficiently.

Review questions

1   Odejayi Ltd produces computer desks. The production manager has collected the following information in order to produce a production budget for the next four months:

(i)   Demand is expected to be 320 desks in April 2018. This should increase by 25% in May and by 20% in the following two months, based on the demand for desks in the previous month.

(ii)   Stock at the end of each month is to be maintained at a level of 25% of the following month's forecast sales.

(iii) The stock at the start of April is 200 desks.

(iv) Sales in August are expected to be 600 desks.

Produce a production budget for the period ending 31 July 2018. Round up, if necessary, to the nearest desk.

Solution

Odejayi Ltd
Production budget for four months ending 31 July 2018

(Desks)	April	May	June	July
Sales	320	400	480	576
Opening stock	200	100	120	144
Closing stock	100	120	144	150
Production	220	420	504	582

2 Bruno produces go-karts which he sells to local retailers. He has decided to produce a sales and debtors budget to help him plan ahead. The following data are available for January to June 2014.

Month	Sales (number of go-karts)
Jan	100
Feb	80
Mar	120
Apr	120
May	150
Jun	180

- Each go-kart will be sold for £50 for the first four months, then the selling price will rise to £60.

- He gives two months' credit to the retailers.

Produce a sales budget and a trade receivables budget for the six months ending 30 June 2014.

Solution

Bruno
Sales budget for six months ended 31 June 2014

Sales	Jan	Feb	Mar	Apr	May	Jun
Units	100	80	120	120	150	180
Revenue (£)	5,000	4,000	6,000	6,000	9,000	10,800

Bruno
Trade receivables budget for six months ended 30 June 2014

	Jan	Feb	Mar	Apr	May	Jun
	£	£	£	£	£	£
Opening balance	0	5,000	9,000	10,000	12,000	15,000
Add Sales	5,000	4,000	6,000	6,000	9,000	10,800
	5,000	9,000	15,000	16,000	21,000	25,800
Less Receipts	0	0	5,000	4,000	6,000	6,000
Closing balance	5,000	9,000	10,000	12,000	15,000	19,800

3 From the following data, construct a cash budget for the six months ending 31 December 2016:

(a) Purchases and sales are expected to be as follows:

Units:	Jul 2003	Aug 2003	Sep 2003	Oct 2003	Nov 2003	Dec 2003
Purchases	170	170	250	210	240	250
Sales	160	180	190	280	300	320

(b) The selling price of each unit is £50.

(c) The purchase price of each unit is £20, but this will rise by 20% on 1 October 2016.

(d) Purchases are paid for one month in arrears.

(e) Twenty-five per cent of sales are for cash, with each sale receiving a 4% cash discount. The remainder will delay payment by one month.

(f) Trade debtors as at 30 June 2006 amounted to £4,500.

(g) Trade creditors as at 30 June 2006 amounted to £2,800.

(h) A new van is expected to be purchased in September, which would cost £18,000. The old van would be traded in at a value of £5,000. However, only half of the net purchase price would be paid then. The remainder would be paid in 2017.

(i) Wages and salaries amount to £3,000 per month, paid in the month incurred.

(j) Overhead expenses will be £900 per month, paid when incurred.

(k) On 1 July 2016 the bank balance was £9,000.

Solution

	Jul £	Aug £	Sep £	Oct £	Nov £	Dec £
Cash inflows						
Cash sales	1,920	2,160	2,280	3,360	3,600	3,840
Receipts	4,500	6,000	6,750	7,125	10,500	11,250
Total	6,420	8,160	9,030	10,485	14,100	15,090
Cash outflows						
Payables	2,800	3,400	3,400	5,000	5,040	5,760
Van			6,500			
Wages and salaries	3,000	3,000	3,000	3,000	3,000	3,000
Overheads	900	900	900	900	900	900
Total	6,700	7,300	13,800	8,900	8,940	9,660
Net cash flow	(280)	860	(4,770)	1,585	5,160	5,430
Opening balance	9,000	8,720	9,580	4,810	6,395	11,555
Closing balance	8,720	9,580	4,810	6,395	11,555	16,985

Working capital management

11

Introduction

A business has two types of capital:

- **fixed capital** in the form of non-current assets, such as premises, machinery and equipment;
- **working capital** to fund the business operations over the short term.

Working capital consists of the current assets and the current liabilities of the business and is calculated as follows:

> Working capital = Current assets (inventory, trade receivables and cash)
> less Current liabilities (trade payables and bank overdraft)

Current liabilities represent the short-term debts of the business which will require payment in the near future. Cash will be the medium by which these short-term debts will normally be repaid and settled, but having assets which are expected to be converted into cash in the near future will also be important. The assets which can be quickly converted into cash without any significant loss in the asset's value – the current assets – are considered to be the firm's liquid assets. Liquidity refers to how quickly an asset can be converted into cash without serious loss in value. Therefore, the business will need to ensure that it has sufficient amounts of working capital (the excess of current assets over current liabilities) in order to pay its debts.

The working capital cycle

The firm will not simply hold cash ready to pay suppliers and other expenses. Cash will be tied up in various categories as working capital, which will be in a state of constant flux and will be constantly moving between different categories in a cyclical matter. This working capital cycle is shown in Figure 11.1.

FIGURE 11.1 The working capital cycle

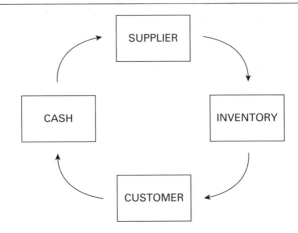

The working capital cycle works (at least in theory) as follows: a firm will purchase inventory (either as finished goods or as raw materials) on credit from its suppliers (appearing as creditors in the working capital). After production has taken place the finished goods will be sold on to customers as either cash or credit sales (now appearing as trade receivables in the working capital). The firm will eventually receive the cash from these credit customers, which in turn can then be used to settle the amounts owing to the credit suppliers as well as any other obligations it has run up during this period, such as wages and other expenses.

A firm will wish to minimize the length of its working capital cycle. The longer a firm holds inventories and the longer a firm takes to collect cash from its customers in respect of credit sales, the more likely a firm will face liquidity problems. Therefore a firm will want to minimize the time cash is tied up in working capital, so as to avoid potential difficulties with cash flow.

The working capital cycle (also known as the firm's operating cycle) can also be measured in terms of the time taken for money to pass through each stage of the working capital. The operating cycle for its working capital will consist of the following timings for cash being tied up in the various stages of the working capital cycle. The information used in calculating the length of the working capital cycle will be obtained from some of the accounting ratios we look at in Chapter 17.

	Inventory days	The average amount of time inventory is held by the firm
+	Trade receivable days	The time taken for a firm to collect its debts from its credit customers
−	Trade payable days	The time taken by a firm to pay its debts to its credit suppliers
=	Working capital cycle in days	

For a firm that manufactures its own products the cycle will be longer than the cycle of those firms that either sell services or purchase inventory ready (or almost ready) for sale.

Example 11.1

Consider the following two businesses – one located in the construction industry and another in the supermarket sector. The length of the operating cycle might appear as follows:

	Construction business (Days)	Supermarket business (Days)
Inventory days	200	20
Trade receivable days	90	0
Trade payable days	(80)	30
Working capital cycle	210	(10)

For the construction business, working capital will be tied up in inventory for a significant amount of time, in terms of bricks and other construction materials. Construction properties will take a significant amount of time (months or even years) to be completed, which means that the full income from a sale may take a very long time before it is realized. For a supermarket, any inventory will be held on the shop shelves for a relatively short period of time until it is sold and shelves are quickly restocked. This means that far less cash is tied up in inventory for the supermarket.

The supermarket industry will usually sell goods for cash or for immediate settlement via debit and credit cards. This means that the supermarket does not have to wait for credit sales to be converted into cash from its customers. This reduces the need for cash to be tied up elsewhere. For the construction industry, it is more likely that sales will be made on credit terms, which means that the operating cycle is lengthened further.

In the case of the supermarket, the length of the operating cycle might even be negative (as shown in the above example). This means that little cash at all is tied up in working capital and cash is therefore free to be used elsewhere in the business for more profitable pursuits.

The ideal size of working capital

The ideal amount of working capital to be held by a firm will depend on many factors. The size of the firm and the industry in which the firm operates will provide useful information in deciding on a prudent level of working capital. However, there are measurements that can provide a guide as to the ideal size for working capital.

Liquidity ratios

The liquidity ratios of the business provide guidance as to whether a firm has sufficient levels of working capital. The two ratios that will be used to assess the firm's liquidity position are as follows:

$$\text{Current ratio} = \frac{\text{Current assets}}{\text{Current liabilities}}$$

$$\text{Acid test ratio} = \frac{\text{Current assets} - \text{Inventory}}{\text{Current liabilities}}$$

Both of these measure the relative size of the firm's current assets. The rationale of these ratios is that a firm will have to repay the current liabilities using the current assets. Therefore it is not the size of the current liabilities that matters but the size of the current liabilities compared with the firm's current assets.

The assumption made with both these ratios is that current liabilities will require payment in the near future and that as long as the firm has more current assets than it has current liabilities it is less likely to face cash flow difficulties. How one interprets the liquidity ratios is covered in Chapter 17.

Having too little working capital means that the firm will risk being forced to cease trading if it cannot meet its monetary obligations. However, holding large amounts of cash generates low returns, and stockpiling large amounts of inventory increases its chance of becoming obsolete as well as resulting in extra storage costs on the firm. Hence, holding excessive amounts of working capital, though less risky than too little, will be inefficient. Management of working capital will therefore focus on how a firm can best manage the individual items contained within the working capital in order to operate as efficiently as possible.

Inventory

Only a firm that sells services will not have to deal with inventory. A firm that sells a physical product is likely to hold inventory in one or more of the following forms:

- finished goods – ready for sale;
- work-in-progress – partly completed goods;
- raw materials – which will be used in the production process.

Inventory will be held by a business for a number of reasons, including the following:

- to deal with erratic patterns of demand for the firm's products;
- so as not to miss out on unexpected sales;
- to benefit from bulk discounts obtained from large orders of inventory;
- to ensure a continuous flow of production;
- as a safety precaution in case of damage or spoilage to inventory in the production process.

However, holding inventory means that cash is tied up in the level of inventory and is not available for other uses within the firm. There are other costs associated with holding inventory as well and these would include the following:

- Storage costs – these will depend on the physical type of inventory but costs associated with storing inventory (such as warehousing, security or even refrigeration costs) may be significant.
- Monitoring costs – as well as security costs, inventory will require supervision, checking and logging, which all impose costs.
- Obsolescence – inventory held by a firm risks becoming out of date and therefore worthless and potentially unsellable.
- Damage and spoilage – inventory held risks the damage of spoilage (especially with food and other perishable materials).
- Theft – even with security, inventory may be stolen by customers and even employees and this imposes a cost on the business.

Optimal inventory levels

As explained above, firms hold inventory for a number of reasons, despite the costs that holding inventory imposes on the firm. Given these costs, it will be useful for a firm to ascertain the ideal average level of inventory to be held by the business that would minimize costs for the firm. By calculating the ideal amount of inventory to hold we would arrive at the ideal amount of inventory that should be ordered that minimizes overall costs associated with inventory. To arrive at this 'ideal' amount the firm will need to consider the following:

- As the quantity of inventory ordered rises, the average level of inventory held at any one time will also rise and therefore the total cost of holding inventory will likewise increase.

- As the quantity of inventory ordered rises, the number of orders made by the firm for inventory will decrease (given that more is ordered each time) and the total reorder costs will decrease.

Figure 11.2 confirms how these costs – the total costs of holding and the total costs of ordering inventory – vary according to the amount of inventory ordered on each occasion. These two costs move in opposite directions but when they are totalled together we can see that there is an optimal amount of inventory to be ordered on each occasion that minimizes overall costs associated with inventory. This ideal amount to be ordered is known as the **economic order quantity (EOQ)** and will remain the same for a given level of annual inventory requirements.

FIGURE 11.2 The costs of inventory

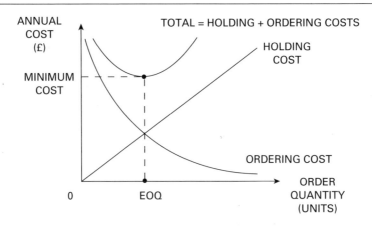

This EOQ can be calculated if we make the following assumptions:

1 Costs of ordering inventory are independent of the size of the order.

2 The unit price paid for inventory is constant.

3 The cost of holding inventory will depend on the size of the inventory in storage – it will normally be calculated as a cost of holding inventory per unit.

4 The demand for inventory by the firm's sales is constant.

5 Constant lead times between placing and receiving an order for inventory.

A constant level of demand for inventory will mean that we can illustrate the pattern of inventory usage by the firm graphically. Figure 11.3 illustrates the typical usage pattern of inventory.

FIGURE 11.3 Constant and uniform demand for inventory

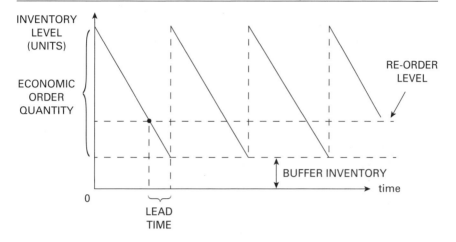

We can see from Figure 11.3 that the level of inventory held by the firm decreases at a uniform rate. The order for the next batch of inventory will need to be placed before the level of inventory is exhausted.

If all these assumptions are met, we can calculate the EOQ for a firm by using the following formula:

$$EOQ = \sqrt{\left(\frac{2 \times C_o \times D}{C_H}\right)}$$

where:

C_O is the cost of each separate order made for inventory (irrespective of the amount ordered).

D is the annual demand for the inventory in units.

C_H is the cost of holding a unit of inventory for one year.

Example 11.2

A firm has an annual demand for units of inventory of 1,000 per year. The cost of placing an order each time is £90 and each item of inventory costs £2 to store. In this case, the optimal amount of stock that should be ordered would be:

$$EOQ = \sqrt{\left(\frac{2 \times £90 \times 1,000}{£2}\right)} = 300 \text{ units}$$

The EOQ means that the firm will need to make just over three orders per year on average (1,000 units/300 units). Therefore inventory will be reordered around every three and half months.

Bulk discounts

There is the possibility that a firm can access bulk purchase discounts if it purchases a large enough batch of inventory. If the minimum number of units to be purchased in order to access the bulk purchase discount is higher than the EOQ, the firm will have to consider whether or not the extra costs in ordering a sub-optimal amount are outweighed by the potential savings. How this would be calculated is illustrated in the following example.

Example 11.3

The annual demand for a product is 5,000 units per year. The purchase price of each unit is £100 and the cost of holding each unit for one year is equivalent to 25 per cent of the purchase price. The cost of placing an order is £400.

The EOQ would be calculated as follows:

$$\text{EOQ} = \sqrt{\left(\frac{2 \times £400 \times 5,000}{£25}\right)} = 400 \text{ units}$$

However, the firm also offers a cash discount of 2 per cent if orders are placed for 1,000 units or more. Should the firm take up this offer or should it stick to ordering the EOQ of 400 units?

The total cost of the EOQ are currently as follows:

	£
Purchase price (5,000 × £100)	500,000
Annual ordering costs (12.5 × £400)	5,000
Annual holding costs (Average holding per year = EOQ/2) × £25	5,000
Total costs	510,000

If we aim for the bulk discount, the amount closest in quantity to the EOQ that we can order would be the 1,000 units that qualifies for the 2 per cent price discount.

The total cost of inventory with the bulk discount are as follows:

	£
Purchase price (5,000 × £98)	490,000
Annual ordering costs (5 × £400)	2,000
Annual holding costs	12,250
(Average holding over year = 1,000/2) × £24.50	
Total costs	504,250

Therefore we can see that the firm should aim for qualifying for the bulk discount rather than choosing to order the EOQ.

Reorder level

How early the order must be placed would depend on the lead time. If suppliers are reliable and can deliver inventory quickly, the order may be placed near the time when inventory levels are close to zero. For example, if a firm uses 10 units of inventory each day and the lead time between an order being placed and the inventory arriving is 4 days, the reorder level would be 40 units. Placing the order for inventory once inventory levels fall below this level risks the firm not having inventory when it is needed. Reordering inventory when levels are above this reorder level means that the firm will have more inventory in stock than it needs and this will impose extra costs on the firm. The reorder level will therefore be dependent on the lead time and the average usage of inventory per day.

Buffer stock

A buffer stock is a level of inventory held for precautionary proposes to cover any shortfall that might arise owing to an uncertain lead time. Ideally a firm would not want to have a buffer stock of a significant size as it represents working capital tied up which could have been used elsewhere. The buffer stock will also impose extra costs in terms of extra holding costs. The size of the buffer stock can be reduced with improved forecasting of actual sales (and subsequent demand for inventory) and improved reliability of suppliers who will deliver within a specified lead time.

Just-in-time

We have already discussed the costs of holding inventory. As an attempt to minimize these costs, some firms have adopted a policy of just-in-time management of inventory. This approach has been largely credited to the management practices in place within the Japanese car manufacturer Toyota. Within the Toyota production facilities, a number of systems were implemented to make the production system a **lean system** which attempted to eliminate waste and errors. Part of this system was the **just-in-time** approach to management of inventory, which was to view the holding of any inventory as a waste.

A firm using a just-in-time approach would only order inventory as and when it is required, eliminating the need for storage costs. This will save the need for cash to be tied up in holdings of inventory. It should also (if it is to be successful) encourage firms to foster closer relationships with their suppliers. The suppliers of inventory to the business will need to be extremely reliable in being able to deliver inventory on demand. The elimination of buffer stocks, which is a feature of the just-in-time system, means that suppliers will need to deliver when required, otherwise the firm will be left with idle production facilities.

In addition, the just-in-time system means that there is very little slack in the system. If spoilage occurs with the existing inventory, the firm will have to reorder more inventory and may be unable to commence production.

This will initially place increased pressure on the management and employees of organizations if they are to attempt to eliminate errors and wastage of inventory.

Just-in-time systems will means that a firm may miss out on extra sales if the lead time for materials to be delivered is too long.

Trade receivables

Trade between businesses is often conducted on the basis of credit terms being offered. This is not the case for retailers selling goods and services to final consumers, which are likely to be are cash sales (ie for immediate payment). Credit may be offered to consumers on large-value purchases, such as cars and consumer durables. The credit terms offered by firms will be an incentive to consumers and other businesses to buy from a particular firm.

By allowing credit sales, a firm will tie up cash in working capital in the form of trade receivables, which may not be realized into cash for a significant period of time (weeks or months). For a small firm, especially a new firm, this period, in which it has engaged in expenditure on the product but has yet to receive any money from the sale, may prove fatal in terms of cash flow problems. A firm that sells on credit will need to ensure that it has sufficient cash flow to allow it to meet its financial obligations before it receives the settlement of cash from its credit customers. Additionally, with credit sales there is also the risk of incurring **bad debts** where no money at all is recovered from the credit sale. Unfortunately, knowing which of the firm's customers are going to turn into bad debts is hard to predict (why would a firm sell on credit if it knew that a particular customer was going to be unable to pay?).

Effective management of trade receivables will focus on two key areas. First, given that trade receivables represents money tied up which cannot be utilized by the firm, it is important that these are controlled efficiently. Second, given the unfortunate existence of bad debts, there are a number of steps a firm can take in order to reduce the risk of bad debts occurring. Strategies for both of these are covered in this section.

Invoice management

Although it may seem obvious, a firm can help itself by ensuring that the invoices it sends to its credit customers are clear and precise in the information that they contain. Correct addresses for the customer and the business should be present as well as an appropriate invoice number and the correct price as agreed for the sale. It will also help a business if they include some or all of the following:

- A clear statement of the length of the credit period offered by the firm, with any discount offered clearly stated.

- Information as to whether any penalties will be incurred by the customer if payment is not received on time. The penalties may include interest charged on the outstanding invoice if payment is late. This is covered later.

- A clause stating that legal title (ie ownership) of the goods remains with the supplier until payment is received (which may help ensure that goods are recovered if the firm faces closure before payment for the goods is made). If this clause does not appear and the customer's business fails, the business is unlikely to receive anything back once the business is liquidated.

A firm should also have systems in place for dealing with outstanding invoices once the credit period has been breached. A reminder letter would be the first step in this process – which may initially appear as a statement of account which just simply states the current financial records between the firm and the customer. If payment is still not forthcoming, further reminder letters may be sent. A letter threatening legal action may seem appropriate if reminder letters (or phone calls) are ignored.

Legal advice is available for firms pursing outstanding trade receivables. However, the advice will not be cheap. A court judgment may help recover the amount outstanding and any legal costs incurred. However, if this is disputed, complications may arise in resolving the dispute and it may take a long period of time before any monies are received.

It will only be worth taking legal action against a customer if it is believed that the customer actually has the resources to make a payment. Otherwise, it will be simpler to write it off as a bad debt.

Aged debtors schedule

Bad debts are more likely to occur with debts that have been outstanding for a long period of time. It should not be too difficult (especially with the use of computers) to produce an aged debtor's schedule. This will be a report of the firm's trade receivables which groups debts together and presents the amounts outstanding by the dates they are due for payment; that is, debts are grouped according to their 'age'.

By being able to analyse trade receivables by the time they have been outstanding it should be easier for a firm to decide how to approach the amounts outstanding. Rather than treating all late balances in the same way, the schedule of debtors would allow a firm to pursue debts according to their age. For example, debtors which are only marginally late could be dealt with through either a phone call or a simple reminder letter. As an outstanding debt becomes 'older' it will pass into a different category, which may involve a more 'threatening' letter. Eventually the debt might become so old that the firm considers whether or not to take legal action or, if it is not an efficient use of the firm's resources, to write off the debt as bad.

Credit checks

Before offering credit to a supplier for the first time it would be sensible to check this business to see if it is able and likely to pay. Checking the creditworthiness of a potential credit customer is a prudent measure which will help prevent bad debts and also help to ensure that payment is received on time. Of course, unexpected events do occur and this cannot eliminate the risk of payment failure completely, but it will ensure that credit is perhaps not offered to high-risk customers. Part of this checking process could involve some or all of the following:

- obtaining bank references – details of the firm's banking and financial details (may be hard to obtain for reasons of confidentiality);
- trade references from other firms that have dealt with the customer before and can vouch for its creditworthiness (ie they have had no difficulties receiving amounts owing in the past);
- financial statements (which may give an advance warning of any financial difficulties the firm may face in the near future);
- security – does the firm possess assets which could act as collateral on any credit offered?

A firm could use a more formal system of checking creditworthiness by obtaining a credit check from an external credit agency. This credit check may provide the business with a credit score for the potential credit customer, which shows the track record of this business in settling and managing its debts.

Cash discounts

Cash discounts are offered by a business to encourage early settlement of an invoice. This means that the firm receives the cash (less the discount) earlier than expected and this will help to minimize the chance of a debt remaining outstanding longer than desired and help with any cash flow difficulties. The discount offered will normally be a percentage of the outstanding invoice (after any trade discount has been deducted). VAT (20 per cent in the UK) is calculated on the assumption that the cash discount is taken.

The level of discount offered will differ from firm to firm, but the discount offered should not be so generous as to seriously erode the profit earned on the sale. In addition, when offering a discount for earlier settlement, the firm should consider whether the benefit from earlier settlement of trade receivables outweighs the costs associated with the discount being offered.

Cash discounts offered for earlier settlement will lead to a loss in revenue if the customer qualifies for and takes the discounts. This will bring in cash flow earlier than it would otherwise have done. If the firm does not require early settlement of these outstanding bills, as cash flow is not a serious concern, the firm should be asking itself whether the cash discount was worth offering in the first place. In addition, offering this discount will create extra costs in the administration of such discounts in terms of managing the sales ledger of the firm. There will also be the problem that some customers will send payment for an outstanding invoice having taken the discount off the amount they are paying but have actually not met the terms to qualify for the discount. This may be an innocent mistake or it may be an attempt by the customer to have the best of both worlds. In this case, the firm will need to decide if it is worth pursuing the customers for the missing amount. Often this amount is small enough not to warrant too much expense in chasing it up.

Late Payment of Commercial Debts (Interest) Act 1998

This UK Act of Parliament was introduced so as to provide compensation for late payments from outstanding trade receivables. This Act enables any business (the original Act was aimed at small businesses) to charge interest on outstanding amounts which are deemed to be late. The 'statutory interest' that can be charged is equivalent to the Bank of England's Base Rate + 8 per cent. This rate is meant to represent the interest that a business would have to pay to obtain money from elsewhere if cash flow difficulties arise out of this late payment of amounts owing.

However, evidence suggests that this Act, though designed to help small businesses, has not been particularly effective. The time taken, on average, for firms to collect payment from trade receivables appears to have increased over the past decade. This may reflect economic difficulties and the associated increased risk of business failure. However, there is evidence that smaller firms are unwilling to enforce the requirements of the Act. This may be due to the fact that smaller firms feel that they do not want to alienate larger firms as potential customers and to some extent are 'bullied' into giving longer periods of 'free' credit.

Debt factoring

Debt factoring can be followed when a firm has trouble collecting monies from outstanding trade receivables. This may be particularly useful for small businesses that are more likely to face cash flow difficulties. A factor is an outside agency that will usually agree to take on the businesses trade receivables. The factor will immediately provide around 80 per cent of the outstanding trade receivables to the business. The balance of trade receivables will then be collected by the factor and paid on to the business less a charge for administration and the service that it provides in collecting these debts.

Factoring can either be *recourse factoring* (where the business carries the risk of the debt turning into a bad debt) or *non-recourse factoring* (where the factor carries the risk of the bad debt). In the case of debt factoring without recourse, it is likely that the commission and other charges will be higher owing to the higher risk borne by the factor.

The main advantage of using a debt factor agency is that it provides an immediate injection of cash into the business. However, the charges made by the factor will often be high and could wipe out any profit that was made on the original sale. The firm considering the use of a factor will need to consider whether the benefits of using a factor outweigh any costs associated with the factor. There is also the issue, which cannot always be measured in financial terms, of the loss of customer loyalty that results when a firm passes on a debt to a factor, which is more likely to use less than friendly means of chasing up outstanding debts.

How to avoid late payments and bad debts

By allowing sales on credit, all firms run the risk of bad debts. Similarly, even with legal action, late payment of trade receivables is likely to happen. Can either of these be avoided?

The easy response to this question is yes. If a firm only allows sales for immediate settlement, that is, cash sales, then the problems of bad debts and late payment are immediately dispensed with. However, the danger in only trading with cash sales is that it will impact on overall sales levels. If potential customers have a choice of where to buy their supplies, then, all other things being equal, it is likely to choose the firm that allows for greater flexibility.

Trade receivables can be monitored and bad debts minimized by employing adequate checks before allowing credit. Late payments can be avoided by follow-up procedures. Legal action may be taken and interest charges applied, but, to maintain harmonious relationships with customers, may well be avoided.

It is worth remembering that trade receivables are part of the firm's working capital cycle and, while it represents amounts of cash tied up elsewhere, the firm should, at the same time, be benefiting from being able to obtain credit terms itself when it purchases inventory from suppliers.

Management of trade payables

Trade payables or creditors represent the amounts owing in relation to credit purchases. Much as the firm will offer credit terms to its customers, the firm can benefit from delaying payments made to suppliers for inventory already acquired. Typical credit periods offered are around 30 days, but may be longer. Being able to defer the payment of trade payables will provided a valuable safety net for firms and acts as a kind of counterbalance to having cash tied up in inventory and in trade receivables. However, there are still issues for a business to consider when managing its payment policy with trade payables.

A firm should attempt to balance the benefits of deferring payment with the penitential benefit of prompt payment discounts. If these are available, a firm can save money and boost overall profits by noticing the cash discounts available. However, these discounts should only be taken and payment made promptly if it does not place too great a strain on the firm's working capital and cash flow position.

Some suppliers will also offer bulk purchase discounts, which may help contribute further to profits. However, these should only be taken if the extra cost of the higher-than-average inventory that may need to be stored does not outweigh the savings made.

As a rule of thumb, firms should monitor the time taken to collect monies from trade receivables and to pay its trade payables. Having similar time periods for both of these will mean that money is leaving the firm but also flowing in at roughly the same time intervals. If these timings diverge significantly, and the difference is caused by a longer time taken to collect trade receivables, the firm is more likely to face cash flow difficulties. These calculations, with further development, are featured in Chapter 17.

Managing cash

A firm will need to ensure that it has sufficient amounts of cash available for meeting day-to-day payments. Suppliers may accept a delay in payment but other creditors of the firm, utility companies, other suppliers who only accept cash payment, and employees may be less willing to wait for the amounts due to them.

The amount of cash available at any one time will be supplemented by the regular receipts of trade receivables. However, a firm will need to ensure that it manages its overall cash flow – cash inflows into the business less cash outflows paid out of the business – so as to avoid financial difficulty.

Although running out of cash poses difficulties for a firm, having too much cash is also inadvisable. Cash and other balances at the bank rarely generate a high return. Hence holding too much cash would be seen as a sign of inefficiency. However, holding too much cash and being inefficient is probably preferable to holding too little cash and risking potential insolvency.

One way of monitoring cash flow in a more systematic way is to construct and update a system of budgets for cash flow. This was covered in the previous chapter.

Review questions

1   A firm has an annual demand for inventory of 240,000 units. Each unit costs £60 to store for one year and the cost of placing an order is £500. Calculate the EOQ and the number of orders that will have to be placed each year.

Solution

EOQ is 2,000 units; number of orders would be 120 per year.

2   A firm has an annual demand for inventory of 36,000 units. Each unit costs £15 to store for one year and the cost of placing an order is £1,200. Calculate the EOQ and the number of orders that will have to be placed each year.

Solution

EOQ is 2,400 units; number of orders would be 15 per year.

3   Give three reasons why a just-in-time policy for management of inventory may lead to problems.

Solution

(i)   Does not allow for spoilage of inventory.

(ii)   Does not allow for late deliveries of supplies.

(iii) Does not allow for faulty production.

Capital investment appraisal

12

Introduction

In Chapter 2 we were introduced to the idea of the business engaging in capital expenditure – the acquisition of non-current assets to be used within the business. In the case of tangible assets, they will be used to facilitate the supply and production of goods and services. Although the capital expenditure does not directly affect profit in any particular year, poor choices made when deciding on capital expenditure will ultimately affect the long-term profitability of the firm.

A firm must be especially careful when deciding to undertake capital expenditure. This is because these items are normally significant amounts of expenditure and will tie up a significant amount of the firm's resources which cannot be used elsewhere, that is, they will carry an opportunity cost. As a result, it is important that the firm makes the correct decision. The decision to undertake capital expenditure cannot easily be reversed – assets may be sold but that will not be a quick process unless the firm is willing to lose money on the sale, and it can take time before a suitable replacement is found and is ready for operations. Capital expenditure is usually a long-term investment that will be expected to last for a number of years.

To ensure that the best decisions are made in terms of capital expenditure, the managers of the firm will need to ensure a rigorous and objective method of assessing and evaluating whether the likely impact of the capital expenditure is utilized. The process of evaluating a potential investment is known as **capital investment appraisal** (or just investment appraisal). This chapter will cover how the firm will begin to appraise investments.

Capital investment

It is worth taking time at this stage to elaborate exactly what we mean by the term capital investment. As mentioned in the opening section, it will normally involve the acquisition of a non-current asset. However, the scale of the investment will depend on the type of firm. For a large company on a multinational level, the investment may be the siting of a new base of operations in a new country. In this case the potential amount of expenditure could run into many millions of pounds. Moving to a new premises or setting up another branch of an existing business would also represent potential capital investment by a firm. For a smaller firm, typical investment decisions will involve the acquisition of machinery, plant or vehicles.

Capital investment appraisal scenarios are likely to include one or more of the following:

- replacement of existing non-current assets, such as machinery and equipment;
- upgrading of existing non-current assets, where the replacement will lead to cost savings for the business;
- deciding between alternative investments – where several options exist, of which only one can selected;
- moving premises – usually either to boost revenues or to reduce costs;
- expansion of the business, through the acquisition of expanded production facilities;
- launching a new product – the costs and benefits associated with the launch of a new product.

In each case, the cost of the investment is known with certainty and this will be incurred at the present time. The investment may be financed by borrowing or may come from internal resources. However, the potential benefits of the investment (either through reduced costs or from increased cash flow and profits) should outweigh the cost of the investment.

Relevant costs and benefits

In evaluating the financial merits of an investment decision, it is vital that we include only the relevant costs and benefits that arise solely out of the investment. Any costs that would be incurred or benefits that would be received regardless of whether the investment goes ahead should not be included in the investment appraisal. For example, costs may have been incurred in researching the suitability of the investment. These are relevant to the whole investment scenario as they are concerned with the idea of whether or not the investment is financially viable. However, these costs would not be considered as relevant costs in the investment appraisal.

This reason for the non-inclusion of any preliminary costs in the investment appraisal is because the cost cannot now be recovered should the investment decision be cancelled. Any cost which is incurred regardless of whether the investment goes ahead is known as a **sunk cost**.

Net cash flow and the investment appraisal

While conducting the investment appraisal it is normal to use cash flows rather than profits that arise out of the investment (the exception to this is the ARR method outlined later in this chapter, which is the only method of investment appraisal to use profits rather than cash flows). The overall appraisal of the investment will be judged by the net cash flow that arises out of the investment going ahead. The net cash flow will be calculated as the difference between the cash inflows and the cash outflows.

The cost of the investment is assumed to occur at the start of the investment project and represents an immediate cash outflow. The cost of the investment plus any additional costs involved in starting the investment, such as installation costs, will also be included.

The cash inflows will be generated by either the extra revenue the investment generates or the cost savings that result from the investment. The cash flows that arise after the investment is undertaken are all estimates. Therefore we are dealing with uncertainty, although some of the estimates may be reasonably certain. For example, if the investment is going to enable a firm to automate part of its production line, the savings made by reducing labour costs can be estimated with reasonable certainty. However, some of the potential benefits will be known with rather less confidence. Extra cash inflows that result from the investment may be contingent on sales being either maintained or improved. Sales estimates should always be treated with caution. A firm cannot guarantee any particular level of sales owing to changes in the economic and market environment in which the firm operates.

Although the investment is likely to be planned on the basis of financial benefits that arise out of it going ahead, there is the possibility that the investment will also generate additional costs. For example, the purchase of a new machine may result in additional savings being made each year. However, the machine itself may generate extra cash outflows in the form of extra maintenance costs or power costs in running the machine. These extra costs should be factored into the net cash flow for each time period by deducting them from the relevant cash inflows for that period.

Investment appraisal is more likely to provide useful and meaningful information for the firm's managers if the cash flow estimates are conducted with as much prudence and caution as possible. It could be that the firm underestimates the benefits of a potential investment. However, given the magnitude of most investment decisions, it would be seen as far more acceptable to turn down an investment because of uncertain returns than for the firm to face failure and insolvency because an overoptimistic forecast of cash benefits arising out of an investment fails to materialize.

The time period by which the investment will be judged is likely to be over a number of years. The estimates of the net cash flows will become less reliable the further into the future the projections are. Forecasting the effect of the investment on the net cash flow during the next year may seem reasonably straightforward. However, estimating the net cash flow for five years in the future will provide an extremely difficult task to achieve with any fair degree of accuracy. Therefore the results gained from the investment appraisal should always be treated with caution. As a result, most investment appraisals will include the net cash flow estimates for only the first few years of a project. The uncertainty of the business environment, coupled with the gradual erosion of the real value of future cash flows due to inflation, mean that it is not particularly helpful to include more than a few years' worth of data.

One of the assumptions made by the methods of investment appraisal is that the net cash flows arising out of the investment will all take place at the end of the financial year (assuming the relevant time period is one year). This is unrealistic, as cash flows are likely to be incurred over the year, but it helps keep examples simple.

Methods of investment appraisal

There are a number of different methods that can be used to appraise any proposed investment. Each method has its own merits. Emphasis placed on the results from a particular method is likely to depend on the motivation and objectives of the particular firm and management conducting the investment appraisal. It is likely that most managers will not rely on the results of only one method and will conduct an investment appraisal utilizing some if not all the methods available.

The investment appraisal methods covered in this textbook are as follows:

1 payback;
2 accounting rate of return (ARR);
3 net present value (NPV);
4 internal rate of return (IRR);
5 discounted payback.

Payback

The simplest investment appraisal method to calculate and to understand is payback. In this method an investment is judged by the time taken to recover the original investment in terms of cash inflows. The time taken for the accumulated net cash inflows to match the original cash outflow of the investment is known as the **payback period**. The payback period will normally be measured in years and an investment is judged as favourable if it has the shortest payback period possible.

Example 12.1

There are two potential investment projects (A and B) which both require an investment of £15,000. The firm will select one of these and will choose the one with the shortest payback period. The net cash flows for each project are estimated as follows:

	Net cash flows	
Year	Project A	Project B
	£	£
0 (now)	(15,000)	(15,000)
1	4,000	2,000
2	5,000	3,000
3	6,000	4,000
4	4,000	6,000
5	3,000	7,000

We can see from the table that project A has a payback of exactly three years (after three years the cash flows will have accumulated to match the original investment). For project B, the payback period will be four years.

It is possible that the payback period will not fall neatly at the end of a financial year as in the above example, and we will be faced with a project which has not reached its payback level at the start of a particular year but receives more than enough in the subsequent year to exceed the payback period. In this case, the payback year can be partly calculated as a fraction of a particular year. Consider the following example.

Example 12.2

A firm is planning to purchase a replacement machine in order to generate cost savings. The machine would cost £15,000 and the estimated costs savings are given in the following table.

Year	Net cash flow
	£
0 (now)	(15,000)
1	3,000
2	4,000
3	5,000
4	4,000

In the above table we can see that the payback period is somewhere between the start and end of the fourth year. After three years, the machine has paid back £12,000 (still £3,000 short of payback) and after four years the machine has paid back £16,000 (£1,000 beyond payback).

We can calculate the proportion of the year that is needed to reach payback by using the following formula:

$$\frac{\text{Amount needed to reach payback} \times 12}{\text{Amount received in year}} = \text{Months needed in year}$$

We know that after three years £3,000 (£15,000 − £1,000) was still needed to reach payback and that in the fourth year £4,000 was received.

Therefore, the months needed in year 4 to reach payback would be (£3,000/£4,000) × 12 = 9. So, the overall payback period is 3 years 9 months.

This is based on the assumption that the net cash flows are generated evenly throughout the year. This is unlikely but makes the calculation far easier. The above technique can be calculated in weeks if the 12 in the equation is replaced by 52.

Payback evaluated

The attraction of the method is its ease of calculation and ease of interpretation. The method would be especially useful for a business that wished to avoid having large amounts of capital tied up in projects for a prolonged period of time. By judging investment projects according to how quickly they recover the amount they cost, they provide an idea as to which investments are less risky than others.

There are limitations of the payback method. The potential profitability of the project is ignored and, as a result, a manager using only this method of appraisal may reject investment opportunities that are more profitable than the project finally selected. Cash flows after payback has been reached are ignored. Ignoring the profits of an investment could be an issue if profit maximization is the main focus of the business. In the first example of this chapter, using payback, the firm would have rejected project B despite its having a greater return than project A (which had the shorter payback period).

The method also takes no account of the time value of money: the fact that the value of money in the future is not directly equivalent to the same value of money in the present. This issue will be explored later in this chapter.

Accounting rate of return (ARR)

With this method an investment project is judged by the profitability of the project. The average profit earned per year is expressed as a percentage of the investment into the project. The formula for this is given as follows:

$$\text{Accounting rate of return (ARR) (\%)} = \frac{\text{Average profit per year}}{\text{Average investment}} \times 100$$

This method uses profits rather than cash flow for the purpose of the calculation. This means that any cash flows present in the data may need adjusting for further non-cash deductions against profits, such as depreciation which would need to be added back.

The total profit of the investment would be calculated as the total of all the profits generated by the investment over its life, less the initial cost of the investment. Estimating the number of years of the project's life may be difficult, so it is appropriate to be prudent here. Once the total profits of the investment have been calculated, this total would be divided by the number of years the investment is expected to last. This figure represents the average profit per year.

The average investment would be calculated as follows:

$$\text{Average investment} = \frac{\text{Initial investment + Residual value}}{2}$$

The calculation is based on the straight-line method of depreciation – in which the investment will lose value in a linear manner. The calculation of the average investment is somewhat counter-intuitive. It may seem logical that we should have calculated it as the initial investment less the residual value divided by two. The rationale for why the two are added together is that we want to show the average value of the investment rather than the net cost of the investment. In many cases, this issue does not arise as the residual value will be assumed to be zero.

Example 12.3

An investment project is available which would cost £250,000, with an expected residual value after four years of £10,000.

The project is expected to generate the following profits for the following years:

	£
Profits in year 1	30,000
Profits in year 2	20,000
Profits in year 3	10,000
Profits in year 4	5,000

The average investment for the project would be (£250,000 + £10,000)/2 = £130,000. The average profit earned on the project would be (£30,000 + £20,000 + £10,000 + £5,000)/4 = £16,250.

The ARR of the project would be calculated as follows:

$$\text{Accounting rate of return (\%)} = \frac{£16,250}{£130,000} \times 100 = 12.5\%$$

ARR evaluated

The ARR does take into account the size of the return of the investment, which will make this method more useful than the payback method for businesses that are aiming to maximize returns and profits. However, the flipside of this is that it treats all profits equally – profits to be earned some years in the future are treated as equivalent to profits earned in the early years of the investment. This means that a business that is aiming to minimize the riskiness of an investment may be misled by an ARR result that suggests a superior return. In addition, the ARR results do not allow comparison of projects with different time periods. If you think about it, a project can be given a higher ARR just by designating a shorter life for the project (the average profit will be higher if the number of years is smaller).

Like the problem with the payback method, the ARR does not take into account the time value of money. The following methods of investment appraisal take into account the time value of money by the utilization of what is known as discounted cash flow.

Discounted cash flow

Given a choice of £100 now or £100 in one year's time, rationally we would choose £100 now. Even if we were not going to spend this money, £100 could be invested and would gain interest. For example, if interest rates are

10 per cent, £100 invested now would be worth £110 in one year's time. For each year invested at an interest rate of 10 per cent, the £100 will continue to grow. For example, after two years, it would have grown to £121 (the £10 interest from the first year plus a further 10 per cent of the £110). This shows the principle of **compound interest** in that the amount of interest gained will increase as the original amount grows through the interest gained. Table 12.1 shows the effect of compound interest on the original investment.

TABLE 12.1 Effect of compound interest of 10 per cent per annum

Time	Investment
Now	£100
1 year	£110
2 years	£121
3 years	£133.10
4 years	£146.41

Therefore, to convert existing amounts into future values we use the principle of compound interest. To convert future amounts into present values we use the concept of **discounting**. Based on the interest rate of 10 per cent, we should be indifferent between the choice of £100 now, £110 in one year's time or £121 in two years' time. We can reverse the logic of calculating compound interest in order to calculate the present values of money generated sometime in the future. In our example, we would say that £121 to be received in two years' time has a present value of £100 (assuming a discounted rate of 10 per cent). Similarly, £110 received in one year's time has a present value of £100 today. The logic of this development is that by discounting cash flows we can see that the further away the money is in the future, the lower will be its present value in today's terms. To calculate the present value of a future amount we use the following formula:

$$\text{Future amount} \times \frac{1}{(1 + i)^n} = \text{Present value}$$

where: i is the interest rate expressed as a decimal (ie 10 per cent would be 0.1)
    n is the number of years away the amount is to be received

For example, the present value of £500 to be received in three years' time with an interest rate of 10 per cent would be calculated as follows:

$$£500 \times \frac{1}{(1 + 0.1)^3} = £375.66$$

To use this concept of discounted cash flow for investment appraisal we need to derive a range of discount factors so that the present value of money can be calculated for various years in the future. For example, using a 10 per cent discount would give us the following discount factors:

After year:	10% Discount factor
1	0.909
2	0.826
3	0.751
4	0.683
5	0.621

To calculate the present value of any amount to be generated (either as a receipt or as a payment) in the future we will multiply this by the relevant discount factors. Discount factors will get progressively smaller the further away they are in the future. In addition, the higher the discount rates to be used, the smaller the discount factors that are used to calculate the present values. Table 12.2 shows discount factors for a variety of time period and interest rates.

TABLE 12.2 A range of discount rates

Year	8%	10%	12%	14%
1	0.926	0.909	0.893	0.870
2	0.857	0.826	0.797	0.756
3	0.794	0.751	0.712	0.658
4	0.708	0.683	0.636	0.572
5	0.650	0.621	0.567	0.497

Choosing discount factors

In an assessment situation it is normal for the discount factors to be provided already calculated. However, the actual rate chosen is meant to reflect the cost of capital to the firm. This could be related to the current interest rates in the economy, as if the firm is relying on borrowed money for the investment, an investment project should generate a rate of return which is generally higher than the cost of this borrowed finance.

The discount rate chosen could also be related to the interest rate available on financial investments if the firm is giving up the chance to use the funds used for the investment elsewhere. Shareholders will also want a return on their capital invested within the business, so the cost of equity should be considered as a cost of financing business operations. Therefore it may be more appropriate to use a weighted average cost of capital (WACC). The WACC reflects that firms will often rely on multiple sources for the investment – for example from debt or equity.

Weighted average cost of capital (WACC)

Those who lend the firm money will require a return on the debt finance they provide for the firm. The interest rate required by lenders will represent a cost of capital to the firm. In addition, shareholders within a company will also require a rate of return on their investment. The rate of return required by shareholders will be related to how risky investors believe investment in the firm's equity capital would be. The riskier the purchase of shares in the company, the higher the return the shareholders will require. This required return by shareholders will also consist of a return equivalent to that available on other risk-free investments.

The WACC for a company can be calculated if we know the capital structure – the proportion of debt finance and equity finance within the firm's overall capital employed, as well as the cost of capital required by both lenders and investors.

Example 12.4

A company has £60,000 of issued share capital and £40,000 of outstanding debentures. The interest rate charged on the debentures is 8 per cent and the required return by shareholders is 12 per cent. This company's WACC would be calculated as follows:

		Cost of capital
Equity	£ 60,000 @ 12%	= £ 7,200
Debt	£ 40,000 @ 8%	= £ 3,200
Total	£100,000	= £10,400

Therefore the weighted average cost of capital will be £10,400/£100,000 × 100 = 10.4%.

In terms of capital investment appraisal, this would act as a guide to the appropriate discount factor to use when assessing potential investment projects. As long as the return achieved by a project exceeds 10.4 per cent, the return will be greater than the cost of the capital used in the investment project.

The above example portrays a highly simplistic model of how the WACC would be calculated. In reality, debt is cheaper the equity because of the fact that interest payments on debt are generally tax deductible. However, this simplified representation of how to calculate the WACC is useful in understanding how a particular discount rate is selected to represent the cost of capital.

In most assessments covering calculations of investment appraisal, the discount factors would be given to you already fully calculated for you to use. The following methods of investment appraisal all make use of discounted cash flow in generating results.

Net present value (NPV)

The net present value (NPV) method of investment appraisal looks at the net cash flows generated by an investment and these are compared with the cash outflows incurred in undertaking the investment – in the form of the costs associated with the project. Each cash inflow (remembering the assumption that the cash flows are generated at the end of the year) is multiplied by the relevant discount factor for that particular cost of capital and for that particular year.

The NPV of an investment project will be calculated by the net total of the present values associated with the project. Normally, the net cash flows arising out of the project will be positive and as long as the present values of the project exceed the cost of the project, we would view the project as a potential investment.

Example 12.5

Carchester United is considering moving to a new football stadium as the current stadium is considered inadequate. There are two options available. One ground in the town area of Greenhill is slightly bigger than the current stadium and would cost £12 million. However, the option for relocating the stadium to the area of Loxden would cost £25 million and that stadium would be twice the size of the current one. A larger stadium would allow a greater inflow of cash as more fans would be able to attend.

The relevant cash flows for both projects are as follows:

		Greenhill £	Loxden £
Cost of stadium		12,000,000	25,000,000
Cash inflows:	Year 1	5,000,000	10,000,000
	Year 2	4,000,000	8,000,000
	Year 3	3,000,000	6,000,000
	Year 4	2,000,000	4,000,000
	Year 5	1,000,000	4,000,000

The cost of capital for this project would be 10 per cent. All cash flows are assumed to be receivable at the end of each year. The NPV calculations for each project would appear as follows:

	Greenhill Stadium			Loxden Stadium		
	Cash flow £	Discount factor	Present value £	Cash flow £	Discount factor	Present value £
Year 1	5,000,000	0.909	4,545,000	10,000,000	0.909	9,090,000
Year 2	4,000,000	0.826	3,304,000	8,000,000	0.826	6,608,000
Year 3	3,000,000	0.751	2,253,000	6,000,000	0.751	4,506,000
Year 4	2,000,000	0.683	1,366,000	4,000,000	0.683	2,732,000
Year 5	1,000,000	0.621	621,000	4,000,000	0.621	2,484,000
Total present values:			12,089,000			25,420,000
Less cost of stadium			12,000,000			25,000,000
Net present value:			89,000			420,000

Based on the calculations, the club should choose the Loxden stadium as it has a NPV of £420,000, compared with the Greenhill stadium's NPV of £89,000.

NPV evaluated

The NPV method of investment appraisal focuses on the profitability of an investment and it also takes into account the opportunity cost of money – the fact that money to be received in the future will be worth less when compared with current amounts of money. This means that it deals with some of the weaknesses of the methods introduced earlier this chapter. However, this does not mean that NPV is without its limitations.

The choice of discount rate may be seen as arbitrary. Choosing an appropriate rate may depend partly on the cost of capital but also on the perceived riskiness of the investment. However, by their very definition, investments are long-term projects and the potential riskiness of the investment may only be known if the external environment takes a turn for the worse. For example, few would have predicted the global economic slowdown in 2008. The discount rate selected may sometimes be seen as too high, meaning that certain projects are turned down. However, if the economic climate deteriorates unexpectedly, the project may appear to be more profitable than the actual outturn.

Internal rate of return (IRR)

As we can see with the NPV method, the profitability of the project will partly depend on the interest rate chosen to provide the discount factors. The higher the interest rate selected, the lower will be the overall profitability of the project when fully discounted. We can see this if we consider the same investment project using two different discount rates.

There will be some interest rate at which an investment project will provide a zero return. This interest rate is known as the internal rate of return (IRR). The IRR may provide more useful information for a manager than the NPV. The IRR shows the yield on the project in the form of a percentage return. As long as the cost of capital does not exceed the IRR, the investment project will generate a positive return. If, for example, the cost of capital for the firm is 10 per cent and the project only generates a positive NPV up to the rate of 11 per cent, the project may be seen as too risky to go ahead. However, if the IRR was calculated at 20 per cent, then, even with an eventual reduction in the overall return, the project will still provide a positive return with the cost of capital at 10 per cent.

Example 12.6

An overhaul of a firm's outdated production facilities is expected to cost £100,000. The improvement to the firm's net cash flow over the next five years is expected to be as follows:

Year 1	£40,000
Year 2	£35,000
Year 3	£30,000
Year 4	£20,000
Year 5	£10,000.

If we calculate the net present value using the discount rates of 10, 12 and 14 per cent, we will arrive at the following results:

	Cash flow	10%	NPV	12%	NPV	14%	NPV
Year 0	(100,000)		(100,000)		(100,000)		(100,000)
Year 1	40,000	0.909	36,360	0.893	35,720	0.877	35,080
Year 2	35,000	0.826	28,910	0.797	27,895	0.769	26,915
Year 3	30,000	0.751	22,530	0.712	21,360	0.675	20,250
Year 4	20,000	0.683	13,660	0.636	12,720	0.592	11,840
Year 5	10,000	0.621	6,210	0.567	5,670	0.519	5,190
			7,670		**3,365**		**(725)**

We can see that the NPV is positive using the discount rates of 10 and 12 per cent but is negative when using the discount rate of 14 per cent. This means that the IRR will be somewhere between 12 and 14 per cent.

To find out the exact IRR we could keep refining our calculations by using a discount rate of 13 per cent or even one of 13.5 per cent and so on. However, this could take time. The IRR can be calculated using the following formula:

$$\text{IRR} = 12\% + \frac{£3,365}{£3,365 + £725} \times (14\% - 12\%) = 13.645\%$$

The above solution is only an approximation to the 'true' IRR but the accuracy of this estimation is nearly always sufficient to use.

Another method of calculating the IRR is by plotting the NPV against the varying discount rates. If we plot the NPV on the vertical axis and the discount rate (as a percentage) generating that NPV on the horizontal axis, the IRR can be found by joining these points together in a line. The IRR will be the point at which this 'curve' crosses the horizontal axis. This is shown in Figure 12.1. The IRR found through this method will only be accurate if the chart is drawn accurately.

FIGURE 12.1 Estimating the IRR graphically

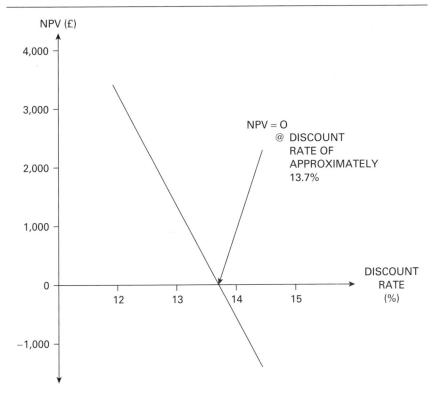

IRR evaluated

A main strength of the IRR method is that it gives a rate of return for any project, which can then be compared with the cost of the capital used to finance the investment project. The IRR can also act as a useful benchmark as to what return a firm requires. A risk-averse manager can then avoid projects that do not produce the required rate of return.

Discounted payback

One of the main limitations of the payback method is that the cash flows used in the calculation of the payback period are not adjusted to reflect the different time periods in which the cash flows are expected to be generated. We know that the further into the future the money is likely to be received, the lower its present value will be. As a result, a hybrid method of investment appraisal – discounted payback – can be used. This method is a modified use of payback with the additional use of discount factors to adjust the cash flows predicted for the future.

Example 12.7

If we use the data for projects A and B from the first example of this chapter we can illustrate the principle of discounted payback. The technique would involve using a discount rate and calculating the present value of the project net cash flows. Once calculated, the discounted figures would then be used for calculating the payback period for each project.

	Project A			Project B		
	Net cash flow	Discounted cash flow	Cumulative discounted cash flow	Net cash flow	Discounted cash flow	Cumulative discounted cash flow
Year	(£)	(£)	(£)	(£)	(£)	(£)
0 (ie now)	(15,000)	15,000		(15,000)	(15,000)	(15,000)
1	4,000	3,636	(11,364)	2,000	1,818	(13,182)
2	5,000	4,130	(7,234)	3,000	2,478	(10,704)
3	6,000	4,506	(2,728)	4,000	3,004	(7,700)
4	4,000	2,732	4	6,000	4,098	(3,602)
5	3,000	1,863		7,000	4,347	745

We can see from the table that project A has a discount payback period of just under four years, whereas for project B the discounted payback period will be close to five years. With discounted payback a greater weighting is given to cash flows received earlier. Projects with similar payback periods would produce different results when using discounted payback if the net cash flows of one project are received earlier than the one with the longer discounted payback period.

Investment appraisal evaluated

For any management tool which relies on estimates and forecasts, the ultimate use of the data will depend on how relevant and reliable the estimates prove to be. If the managers conducting the investment appraisal use overly optimistic cash flow predictions, the results that the investment appraisal methods generate will not be particularly useful and may actually lead to the firm committing large amounts of capital investment into projects which may not warrant such investment. Therefore the validity of investment appraisal will ultimately depend on the reliability of the data used within the calculations. It may be prudent to use a variety of different scenarios for the forecast of cash flows, thus producing a range of results. As always, managers should be prudent when making these estimates. Even if the cash flows are realistic estimates, there are other factors that should be considered when conducting investment appraisal.

Capital budgets

Capital expenditure usually involves the expenditure of large amounts of money. The capital budget for a firm may not permit all the potential investment projects to go ahead. In this case, decisions will have to be made as to which projects are priorities. This will depend on the nature of the project and the nature of the firm's overall aims.

Economic climate

The success of a particular investment project could well depend on the prevailing economic climate at the time of the investment. During periods of low economic activity and low business and consumer confidence, the success of a project may be in some doubt. Even if the economic conditions are fairly benign, the situation can change rapidly, thus making any investment appraisal projections largely meaningless. The financial crisis which began in 2007–08 was not expected to be as severe or as prolonged as it turned out to be. Similarly, the downturn and crisis in the eurozone that emerged from 2010 onwards was not foreseen a few years earlier.

Review questions

1   Richardson Ltd is trying to decide which project should be taken up, out of three possible investments. The initial investment would amount to £40,000. Scrap value at the end of use would be nil.

The cost of capital is 9 per cent, for which discount factors are as follows:

Year	Present value of £1
1	0.917
2	0.842
3	0.772
4	0.708
5	0.650

The net cash inflows from the three projects under consideration are:

	XC1	VB93	IPR2
	£	£	£
Year 1	5,000	14,000	11,000
Year 2	8,000	16,000	12,000
Year 3	6,000	21,000	13,000
Year 4	12,000	–	14,000
Year 5	18,000	–	–

For each possible project you are required to calculate:

(i)   payback;

(ii) net present value.

Solution

(i)   Payback periods

XC1	4 years 6 months
VB93	2 years 5.7 months
IPR2	3 years 3.4 months.

Based on payback, the firm should choose the VB93 project.

(ii) Net present value

XC1	Net cash flow	Discount factor	Present value
	£	£	£
Year 0	(40,000)	1.000	(40,000)
Year 1	5,000	0.917	4,585
Year 2	8,000	0.842	6,736
Year 3	6,000	0.772	4,632
Year 4	12,000	0.708	8,496
Year 5	18,000	0.65	11,700
			(3,851)

VB93	Net cash flow	Discount factor	Present value
	£	£	£
Year 0	(40,000)	1.000	(40,000)
Year 1	14,000	0.917	12,838
Year 2	16,000	0.842	13,472
Year 3	21,000	0.772	16,212
Year 4	–	0.708	0
Year 5	–	0.65	0
			2,522

IPR2	Net cash flow	Discount factor	Present value
	£	£	£
Year 0	(40,000)	1.000	(40,000)
Year 1	11,000	0.917	10,087
Year 2	12,000	0.842	10,104
Year 3	13,000	0.772	10,036
Year 4	14,000	0.708	9,912
Year 5	–	0.65	0
			139

Based on NPV calculations, the firm should go ahead with project VB93.

2   Throup Ltd is considering extending its operations into the production and sale of components used in the making of lawnmowers. The components cost £7 to manufacture and would be sold on to the lawnmower manufacturer for £12. A new machine will be needed, costing £10,000, which is payable on 1 January in year 1.

The expected sales of these components are as follows:

	Units
Year 1	600
Year 2	650
Year 3	720
Year 4	800
Year 5	850

The cost of capital is 10 per cent.

The following is an extract from the present value table for £1:

	10%
Year 1	0.909
Year 2	0.826
Year 3	0.751
Year 4	0.683
Year 5	0.621

It is assumed that revenues are received and costs are paid off at the end of each year, and that everything produced is sold.

(a)   Calculate the annual net cash flows for each year which are expected to result from the purchase of the machine.

(b)   Using the expected annual net cash flows, calculate the net present value for the machine.

Solution

	Cash inflow £	Cash outflow £	Net cash flow £
Year 1	7,200	4,200	3,000
Year 2	7,800	4,550	3,250
Year 3	8,640	5,040	3,600
Year 4	9,600	5,600	4,000
Year 5	10,200	5,950	4,250

	Discount factor	Net cash flow	Present value (£)
Year 1	0.909	3,000	2,727
Year 2	0.826	3,250	2,684.5
Year 3	0.751	3,600	2,703.6
Year 4	0.683	4,000	2,732
Year 5	0.621	4,250	2,639.25
			13,486.35
		Less costs	10,000
		Net present value =	**3,486.35**

3 The assembly machine of Tahoulan Ltd could be replaced. A replacement machine will cost £400,000, which is payable on 1 January in year 1. The new machine will be able to assemble 24,000 units a year. However, this is expected to rise by 25 per cent from the start of year 4.

- The cost of capital is 10%.
- The following is an extract from the present value table for £1:

	10%
Year 1	0.909
Year 2	0.826
Year 3	0.751
Year 4	0.683
Year 5	0.621

- It is assumed that revenues are received and costs are paid off at the end of each year.
- It is assumed that everything produced is sold.
- Each unit of production costs £25 to manufacture, but will rise to £32 in year 3 and £35 in year 4 onwards.
- Each unit is expected to sell for £35 in years 1 and 2, increasing by 10% in year 3 onwards.

Solution

	Units	Cash inflow	Cash outflow	Net cash flow
		£	£	£
Year 1	24,000	840,000	600,000	240,000
Year 2	24,000	840,000	600,000	240,000
Year 3	24,000	924,000	768,000	156,000
Year 4	30,000	1,155,000	1,050,000	105,000
Year 5	30,000	1,155,000	1,050,000	105,000

	Discount factor	Net cash flow	Present value
		£	£
Year 1	0.909	240,000	218,160
Year 2	0.826	240,000	198,240
Year 3	0.751	156,000	117,156
Year 4	0.683	105,000	71,715
Year 5	0.621	105,000	65,205
			670,476
		Less Cost	400,000
		Net present value	270,476

An introduction to limited companies

13

Introduction

As countries began to industrialize during the 18th and 19th centuries, business ventures generally expanded in size owing to increasing reliance on mechanized forms of production. This led to an increased need for capital in order to finance these operations. Potential investors in these business ventures would have been reluctant to risk much of an investment because the owners of such enterprises faced **unlimited liability**. This meant that owners of businesses would not only lose their original investment in the business but might also have to resort to selling off their own resources not used within the business in order to settle any outstanding debts that the business had incurred if it was unable to pay out of its own resources.

Unlimited liability still exists for business ventures for both sole traders and partnerships. These business organizations may bear the risk of un-limited liability but they are normally small-scale operations that have not acquired significant levels of debt. As small-scale ventures, the need to attract external investment is not as pressing an issue. Even with partner-ships, which are normally larger-scale organizations than sole traders, changes in regulation have allowed for the existence of a limited liability partnership, which means that this form of organization no longer has the risk of the owners of the business having to lose personal resources.

Limited liability

As the need for capital increased as the early industrial revolution progressed, it was recognized that to encourage investors to take risks by investing into business ventures, a change in the legal status of business organizations was needed. The introduction of the **limited company** as a new form of business organization allowed companies to raise capital from investors without the risk of the investors losing their own personal resources.

A limited company is characterized by the owners of the company benefiting from **limited liability**. This means that the owners of the company can lose no more than their original investment into the company. This is because the company, once set up, exists in the eyes of the law as a **separate legal entity**. For example, if legal action is to be taken against a company, it is the company that will face the action and not the owners of the company. The company exists separately from the owners of the company.

Setting up a limited company

Setting up a company in the UK requires the completion of a number of documents which must be submitted to Companies House. These documents are:

- *Application form IN01*. This includes details of the company's registered office, the names and addressors of the directors – the officers and, where appropriate, the company secretary – as well as a statement of the capital of the company and the initial shareholdings.
- *Memorandum of Association*. This contains details of the members of the company as well as their agreement to form a company and a commitment to buy a minimum number of shares within the new company.
- *Articles of Association*. This contains the 'rules' of how the company is to be run. These rules must not contradict the requirements of the Companies Act 2006. They can cover arrangements such as the rights of shareholders and details of the directors' powers.

Types of limited company

There are two main types of limited company in the UK: a public limited company and a private limited company.

Public limited companies

A public limited company will raise capital by issuing shares. Each member or shareholder will be limited in their liability to the value of their shareholdings (the total value of the initial share capital held by each member). Compared with other types of limited company, a public limited company has the following features:

- A minimum value of the share capital of £50,000.
- The company must have at least two directors and one company secretary.

- Shares in the company can be sold on the stock market in order to raise capital.

The ability to buy and sell shares in the public limited company is often seen as the key difference between this and a private limited company. Being able to 'trade' shares on the stock market means that company is capable of raising much greater levels of investment than a private limited company. This also has the implication that control of the public limited company may change hands over time – who owns the shares and has ultimate control can vary. If the original owners of the company wish to maintain control, they must ensure that they control a significant proportion of the voting shares of the company.

To signify that a company is a public limited company, it will have the abbreviation 'plc' at the end of its name.

Private limited companies

Although the private limited company is still set up by directors, it can be set up by one person alone who can operate as the sole director of the company as well as being the company secretary.

As with a public limited company, the private limited company will also raise capital by issuing shares. However, these shares will not be traded publicly. The shares in the company cannot be traded with non-shareholders unless prior agreement from existing shareholders is reached. This means that the size of the private limited company's capital is likely to be much smaller than that of a public limited company.

Although public limited companies are more likely to feature in news stories, the private limited company is much more commonplace. Many private limited companies are set up as small family-based businesses that wish to benefit from the limited liability the company status gives.

To signify that a company is a private limited company, it will have the abbreviation 'ltd' or the word 'limited' at the end of its name.

Other types of company

There are other types of limited company that exist. These are as follows:

- **private company limited by guarantee** – this type of organization does not have shareholders and is often favoured by charities as a business structure;
- **private unlimited company** – a rare type of organization where members' liability is unlimited.

Share capital and dividends

Each share issued will be sold to an investor for an amount of money which can then be used within the business. The total value of all the shares issued is referred to as the **share capital** of the business. The owners of these shares are referred to as **shareholders** and these are the real owners of the company. It is quite acceptable for the shareholders of the company to have no direct interest in the running of the company. This is referred to as a '**separation of ownership from control**'; the company will be run by a board of directors and the various managers of the various sections of the business. However, the owners are the shareholders, who usually purchase shares in order to generate a positive financial return.

As set out in either the IN01 form or the Memorandum of Association, the size of the company will be determined by the size of the share capital which can be issued by the firm. This maximum limit of share capital that can be raised is known as the **authorized share capital**. This will consist of the nominal value of each share (often £1 or some other small denomination) and the total number of shares that the company is permitted to issue. However, it is the **issued share capital** of the company that will appear on the balance sheet. This is the amount of share capital that has been 'sold' to investors. For public limited companies, the stock exchange helps facilitate trade in a company's shares. In effect, the stock exchange represents a second-hand market for the buying and selling of shares that have already been issued by the company. The current price of the share may well be significantly different from the value at which the share was originally issued.

Dividends are paid to shareholders out of company profits. The level of dividends will be determined by the size of the profits and the amount of the profits that the directors decide to retain within the company for future business use. Dividends are usually paid at the end of the financial year. However, a firm may also pay interim dividends which are paid during the year – often on declaration of the interim or halfway trading results of the company. The amount of dividend received by the shareholder will depend on the type of share held. There are different types of shares as follows.

Ordinary shares

Ordinary shares are the most common type of share on a company's balance sheet. Although there are often different classes of ordinary share, a common feature of the ordinary share is that the owner will be entitled to vote at the company's **Annual General Meeting (AGM)**. Voting will usually be concerned with the election of the directors of the company as well as any major changes in the company's future policy. Votes are proportionate to the number of shares held by the shareholder. It may not be a surprise to find that it is commonplace for the directors who have been elected to run the company to have substantial shareholdings.

If the company faces liquidation (often because of the firm's inability to settle its debts), the assets of the company will be sold off to settle, as far as possible, any outstanding debts of the business. It is the ordinary shareholder that is ranked lowest in terms of receiving money – they will only receive any money back in return for their investment if there are sufficient funds available once all other debts have been settled. However, the liability of ordinary shareholders is limited to the value of their investment (ie they can lose the investment but no more).

Ordinary shareholders have no automatic rights to dividends. However, they may receive dividends depending on how successful the company is each year. This means that in years when profits are high, the dividends paid to the ordinary shareholders might be quite high. However, in years of low profits, dividends may be low or non-existent.

Dividends will be normally be declared as an 'amount' per share.

Example 13.1

A firm has issued 500,000 £1 ordinary shares. At the AGM, the directors declare that an ordinary dividend is to be paid out of the profits, amounting to 6p per ordinary share. In this case, the total dividend to be paid will be 6p for each £1 share × 500,000 = £30,000.

Preference shares

Preference shares may also be issued by the company. These shares do not normally have any voting rights. They are termed preference shares because they take priority over ordinary shareholders in the case of the company being liquidated and money from the realization of the assets of the company being paid out to the various stakeholders of the company. In addition, the dividends of the preference shareholder will be paid before the ordinary divided is paid.

The dividend on the preference shares is fixed. This is often expressed as a percentage of the nominal value.

Example 13.2

A firm has preference share capital of 300,000 50p shares which carry a dividend at the rate of 5 per cent.

The dividend will be 5% × 50p = 2.5p × 300,000 = £7,500.

Another type of preference share is a **cumulative preference share**. If these are issued, then when a company has insufficient profits to pay its preference dividends, that year's dividend will be carried forward and paid out the next year along with that year's dividends as well. The extra dividend paid as a result of the accumulation of unpaid dividends may also mean that there are insufficient profits to pay the ordinary dividend.

The value of a preference share will fluctuate according to returns available elsewhere. For example, if a preference share carries a dividend of 6 per cent of the face value of the share but returns on other financial investments are higher, the market price of the preference share would fall until the return on the preference share is of a comparable size. So, if the face value of the preference share was £1 with a 6 per cent dividend, but other returns were available elsewhere equivalent to 10 per cent, the preference share would, all other things equal, look unattractive until its value fell to £0.60 when the 6 per cent dividend is equivalent to 10 per cent on the actual price for the share.

There are other types of share, such as convertible shares, which are shares which can be converted into loans. Similarly, there are non-current liabilities that may be converted into shares at a later date.

Financial statements of the limited company

Before we consider the financial statements of the limited company it is worth making the distinction between the internal financial statements and the external versions of the statements. Internal financial statements are drawn up for the user groups within the company, such as managers and directors. The external financial statements are those that are published for user groups outside the company. External financial statements must meet the requirements set out by legislation and the accounting standards relevant to the business organization. Financial statements produced for internal use do not have to conform to any agreed standard or format. This means that they can contain as much or as little detail as required. It is the internal statements we will consider initially.

Income statements

The principles applied to the construction of an income statement for a sole trader will also apply to a limited company or other forms of business organization. The accruals concept is still applied to the incomes and expenses that are incurred by the company. Other accounting concepts should also be applied, such as the concepts of prudence, consistency and going concern.

There are also items which will appear in the income statement which would not appear in those of partnerships or sole traders:

- **Director's remuneration** will appear as an expense in the income statement and represents the amounts paid to the directors of the company.

- **Debenture interest** may also appear as an expense. Debentures (a form of long-term liability) will only be issued by companies and the interest on any outstanding debentures will be charged on an annual basis.

- **Corporation taxation** will appear as a deduction in the income statement. Individuals and other unincorporated businesses will pay income tax. Companies, which exist as entities separate from their owners, will pay corporation tax, which is based on the profit earned by the company.

In addition to the income statement, there is a further statement which follows on from the final profit calculation. This is known as the **statement of changes in equity** and it shows how profits have been allocated within the business. This will often consist of the level of dividends paid and any transfers to reserves, which are covered later in this chapter. For the published accounts prepared for external users, the statement of changes in equity will contain more items and more details, which are covered in the following chapter.

Balance sheet of a limited company

The balance sheet of a limited company prepared for internal usage, as with the income statement, is not significantly different from that of a sole trader. Assets are classified into non-current assets and current assets. Liabilities are classified into non-current and current liabilities. Explanations of these categories of assets and liabilities were given earlier in this book. The main differences between the balance sheet of a sole trader and the balance sheet of a limited company are found in the capital section.

Capital of a limited company

Capital in a limited company will arise out of shares sold to potential investors. These could consist of both ordinary and preference shares. If all the profits earned by the company for a particular period were distributed as dividends to the shareholders, the capital of the company would not grow. However, it is likely that not all profits will be distributed by the company and this will lead to the creation of reserves.

Reserves

Reserves will appear on the balance sheet of the limited company as part of the equity. **Equity** refers to the combined total of issued share capital and these reserves (also known as **shareholders' funds**).

The term 'reserves' is often misunderstood by accounting students. This is because the term 'reserve' conjures up the idea that it corresponds to an amount of money. It is important to shed any assumptions that reserves correspond to actual amounts of money put aside somewhere in the company for use at a later date. The reserves that exist on the company balance sheet arise from a number of sources, such as the profits retained within the business as well as other changes to the firm's capital. There are two types of reserves that appear on the company balance sheet: **capital reserves** and **revenue reserves**.

Revenue reserves

These reserves are 'created' out of profits which are retained within the company to help the business expand. For the sole trader, any net profit which is not taken out of the business in the form of drawings is added on to the capital of the sole trader, which would gradually increase over time (assuming that the business was successful) as increasing amounts of profits built up capital over time.

For the company, the profit which is retained within the business is kept in its own reserve, referred to as **retained earnings**. This reserve will grow over time as more profit is retained within the company. However, this reserve can also be used to distribute dividends. For example, if the profit of the company is particularly low one year, the directors may decide to declare a dividend for shareholders in excess of the profits actually earned. This dividend payment would reduce the size of the retained earnings (it is more probable, though, that companies would prefer not to reduce the size of their revenue reserves in this case and would declare either no dividend or a reduced dividend).

Another revenue reserve which may appear on the balance sheet is known as the **general reserve**. Amounts can be transferred to this general reserve from the profits earned by the company. Likewise, amounts can be transferred out of the general reserve so as to free them up for use as dividends.

Capital reserves

As well as revenue reserves, capital reserves may also appear within the equity section of the balance sheet. These reserves arise out of one-off adjustments to the capital of the company. The capital reserves cannot be used for distribution as dividends. Two frequently appearing capital reserves are as follows.

Revaluation reserve

If the current fair value of a non-current asset (an amount that the asset could be sold for) is significantly higher than the existing balance sheet value of the asset, it is usually permissible for a company to increase the value for that asset on the balance sheet. So that the balance sheet maintains its 'balance', the increase in valuation would appear as an entry (or creation if this is the first time this process has occurred) in the revaluation reserve.

Example 13.3

Property valued by the business at its historical cost of £250,000 is now considered to be significantly out of date. The directors have had the property valued by an external agency and would now like to raise the value of the property on the balance sheet to £1 million.

The change in the valuation is £750,000 so it is this amount that would appear in the revaluation reserve:

Assets	*Equity*
Restate value of property at £1,000,000 (ie increases by £750,000)	Increase size of revaluation reserve by £750,000

Given that the business now has a more valuable asset, it might have seemed appropriate to record this as a profit on revaluation in the income statement. However, given that the company is unlikely to sell this asset in the near future, it is not included as a profit that can be realized.

Share premium account

As mentioned earlier, a company may choose not to issue all of its authorized share capital at one time. If a company makes a further share issue at a later date, the market price of the share may have risen above the original nominal value. Companies can sell the new shares for a higher price which is more in line with the current market price. However, the share capital that appears on the balance sheet must reflect the nominal value. The 'excess' value that is generated when shares are sold is known as the share premium.

Example 13.4

When a company was formed it issued 500,000 £1 ordinary shares as its share capital. A few years later it wishes to raise additional funds, so it issues an additional 200,000 shares but these are sold at a value of £2.50.

The 'excess' amount of £1.50 (£2.50 − £1 original value) represents the share premium. Based on the number of shares being issued, this will raise:

$$£2.50 \times 200,000 = £500,000$$

The effect on the company's balance sheet would be as follows:

Assets	Equity
Bank should increase by £500,000	Share capital will rise by 200,000 × £1 = £200,000
	Share premium will rise by 200,000 × £1.50 = £300,000

Example 13.5

The following is a worked example of a set of financial statements for a limited company produced for internal use:

Shortland plc
Trial balance as at 31 Dec 2018

	£	£
Issued ordinary share capital (£1 shares)		250,000
5% Debenture 2024		40,000
Retained earnings		15,600
Property	300,000	
Plant and equipment	62,000	
Sales revenue		178,000
Purchases	87,500	
Inventory as at 1 January 2018	14,750	
Distribution costs	12,110	
Administration costs	7,676	
Debenture interest	2,000	
Directors remuneration	18,900	
Trade receivables and payables	6,456	5,341
Cash and cash equivalents	1,549	
Provision for depreciation on property		13,000
Provision for depreciation on plant and equipment		22,000
Dividends paid	11,000	
	521,941	521,941

Additional information:

1 Inventory at 31 Dec 2018: £8,950.

2 Tax charge for the year: £7,740.

3 Depreciation is to be provided for as follows:

   a Property: 1% on cost

   b Plant and equipment: 20% on cost.

Shortland plc
Income statement
for year to 31 December 2018

	£	£
Sales		178,000
Less Cost of goods sold:		
Opening inventory	14,750	
Add Purchases	87,500	
	102,250	
Less Closing inventory	8,950	93,300
Gross profit		84,700
Less Expenses		
Distribution costs	12,110	
Administration costs	7,676	
Depreciation on property	3,000	
Depreciation on plant and equipment	12,400	
Debenture interest	2,000	
Directors' remuneration	18,900	56,086
Profit before tax		28,614
Tax		7,740
Profit for year		20,874

Statement of changes in equity

	£
Retained earnings:	
Balance at start of year	15,600
Add Profit for year	20,874
	36,474
Less Dividends paid	11,000
Balance at end of year	25,474

Shortland plc
Balance sheet as at 31 December 2018

Non-current assets	Cost	Depreciation	Net book value
	£	£	£
Property	300,000	16,000	284,000
Plant and equipment	62,000	34,400	27,600
	362,000	50,400	311,600
Current assets			
Inventory		8,950	
Trade receivables		6,456	
Cash and cash equivalents		1,549	
		16,955	
Current liabilities			
Trade payables		5,341	
Tax owing		7,740	
		13,081	
Working capital			3,874
			315,474
Non-current liabilities			
5% Debentures 2024			40,000
			275,474
Equity			
Ordinary share capital			250,000
Retained earnings			25,474
			275,474

Rights issues

A company may wish to raise additional share capital in order to fund the acquisition of additional assets or to repay loans. If the company has not yet issued all of its authorized share capital, it is possible to issue further share capital through a rights issue (it could engage in a 'normal' issue but this is likely to be more expensive).

A rights issue takes place when the company initially offers the right to purchase additional shares to existing shareholders. These new shares would normally be offered to existing shareholders in proportion to their existing holdings. The right to take up this offer is usually made more attractive by the offer of the new shares being at a discount to the current market price. In effect, as long as the market price is not about to collapse, it would prove profitable for an existing investor to exercise their right to purchase these shares even if they were to sell them on immediately at the current (higher) market price.

A rights issue will normally be cheaper for a company to arrange than a traditional share issue, where a prospectus has to be arranged with a potentially expensive advertising campaign. However, the effect of a rights issue, even if successful, is likely to lead to a slight fall in the market price to reflect these new discounted shares appearing on the market.

In 2008, as the financial crisis developed, many companies attempted to undertake rights issues. Banks and other financial institutions attempted to increase the liquidity of their balance sheets by organizing rights issues. Most of these were unsuccessful. The reason was that although the rights issues shares were offered at a discount, the current market prices of the companies' shares were already falling – what would be the point in buying shares at a discount if you knew that they are likely to be worth even less in a matter of a few weeks?

Example 13.6

The market price of the shares of Hardy plc is currently £6.

In order to raise additional finance the company decides to raise finance through a rights issue. Existing shareholders are offered shares in the proportion of one new share for every ten already held at the discounted price of £5.

Equity	£
Ordinary shares of £1 each	10,000,000
Revaluation reserve	2,000,000
Profit and loss account	3,000,000
	15,000,000

One in ten new shares being issued means 1,000,000 new shares. This will raise £5 × 1,000,000 = £5,000,000 extra money.

Assuming the rights issue was successful, the equity section of the balance sheet of Hardy plc would appear as follows:

Equity	£
Ordinary shares of £1 each	11,000,000
Share premium account	4,000,000
Revaluation reserve	2,000,000
Profit and loss account	3,000,000
	20,000,000

Bonus issues

A bonus issue (also known as a **scrip issue**) involves giving 'free' shares to existing shareholders in proportion to their existing shareholdings. The bonus shares that are issued do not raise capital for the company as the shares are given to the shareholders. These free shares are created out of the existing reserves of the company. The value of the bonus shares created must be equally offset by the reduction in the reserves of the company. The company can choose which of its reserves to utilize for the creation of the bonus shares.

Example 13.7

The directors decide to make a bonus issue of shares on the basis of one share for every four shares held. The directors have decided to utilize all the company's reserves equally.

Equity	£
Ordinary shares of £1 each	12,000,000
Revaluation reserve	2,000,000
Profit and loss account	5,000,000
	19,000,000

This means that the company will be creating ¼ × 12,000,000 = 3,000,000 bonus shares of £1 each. It will also mean that the company has to reduce its reserves by an equivalent amount.

After the bonus issue, the equity section of the balance sheet will appear as follows:

Equity	£
Ordinary shares of £1 each	15,000,000
Revaluation reserve	500,000
Profit and loss account	3,500,000
	19,000,000

In theory, the market price of the share would adjust immediately after the bonus issue so as to leave the total value of any shareholdings unaltered. For example, a shareholding of five shares with a market value of £4 each would give a total value of £20. If three additional bonus shares were included, the total holding of eight shares (five plus the three bonus shares) would still be worth £20. This means that the market price would be expected to fall to £2.50 (£20/8). However, the market does not always behave in a perfectly rational manner.

The motivation for a bonus issue may include the following:

- It shows that the managers are confident that they will have no problem paying future dividends. If revenue reserves have been used to create the bonus shares, the managers of the company must be confident that the company will grow and the existing reserves would not be needed for the purpose of dividend distribution.

- The bonus issue should improve the ease of being able to sell an individual share (or group of shares). If the current market price of a share is very high, it may be hard to sell if investors are generally looking to buy shares in smaller 'denominations' – for example, a share worth £400 may be hard to sell if an investor is only looking to invest, say, £200. However, after the bonus issue, the market price should fall, so making it easier for a current shareholder to sell their shares.

- The creditors (lenders) of the company might want the bonus issue to occur. For example, a bank may stipulate that a company undertakes a bonus issue so as to ensure that reserves are made part of the 'permanent capital' of the business and cannot be used for dividends (with the assumption that a lower level of dividends is better for the long-term growth prospects of the business).

Review questions

1   Stoddard plc started in business on 1 January 2012. Its issued share capital
    was 120,000 ordinary shares of £1 each and 30,000 6% preference shares of
    £1 each. The following information is available:

    • Net profits for the first two years of business were as follows: 2012 £58,911;
      2013 £72,344.

    • Corporation tax was as follows: 2012 £15,890; 2013 £26,750.

    • Transfers were made to the general reserve: 2012 £5,000; 2013 £10,000.

    • Preference dividends were always paid, whereas the ordinary dividends
      paid were 5% in 2012 and 7% in 2015.

    Produce a balance sheet extract for each of the three years of trading, showing
    the equity section.

Solution

Stoddard plc
Balance sheet extracts as at 31 December

	2012	2013
Equity	£	£
Ordinary share capital £1 shares	120,000	120,000
6% Preference shares	30,000	30,000
General reserve	5,000	15,000
Retained earnings	30,221	55,615
	185,221	220,615

2 Carlin plc started trading on 1 January 2014. The issued share capital was as follows:

- Ordinary share capital: 80,000 £1 shares.

- Preference share capital: 20,000 £1 shares (4%).

Details relating to trading for the first three years are as follows:

	2014	2015	2016
Net profits	£18,300	£21,456	£24,360
Taxation	£6,700	£7,650	£9,860
	£11,600	£23,006	£30,306
Transfers to reserves:			
General reserve	–	£4,000	£10,000

Preference dividends are provided as expected and ordinary shares are provided for as follows:

2014	2%
2015	3%
2016	5%.

Produce a balance sheet extract for each of the three years of trading, showing the equity section.

Solution

Carlin plc
Balance Sheet extracts as at 31 December

	2014	2015	2016
Equity	£	£	£
Ordinary share capital £1 shares	80,000	80,000	80,000
4% Preference shares	20,000	20,000	20,000
General reserve		4,000	14,000
Retained earnings	9,200	15,806	15,506
	109,200	119,806	129,506

Published accounts of the limited company

14

Introduction

When preparing financial statements for internal user groups the important issue is not whether the financial statements follow a prescribed format but whether the statements produced are fit for the purpose of the user. For example, if the user is a manager of the business who is interested in controlling expenditure and increasing profits, an important feature of the financial statements will be whether there is sufficient information about the types of, and levels of, expenditures contained within the statements to enable the manager of the business to achieve the objective of controlling expenditure.

For a company that is publishing its financial statements for external user groups, it will need to ensure that published statement follow certain formats and that certain information has been provided. All companies that sell their shares on the stock exchange (known as **listed companies**) are required to publish an annual report.

Annual return

All companies will have to submit an **annual return** to Companies House each year. The return will confirm many of the details that were submitted when the company was originally incorporated. Increasingly, companies are choosing to file their return online. If there are no changes to the members (directors) of the company or the share capital of the company, this can be relatively straightforward. However, if there is a change in the share capital or the directors of the firm, the change must be submitted separately.

For private companies, each shareholder and each debenture holder should receive a copy of the annual report or annual set of accounts of the company. These accounts will consist of the following:

- a set of financial statements plus notes to explain these statements;
- a directors' report;
- an auditor's report (some exemptions are made for small companies).

Depending on the size and nature of the company, the level of detail required for the annual accounts will vary. The size and nature of the company will determine which framework of accounting standards should be applied.

For public limited companies, an annual report will contain all of the items stated above but is also likely to contain additional information. In this chapter we will focus on the annual reports produced by public limited companies.

Contents of the annual report

Those making decisions about whether to purchase shares in a company will want confidence that the financial statements have been prepared in a manner which does not mislead the potential investors as to how successful the business actually is. In addition to the annual return and annual accounts, many large companies will publish an annual report which is designed to give the firm's shareholders information to enable them to assess their investment and to enable future investors to make a decision as to whether to purchase shares in the firm.

The annual accounts are often published and made available for shareholders as a summarized set of financial statements. As stated earlier, the quantity of information provided will depend on the size and type of company. For public limited companies the annual reports will often consist of glossy brochures designed to give out information to attract investors and to inform current investors, but also partly as a public relations exercise. These often contain details not legally required but designed to give useful information about the firm's activities and also to serve to establish a certain image of the company in the eyes of the general public and the media.

A typical annual report would contain some or all of the following:

- financial statements, consisting of the following:
  - income statement
  - balance sheet
  - statement of cash flows
  - statement of changes in equity
  - notes to the financial statements;

- a financial summary – based on the above financial statements;
- list of directors – and their roles within the business;
- directors' report – a board review of business performance and an outline of future plans;
- chairperson's report – a further commentary provided by the chair of the board of directors;
- remuneration report – the payments made to the executive and non-executive directors;
- historic review – a summary of the financial results of the firm over a longer period of time (usually five years);
- corporate governance report – a report on whether the company is complying with the Code of Best Practice on the board of directors and the remuneration package available for the directors;
- auditor's report.

Auditor's report

In order to protect shareholders, most companies must have an auditor. Auditors are professional accountants who are independent of the firm (so as to ensure objectivity and no vested interest) and are employed to check the reliability of the accounting records produced by the firm.

The auditor's report will comment on the assumed responsibility of the auditors and whether the auditors believe that the financial statements of the company have been produced in accordance with the appropriate accounting framework and relevant legislation.

If the auditors are satisfied that the financial statements have been produced in the appropriate manner, the auditor's report is likely to contain a comment suggesting that the statements are a *'true and fair view'* of the firm's overall financial performance (ie the financial statements are not misleading to potential or current investors). Other phrases which are used to indicate that the statements have been produced in an appropriate manner are that the statements are a *'fair presentation'* or that they *'present fairly, in all material aspects'*.

If the auditor is not satisfied that the financial records have been presented in an appropriate manner, they may present a **qualified report**. A qualified audit report is likely to appear where the auditors and the managers of the company disagree over some aspect of the financial records – this could include a change to an accounting policy, or an interpretation of a particular accounting standard. The disagreement may be over a relatively minor issue. However small the disagreement is, the auditors may feel they have a duty to bring the disagreement to the shareholders' (and potential shareholders') attention by making this qualified report. If they are satisfied with the financial statements, they will 'sign off' the statements.

Small companies (defined in the following chapter) can be considered to be exempt from having their annual accounts audited. This exemption does not apply to public limited companies or to private companies where a shareholder holding at least 10 per cent of the issue share capital demands an audit of the accounts.

Well-known examples of auditors are:

- PricewaterhouseCoopers
- Deloitte Touche Tohmatsu
- Ernst & Young
- KPMG
- BDO International
- Grant Thornton.

After a number of high-profile business failures occurred in the 1990s, some authorities took legal action against auditors where it was felt that the audit report had not given a warning that the financial statements were not a true and fair view of the business. The **Bannerman ruling** (based on the successful legal action taken against an auditing firm) means that auditors are now likely to provide a statement within their audit report that the auditors do not accept responsibility for any other parties using the annual report.

In the United States the failure of some businesses was blamed on auditors not doing their jobs properly and this partly led to legislation known as the **Sarbanes–Oxley Act** being passed. This was designed to make corporate reporting more transparent so as to protect investors.

Directors' report

The directors are elected by the shareholders of the company to oversee the overall running of the business. They are responsible for ensuring that the company complies with the relevant legislation applicable to the type of company that the directors represent, such as the need for filing the accounting statements produced by the company with the **Registrar of Companies** at Companies House.

It is a legal requirement to produce the statement known as the directors' report. This will contain details such as:

- the principal activities of the company;
- the name of each director and their shareholdings;
- the proposed dividends recommended by the directors to be paid to shareholders.

Business review

With the exception of small companies, the directors' report should also contain a **business review**. This will contain commentary on the performance of the business over the past year, its financial position at the end of that year and details of the principal risks and uncertainties that the business is likely to face during the coming year.

For quoted companies this business review should also contain details concerning the following:

- trends the business is likely to face and the likely effect on the performance of the company;
- the impact of business activities on the environment;
- details of company employees – such as employment data regarding people with disabilities;
- social and community issues;
- details of the employee pensions.

The directors' report should not be confused with any report included from the chairperson. The chairperson's report is not a statutory requirement for inclusion in the annual report and is more likely to focus on the positive aspects of the company's performance than the requirements of the directors' report.

Published financial statements – IAS 1

Published financial statements must comply with the guidance given by the relevant accounting standards set out by the country's accounting authority. Following a common approach to the presentation of financial statements should mean that accounting transactions and their effects on the financial statements should be recorded and presented in a way that does not mislead users as to the interpretation of such transactions.

All EU (including the UK) companies which have shares quoted on a recognized stock exchange (such as the FTSE100) are required to comply with **International Accounting Standard (IAS) 1: Presentation of financial statements**. This standard states that a complete set of financial statements would consist of the following:

- statement of financial position (the IFRS term for the Balance Sheet);
- statement of comprehensive income (the IFRS term for the Income Statement);
- statement of changes in equity;
- statement of cash flows;
- notes to the accounts and accounting policies.

IAS 1 makes use of different titles for the financial statements we have already covered earlier in the book. However, although IAS 1 refers to these different titles, it still allows the use of alternative titles for the financial statements, such as balance sheet and income statement.

Companies will need to state explicitly that their financial statements have been constructed according to IAS1 where this is the case. If a company has reason not to want to comply with all the requirements of IAS 1 (which may be appropriate if following the standard means that information presented may be misleading), this must also be stated with detailed reasons and/or explanation given for the divergence from the standard.

All financial statements should be produced, as a minimum, on an annual basis. This period of time between successive sets of financial statements is known as the **reporting period**. If a business wishes to change its reporting period, it is allowed to do so, provided that a warning about potential problems of comparability between earlier periods, and a reason for the switch, are given. Other requirements made by IAS 1 are that certain concepts are applied, such as the following.

Accruals concept
It is assumed that, apart from the statement of cash flows, the financial statements will have been prepared on an accruals basis.

Consistency
Unless there is a change in accounting standard requirements, the presentation and classification of items in the financial statements should remain the same in successive periods. Changes are permitted but this should be avoided unless necessary.

Going concern
The assumption is made that the business will continue to trade as a business into the future. If the business is not a going concern, or there is doubt that the business will remain a going concern, this must be disclosed as part of the financial statements.

Materiality and aggregation
Similar items must be grouped together to represent a class of items. For example, expenses of a similar nature should be aggregated and presented as one 'total' expense for the period. However, if disparate items exist which are not of material amounts, it is permissible to aggregate these together in order to produce a material amount.

Statement of financial position

As stated above, the statement of financial position is what we have previously termed the balance sheet of the business. This will show the information relating to the assets, the liabilities and the equity (the capital) of the business.

According to IAS1, assets would normally be categorized into current and non-current assets. Likewise, liabilities should be categorized into current and non-current liabilities. Definitions of what constitutes a non-current or current asset or what constitute non-current or current liabilities are similar to those given in Chapter 3. The distinction between non-current and current assets can be ignored if it is felt that it is not appropriate. In this case it may be appropriate to present the assets and liabilities in order of liquidity.

Content of the statement of financial position

The following contains the minimum requirements for inclusion within the statement of financial position:

- **(a)** property, plant and equipment;
- **(b)** investment property;
- **(c)** intangible assets;
- **(d)** financial assets;
- **(e)** investments accounted for by the equity method;
- **(f)** inventories;
- **(g)** trade and other receivables;
- **(h)** cash and cash equivalents;
- **(i)** assets classified as 'held for sale';
- **(j)** trade and other payables;
- **(k)** provisions;
- **(l)** financial liabilities;
- **(m)** current tax assets and liabilities;
- **(n)** deferred tax assets and liabilities;
- **(o)** liabilities included in disposal groups held for sale;
- **(p)** non-controlling interests;
- **(q)** issued equity capital and reserves.

Many of the items featured on the statement of financial position were explained in Chapter 3 when we looked at the balance sheet of a sole trader. Many of the terms and explanations that appear there will also apply here. However, financial statements published in accordance with IAS 1 will contain items which have not been previously explained, and further explanation of these items is given below.

Tangible assets

The standard that deals with many of the tangible non-current (or fixed) assets of the business is **IAS 16: Property, plant and equipment**. According to this standard, items of property, plant or equipment should be recorded on the statement of financial position at their original (historical) cost. This cost may also include other items of expenditure that have been capitalized, such as legal costs involved in the acquisition of the asset. Once the assets appear on the statement, the future value of the asset can follow one of two models: the cost model or the revaluation model.

The cost model involves the asset being shown at its carrying amount (or net book value), which would be the difference between the cost of the asset and the accumulated depreciation for that asset. As covered in Chapter 4, the depreciation of the asset represents the economic benefits gained from the consumption (ie use) of the asset. The depreciable amount of the asset (the cost less any expected residual value of the asset at the end of its useful life) would therefore be charged against the profit of the business over the lifetime of the asset. The method of depreciation chosen by the firm should reflect how the firm benefits from the asset over its life. Straight-line depreciation is a commonplace method – based the assumption that the firm benefits equally from each year's use of the asset.

The revaluation model for assets involves regular revaluation of the assets. The value of an asset on the statement should reflect a **fair value** of the asset less any depreciation or impairment losses. The fair value is the value at which an asset could be exchanged with a third party (assuming no vested interest from either party). Any revaluations of assets should be applied to all assets within the same class. For example, if one item of machinery is revalued upwards, all items of machinery held by the firm should be revalued.

Investment property is property held by the business for the purpose of earning rental incomes or for capital gain (through selling the property for a higher value than that originally paid). This investment property cannot be used for production of goods and services by the firm. Valuation of such property is fairly similar to the guidelines given in IAS 16. However, further information for the treatment of investment property comes under **IAS 40: Investment property**.

Intangible assets

The standard **IAS 38: Intangible assets** sets out the requirements made on a company for the treatment of intangible assets. An intangible asset is a *non-monetary asset that possesses no physical substance*. As with other definitions of assets, the intangible asset will generate future economic benefits for the business and it is under the control of the business. The business should also be able to identify the intangible asset separately from the business so that it could be sold or transferred by the business if it so wished. This gives us three criteria which can be used to judge whether an intangible asset exists:

- *Control* – does the business have control over the asset?
- *Identifiable* – can it be separated from the business and, if need be, sold?

- *Future economic benefits* – will the possession of the intangible asset generate future benefits to the business?

The intangible asset can either be acquired externally (ie by purchase from an outside agent) or created internally by the business. If the cost of the asset can be ascertained and the benefits that will flow to the business as result of the intangible asset can be quantified (ie future profit or future revenue streams), the asset can be recognized as an asset and appear on the statement of financial position.

Whether the intangible asset is acquired externally or generated internally does not prevent the asset being capitalized on the statement of financial position as long as the cost of the asset can be reliably measured and it is probable that benefits will flow to the business as a result. If neither of these criteria can be met, the intangible asset must not appear on the statement of financial position and should appear instead as an expense in the statement of comprehensive income. Common examples of intangible assets include the following:

- computer software;
- patents;
- copyrights;
- franchises;
- marketing rights.

If any of these fulfil the definition of an intangible asset, they can be capitalized. For some of the above examples, the decision on whether to include them as an asset or to treat them as an expense will depend on the circumstances. For example, externally purchased computer software can be measured in terms of cost, can be identified separately and the generation of future benefits can be measured. This would mean that the software fulfils the definition of an intangible asset. However, for internally generated computer software, it might be harder to show how it can be separated. The business would have to show that the internally generated software could be sold on to an outside agent before it could be treated as an intangible asset. In fact, IAS 38 states that internal development of software should be treated as an expense until it can be clearly established that the software could be sold.

Internally generated intangible assets would seem less likely to meet the criteria for the asset to be placed on the statement of financial position. For example, IAS 38 clearly states that internally generated goodwill, brand names generated internally and other types of intangible asset cannot be capitalized and should be written off as revenue expenditure.

Research and development refers to expenditure on generating new products and new processes by the business. Although the terms research and development frequently appear together as if it is simply one type of expenditure, the accounting treatment for research and development is quite clear in separating out **research expenditure** from **development expenditure**.

Research expenditure

Research involves expenditure in the hope of generating new scientific or technological advances for the business. Given that research expenditure is largely theoretical and does not involve any definite promise of future economic benefits for the business, it must be classified as revenue expenditure.

Development expenditure

Development expenditure involves taking the findings acquired from prior research and putting the research into practice in the form of new products, new processes and the like which can be exploited for commercial gain. This expenditure, which involves the business in seeking to make commercial gain from theoretical research, can be capitalized if the potential commercial gains from the development expenditure can be clearly identified and the business can show how it will gain economic benefits from the expenditure. Otherwise, the development expenditure will also be treated as revenue expenditure.

Where research and development expenditure cannot reliably be separated, the expenditure should not be capitalized.

Intangible assets should be shown on the statement of financial position at the point of acquiring the asset at cost value. However, as with tangible non-current assets, the intangible assets can be shown on the statement using either the cost model or the revaluation model.

Intangible assets are assumed to have either an infinite or a finite life. An intangible asset with a finite life should be **amortized** over its expenditure life. Amortization is the term used to describe the depreciation of intangible assets. A method of amortization should be chosen which reflects how the business will benefit from the intangible asset. This may be harder to judge than with tangible assets and so the straight-line method would normally be used. A key difference between the depreciation of a tangible asset and the amortization of an intangible asset is that it is highly unlikely that an intangible asset with a finite life would have any residual value. If the intangible asset is deemed to have an infinite life, the business should undertake regular impairment reviews to see whether the asset is still assumed to have an infinite life. If it is no longer assumed to have infinite life, it should revert to the accounting treatment for intangible assets with finite lifespans.

Assets classified as 'held for sale'

A non-current asset is deemed to be 'held for sale' if the business is actively seeking to sell the asset within the next year. Even if the asset is not actually sold, it must be available for immediate sale and the management of the business should be actively looking for a buyer for the asset. For example, if the management of a business were looking to sell part of the premises, they should ensure that the premises are not in use within the business, as this would prevent the asset being available for immediate sale. The selling price of the asset must be in relation to the current fair value of the asset as shown on the statement of financial position. If the firm is looking to sell the asset for a significantly higher amount than its fair value would imply, it should not class the asset as 'held for sale', as it is unreasonable to expect this asset to be sold in the near future.

The value of the asset held for sale on the statement of financial position should be the lower of the carrying amount on the statement or the fair value of the asset (less any costs involved in the sale of the asset). In most cases, the fair value will be lower than the carrying amount and therefore this should be the value at which the asset appears. Assets held for sale should be shown as a separate category on the statement of financial position and these assets should not be depreciated. The standard dealing with assets held for sale is **IFRS 5: Non-current Assets Held-for-sale and Discontinued Operations.**

Investments

A firm may hold investments in the form of shares within another company. How these appear on the statement of financial position will depend on the proportion of shares that are held by the investing company. The proportion held will connect with the degree of control the investor holds over the company in which it holds shares – obviously the greater the proportion of shares held, the greater the control.

Where a firm owns less than 20 per cent of the voting shares in another company, this investment would normally appear on the statement of financial position at cost or fair value.

Investments in associates

If a company owns more than 20 per cent of a company's shares, the firm would class the company in which it owns shares as an **associate**. This means that it has significant influence but not complete control over this company; it can influence policy decisions of the company but cannot directly dictate policy.

The valuation of the investment would originally have been at the cost of the investment (ie the purchase price of the shares). After the initial valuation, the investment in the associate would appear on the balance sheet using the **equity method**, which means that value would be adjusted according to the investor's shares in the profits and losses made by the associate company. The accounting standard dealing with associate companies is **IAS 28: Investments in associates.**

Investments in subsidiaries

If a company owns at least half of the voting shares of another company, the company in which the shares are held is said to be a **subsidiary** of the investing company. The investing company is said to be the **parent company**. If all the shares in the subsidiary are held, the subsidiary is said to be a 'wholly owned' subsidiary, and if more than 50 but less than 100 per cent are held, the subsidiary is said to be 'partly held'.

In the case of subsidiaries, a parent company is expected to present **consolidated accounts** where the financial statements of the parent and its subsidiary company (or companies) are presented as if they are from a single business entity. Where the subsidiary is wholly owned, the parent company can easily assimilate the profit or loss made by the subsidiary into its consolidated accounts. However, if the subsidiary is partly owned, in which case the shareholders outside the control of the parent company are known as **minority shareholders**, the parent company will not have the right to all the subsidiary firms' profits and losses. Any profit earned by the subsidiary firm, which is part attributable to the minority shareholders, will appear as a deduction in the statement of comprehensive income as a **minority interest**.

The subsidiary companies can still present their own single financial statements made available for their own shareholders. The accounting standard for dealing with subsidiaries' accounting is **IAS 27: Consolidated and Separate Financial Statements**.

Inventories

Inventories are goods that are held by the business for sale as part of the normal operations of the business. It will also include any partly finished goods (work-in-progress) and any raw materials held by the business in order to be converted into finished goods for resale at a later date.

The rule for the valuation of inventories is that they should appear on the statement of financial position at the lower of cost or net realizable value. The cost value of the inventories will include both direct and also some indirect costs of production. Procedures for the treatment of inventory are dealt with in **IAS 2: Inventories**.

A further calculation must be made for inventory where a business makes multiple purchases of identical inventory over a period and has inventory remaining unsold at the end of the period. The cost value of this inventory would vary if the cost value of the goods purchased had varied over the year. In this case an assumption has to be made over which cost value to use for the remaining inventory.

There are two methods which can be used to provide the value of inventory held by the business on the statement of financial position. These are as follows:

- **FIFO (first in, first out method)** – this method assumes that inventory remaining is of more recent purchases of goods.
- **AVCO (average cost method)** – this method takes a weighted average of the different cost values used to purchase inventory over the period.

Either of these methods is acceptable under IAS 2. If we make the assumption that inventory prices are rising over time, then out of the two methods of valuation it is the FIFO method which will give a higher value for inventory at the end of the reporting period. Once selected, a firm should continue to the use the same basis for valuing inventory on a consistent basis.

Tax assets and liabilities

Companies pay tax based on their profits. In the UK this is known as corporation tax. Given that this will not be known until some time after the end of the financial year, this will mean that any taxation will almost certainly appear under a current liability on the statement of financial position.

In addition, a company may have to show amounts owing or owed for deferred taxation. If depreciation rates charged by the company differ from capital allowances allowed under the tax regime followed by the company, there may be a difference between the actual profit appearing on the statement of comprehensive income and the profit that the tax payable will be based on. The tax deducted against the current profit will not necessarily be the amount of tax that is paid by the company in that period. It may also not be the same as the tax actually due for that period. Deferred taxation explains these differences in the amounts. Because of timing differences, the tax can appear as both an asset and a liability on the company's statement of financial position.

Provisions

Earlier in this book we referred to provisions – those for doubtful debts and those for depreciation of non-current assets. Strictly speaking, these are not provisions but can be thought of as 'allowances' rather than provisions.

According to **IAS 37: Provisions, Contingent Liabilities and Contingent Assets,** a provision is a liability whose timing and/or size is uncertain. If it is fairly likely that a firm will incur a debt or obligation to make a future payment, but it is uncertain how much this will amount to or what the exact timing of this obligation will be, the company should reflect this on the statement of financial position as a provision. This is not the same as a future planned amount of expenditure, as the liability must arise out of past events. Examples of items for which a provision may be made include the cost in cleaning up contaminated land, the cost of customer refunds, and the restructuring costs after the sale of a business operation. If a provision is recorded, the corresponding entry required to record the provision would be made either as an expense or as a cost to a new asset. For example, clean-up costs could be associated with the purchase and installation of a new oil rig.

A contingent liability occurs where there is a possible obligation due to some uncertain future event. Whereas a provision can appear on the statement of financial position, a contingent liability should not appear on the statement but should be disclosed. Contingent assets – a possible economic benefit from an uncertain future asset – should not be recognized but should be disclosed if probable.

Equity

The company's equity – its issued share capital and any reserves – will appear on the statement of financial position. The following disclosures are also required:

- number of shares both authorized and issued by the company, including those fully paid and those not fully paid;
- the par value of the company's shares (ie the face value);
- reconciliation of shares outstanding at the start and end of the period;
- treasury shares – those shares 'bought back' by the company;
- shares reserved for issue under share options and contracts;
- description of the nature and purpose of each reserve appearing within the equity section, such as that for share premium and for retained earnings.

If the company is a parent company with control over subsidiary companies, any minority interest would also appear here at its nominal value. This represents the nominal value of the share capital which is not owned by the investing company but is owned by the minority shareholders.

Presentation of the statement of financial position under IAS 1

The order of the items can be altered if the business feels that a different order would be appropriate. If appropriate, further items can appear, as categories may be subdivided. For example, inventories may be classified into further groups, such as finished goods inventory and raw materials inventory.

A common format of the statement of financial position is as follows:

Typical statement of financial position (balance sheet) at 31 December 2016		
	2016	2015
	£000	£000
ASSETS		
Non-current assets	XXX	XXX
Property, plant and equipment	XXX	XXX
Investment property	XXX	XXX
Intangible assets	XXX	XXX
Financial assets	XXX	XXX
Investments accounted for by the equity method	XXX	XXX
Current assets		
Inventories	XXX	XXX
Trade and other receivables	XXX	XXX
Cash and cash equivalents	XXX	XXX
Total assets	XXX	XXX
EQUITY AND LIABILITITES		
Equity	XXX	XXX
Issued share capital	XXX	XXX
Retained earnings	XXX	XXX
Other reserves		
Total equity		
Non-current liabilities		
Long-term borrowings	XXX	XXX
Deferred tax	XXX	XXX
Current liabilities		
Trade and other payables	XXX	XXX
Short-term borrowings	XXX	XXX
Current tax owing	XXX	XXX
Total liabilities	XXX	XXX
Total equity and liabilities	XXX	XXX

However, there is no prescribed format for the statement of financial position. Many UK companies present their details on the statement of financial position using the following identity:

Non-current assets + Current assets − Current liabilities
= Equity + Non-current liabilities

Statement of comprehensive income

The statement of comprehensive income is the term used within IAS 1 for the income statement (or profit and loss account). This is meant to present the flows of incomes and expenses for the reporting period for the business, which will lead to the calculation of the profit or loss for the period. This profit or loss is then supplemented by 'other comprehensive income' for the same period.

IAS 1 permits two formats for the statement of comprehensive income:

- a single statement of comprehensive income; or
- two statements comprising:
  - income statement showing profit or loss for the period;
  - statement of comprehensive income including profit or loss for the period but also including other comprehensive income.

Although the profit or loss calculation will appear similar to work covered earlier in this text, the inclusion of other comprehensive income will mean that the income statement of a company following IFRS appears very different from that of a sole trader.

Other comprehensive income will consist for the following components:

- changes in the revaluation surplus;
- actuarial gains and losses on defined benefit plans;
- gains and losses made from translating financial statements of a foreign operation;
- gains and losses on measuring available-for-sale financial assets;
- the effective portion of gains and losses on hedging instruments in a cash flow hedge.

As with the statement of financial position, IAS 1 stipulates a minimum number of entries that should appear where relevant on the statement of comprehensive income. These are as follows:

(a) revenue (ie sales revenue);
(b) finance costs;
(c) profits or losses accounted for by the equity method;
(d) tax expense;

(e) profit or loss (after tax) for any discontinued operations;

(f) profit or loss for the period;

(g) each component of other comprehensive income;

(h) total comprehensive income.

If the statement of comprehensive income is for a group of companies rather than a single company, additional entries will needed in the statement to account for:

- the profit or loss attributable to non-controlling interest (ie associates and joint ventures) of the business to the owners of the parent company;

- any other comprehensive income attributable to non-controlling interest (ie associates and joint ventures) of the business to the owners of the parent company.

Expenses that appear in the calculation of the profit or loss for the period can be analysed by either their nature (eg raw materials, staffing costs, depreciation, etc) or their function (eg cost of sales, selling costs, administration costs, etc). Additional information would need to be provided if the business chose to analyse expenses by function rather than by nature.

Some of the items appearing in the statement of comprehensive income correspond to an asset or liability on the statement of financial position. However, some of the items require a closer look.

Revenue

The first entry in the statement of comprehensive income will be the sales revenue for that period. The level of sales would normally (but not always) appear net of sales taxes (such as VAT) and should be shown net of any returns sent back to the company. Given the existence of sales made on credit – where the sale of goods and the payment received for the sale of goods are in different time periods – we need to consider carefully how we are going to recognize a sale. The realization concept will act as a guide and further requirements on how and when a sale is recognized is given in the standard **IAS 18: Revenue.**

Given the importance of revenue in generating profit for the business, there have been cases where businesses have included sales that perhaps should not have been included in the revenue for that period. Examples of sales that might mislead users as to the true extent of the sales figures would include firms making sales on a 'sale or return basis', whereby a customer can return the goods at a later date and expect a full refund without any conditions attached to the return. Similarly, including sales before the order has been received would give a false impression that a sale has taken place as, being prudent, we should not anticipate income before it is earned. Both of these examples would fail to meet the criteria given by

IAS 18 as to what should be included as a sale. The standard states that certain conditions have to be met before a sale is recognized. These include the following:

- The buyer has taken on the risk and reward of the ownership of the good or service sold.
- The seller retains no involvement or control over the goods sold.
- The transaction will probably generate economic benefits that flow to the business making the sale.
- The amount of revenue generated by the sale can be reliably measured.

Cost of sales

The cost of sales figure is equivalent to the cost of goods sold figure covered within Chapter 3 on the balance sheet. This will cover the costs incurred in the purchase or production of goods which are made available for sale. The costs incurred in the cost of sales calculation will include the direct costs involved in production as well as direct production overheads. Any change in the inventory levels of finished goods would be adjusted for. The adjustment that we previously showed in full in the income statement of a sole trader will not normally be present on the statement of comprehensive income, though the details of the adjustment may be present in a note to the statement.

Continuing operations

A statement of comprehensive income will contain the profit earned by the company on both **continuing operations** and **discontinued operations**. A discontinued operation occurs when a business sells off or disposes of part of the operations of the business during the most recent period. In the year-end results it makes sense to categorize any profits or losses on this part of the business separately from the continuing operations of the business. This is because a user of the statements can then assess how the business is likely to perform in the following year by focusing on the areas that will still be part of the business in the future.

Share of profit in associates or joint ventures

As mentioned earlier, the company may have a significant influence over other companies through share ownership. Any profits earned from investments in associates would be included as a separate income (and losses would appear as a separate deduction). This will also apply to profits earned on **joint ventures**. A joint venture occurs where a company enters into a contractual agreement with another company. The profits or losses on this enterprise (which is often a temporary coming together of two companies which may have complementary expertise for a particular business operation) will be accorded to the company in proportion to its investment in the joint venture. The profits from the joint venture will appear as a separate entry distinct from the company's overall profits and are not consolidated into the company's overall income as the company does not have complete control over this venture.

Layout of the statement of comprehensive income

The following examples illustrate a typical layout of a statement of comprehensive income based on the two formats allowable by IAS 1.

On the first statement – the single statement of comprehensive income – we have analysed (ie presented) expenses according to their function:

Typical company plc Single statement of comprehensive income for year to 31 December 2015		
	2015	2014
	£	£
Revenue	XXX	XXX
Cost of sales	(XXX)	(XXX)
Gross profit	XXX	XXX
Other incomes	XXX	XXX
Selling expenses	(XXX)	(XXX)
Administration expenses	(XXX)	(XXX)
Other expenses	(XXX)	(XXX)
Operating profit	XXX	XXX
Finance costs	(XXX)	(XXX)
Share of profit in associates or joint ventures	XXX	XXX
Profit before tax	XXX	XXX
Tax (charged on profit)	(XXX)	(XXX)
Profit for the year from continuing operations	XXX	XXX
Profit on discontinued operations	XXX	XXX
Profit for the year	XXX	XXX
Other comprehensive income	XXX	XXX
Exchange differences on translating foreign operations	XXX	XXX
Gain on revaluation of property	XXX	XXX
Tax on other comprehensive income	(XXX)	(XXX)
Other comprehensive income after tax	XXX	XXX
TOTAL COMPREHENSIVE INCOME	XXX	XXX

The following single income statement contains expenses which are analysed according to their nature:

Typical company plc **Separate income statement for year to 31 December 2015**		
	2015	2014
	£	£
Revenue	XXX	XXX
Investment income	XXX	XXX
Changes in inventories	XXX	XXX
(of finished goods and work-in-progress)		
Raw materials used	(XXX)	(XXX)
Depreciation and amortization charge for period	(XXX)	(XXX)
Employee expenses	(XXX)	(XXX)
Finance costs	(XXX)	(XXX)
Profit before tax	XXX	XXX
Tax (charged on profit)	(XXX)	(XXX)
Profit for the year	XXX	XXX

The income statement would then be followed by a statement of comprehensive income for the business.

Typical company plc **Statement of comprehensive income for year to 31 December 2015**		
	2015	2014
	£	£
Profit for the year	XXX	XXX
Other comprehensive income	XXX	XXX
Exchange differences on translating foreign operations	XXX	XXX
Gain on revaluation of property	XXX	XXX
Tax on other comprehensive income	(XXX)	(XXX)
Other comprehensive income after tax	XXX	XXX
TOTAL COMPREHENSIVE INCOME	XXX	XXX

Statement of changes in equity

A company's equity represents the residual interest of the shareholders of the company in the assets of the company after liabilities have been deducted. Equity will consist of issued share capital and any reserves of the company. The statement of changes in equity will show how each component that makes up the equity of the company has changed over the most recent reporting period.

For the internal statement of comprehensive income produced by a business, the statement of changes in equity can be a short addition to the overall calculation of profit for the year (as covered in the previous chapter). However, when publishing financial statements, IAS 1 stipulates that the statement of changes in equity should appear as a separate statement. IAS 1 also stipulates the minimum amount of information that should appear in this statement:

- Total comprehensive income for the period (split into amounts for the owners of the parent company and those of non-controlling interests).

- If the accounting policy has changed, the effects of any retrospective application of the change in policy should be shown.

- Reconciliation showing the carrying amounts for each component of equity between the start of the period and the end of the period – with separate adjustments for:
  - profit or loss;
  - other comprehensive income;
  - transactions with the owners of the company in the form of dividends distributed to the owners of the company and any share issues made by the company.

A typical statement of changes in equity would appear as follows:

Typical company plc Statement of changes in equity for year to 31 December 2015			
	Share capital £000	Retained earnings £000	Capital reserves £000	Equity £000
Balance at 31 Dec 2014	XXX	XXX	XXX	XXX
Changes in equity for 2015:				
Issued share capital	XXX			
Total comprehensive income		XXX		XXX
Dividends		(XXX)		(XXX)
Balance at 31 Dec 2015	XXX	XXX	XXX	XXX

Example 14.1

As at 1 January 2014 the equity of Masters plc comprised the following:

	£000
Issued share capital	500
Share premium account	100
Retained earnings	89
Total equity	689

During the year a further 100,000 £1 shares were issued at a premium of 75p. Profit for the year was £37,200 and the level of dividends paid totalled £12,000.

The statement of changes in equity would appear as follows:

Masters Plc
Statement of changes in equity for year to 31 December 2014

	Issued share capital (£)	Retained earnings (£)	Share premium account (£)	Equity (£)
At 1 January 2014	500,000	89,000	100,000	689,000
Issue of shares	100,000		75,000	175,000
Profit for the year		37,200		37,200
Dividends		(12,000)		(12,000)
As at 31 December 2014	600,000	114,200	175,000	889,200

Statement of cash flows

The standard applicable to the statement of cash flows is IAS 7 and this is covered separately in Chapter 16.

Notes to the financial statements

The notes to the financial statements will contain the details of the company's accounting policies. For example, property, plant and equipment will be subject to depreciation for each separate category of asset. The depreciation policy used would be stated for each class of asset. The methods used to value inventories would also appear.

Many of the accounting standards which have been used to present and construct the financial statements will make requirements on a company to make various disclosures which would otherwise not show up in the financial statements. For example, disclosures concerning contingent liabilities and contingent assets should be made here.

For large companies, the notes to the financial statements will often be lengthy and will contain useful information for a potential investor. For example, if there has been a change in policy, the notes may give an explanation of why such a change was thought necessary. One common inclusion is a **schedule of non-current assets**. This outlines the changes to the various classes of non-current assets held by the company. An example appears here.

Example 14.2

Gibbon Plc had the following fixed assets as at 31 December 2015:

	Cost	Provision for depreciation to date
	£	£
Freehold land	300,000	n/a
Buildings	250,000	50,000
Plant and machinery	120,000	40,000

The depreciation policy of the firm is to provide for depreciation as follows:

- buildings: 10% per year straight line;

- plant and machinery: 20% per year straight line.

No depreciation is to be provided for freehold land. All depreciation is based on the values of assets held at the end of the financial year.

During the year to 31 December 2016, the following events occurred:

1   Land was revalued to £500,000.

2   New buildings were purchased at a cost of £200,000.

3   Plant and machinery which had cost £40,000 were sold for £30,000, which generated a profit on disposal of £10,000.

4   Plant and machinery was purchased for £60,000.

The schedule of non-current assets at 31 December 2016 for inclusion in the notes to the accounts for the year end would appear as follows:

Schedule of non-current assets
for year ending 31 December 2016

	Freehold land £	Buildings £	Plant and machinery £
Balance as at 31 Dec 2005	300,000	250,000	120,000
Increase in revaluation	200,000		
Additions at cost		200,000	60,000
Disposals at cost			(40,000)
	500,000	450,000	140,000
Depreciation:			
Provisions as at 31 Dec 2004	n/a	50,000	40,000
Provisions on disposals			(20,000)
Charge for year	n/a	45,000	28,000
		95,000	48,000
Net book value at 31 Dec 2015	300,000	200,000	80,000
Net book value at 31 Dec 2016	500,000	355,000	92,000

The provision for depreciation on the plant and machinery sold would be calculated as follows: the profit on disposal means that the plant was sold for £10,000 more than its net book value. Therefore the net book value must have been £20,000. Therefore the depreciation on this asset must have been £20,000 (cost less net book value).

Example 14.3

Here is a worked example of the financial statements being produced from the trial balance of a company. The principles applied in the construction of the statement are identical to those used to construct the statements of a sole trader. However, the requirements of IAS 1 mean that the format of the statement must comply with a prescribed layout.

Hallsworth plc
Trial balance as at 31 December 2019

	Dr £000	Cr £000
Ordinary share capital (£1 shares)		800
Plant and equipment at cost	420	
Depreciation on plant and equipment		95
Investments (non-current)	330	
Property at cost	1,000	
Depreciation on property		150
Inventories as at 1 Jan 2019	48	
Revenue		1,100
Purchases	715	
Dividends paid	87	
Dividends received		28
Retained earnings		195
Distribution costs	105	
Trade receivables	85	
Trade payables		62
Accruals		
Administration costs	99	
Share premium		300
Cash and cash equivalents	81	
10% Debentures		250
Interest paid	10	
	2,980	2,980

Additional information:

1   The taxation due on the company's profits for the year is £76,000.

2   Distribution costs accrued at 31 Dec 2019 total £8,000.

3   Administration costs prepaid at 31 Dec 2019 totalled £4,000.

4   Only £10,000 of the interest due on the debentures had been paid by the end of the year.

5   Inventory in trade at the year end totalled £76,000.

6   The company engaged in a bonus issue of shares during the year which is not recorded in the trial balance. The bonus issue was made on the basis of one new share for every four already held. Reserves were to be mentioned in the most distributable form.

Solution

It may take time to commit the IAS 1 layout to memory. You should check to see if knowledge of the format is required for any assessment questions.

In our example, the statement of comprehensive income is produced as one overall statement as it is not detailed enough to warrant the two statements being presented separately.

The statement of comprehensive income would appear as follows:

Hallsworth plc
Statement of comprehensive income
for year ending 31 December 2019

	£000
Revenue	1,100
Cost of sales	(700)
Gross profit	400
Distribution costs	(113)
Administration costs	(95)
Profit from operations	192
Income from investments	28
Finance costs	(25)
Profit before tax	195
Tax	(76)
Profit for the year	119

Note that the adjustments for inventory are no longer shown in the statement (though the workings for this are still incorporated into the cost of sales figure). In addition, the adjustments for interest owing and other outstanding balances are factored into the data.

Hallsworth plc
Statement of changes in equity for year ending 31 December 2019

	Share capital £000	Retained earnings £000	Capital reserves £000	Equity £000
Balance at 31 Dec 2018	800	195	300	1,295
Changes in equity for 2019:				
Issued share capital	200		(200)	
Total comprehensive income		119		119
Dividends		(87)		(87)
Balance at 31 Dec 2019	1,000	227	100	1,327

We can see the effect of the bonus share issue is to increase share capital by £200,000 but also to reduce the share premium account by £200,000.

Hallsworth plc
Statement of financial position as at 31 December 2019

	£000
Non-current assets	
Property, plant and equipment	1,175
Investments	330
	1,505
Current assets	
Inventories	63
Trade and other receivables	89
Cash and cash equivalents	81
	233
Total assets	1,738
Equity and liabilities	
Equity	
Ordinary share capital (£1 shares)	1,000
Share premium	100
Retained earnings	227
Total equity	1,327
Non-current liabilities	
10% Debentures	250
Current liabilities	
Trade and other payables	85
Tax	76
	161
Total liabilities	411
Total equity and liabilities	1,738

Review question

1 The trial balance of Fender plc is as follows:

Fender plc
Trial balance as at 31 December 2017

	Dr £000	Cr £000
Ordinary share capital (£1 shares)		400
Plant and equipment at cost	480	
Depreciation on plant and equipment		95
Investments (non-current)	200	
Inventories as at 1 Jan 2017	74	
Revenue		965
Purchases	695	
Dividends paid	45	
Dividends received		22
Retained earnings		75
Selling and distribution costs	75	
Trade receivables	38	
Trade payables		27
Administration costs	49	
Share premium		60
Cash and cash equivalents	28	
5% Debentures		80
Interest paid	40	
	1,724	1,724

Based on the above trial balance, produce a statement of comprehensive income for the year ended 31 December 2017 and a statement of financial position as at that date.

Additional information:

1 Inventory as at 31 December 2017 was valued at £55,000.

2 Taxation for the year was assessed to be £30,000.

The format of the financial statements should follow the requirements of IAS 1 as closely as the information permits.

Solution

Fender plc
Statement of comprehensive income
for year ending 31 December 2017

	£000
Revenue	965
Cost of sales	(714)
Gross profit	251
Selling and distribution costs	(75)
Administration costs	(49)
Profit from operations	127
Income from investments	22
Finance costs	(40)
Profit before tax	109
Tax	(30)
Profit for the year	79

Statement of changes in equity
for year ending 31 December 2017

	£000
Retained earnings:	
Balance as at 1 Jan 2017	75
Profit for the year	79
	154
Dividends paid	(45)
Balance as at 31 Dec 2017	109

Fender plc
Statement of financial position
as at 31 December 2017

	£000
Non-current assets	
Plant and equipment at cost	385
Investments	200
	585
Current assets	
Inventories	55
Trade and other receivables	38
Cash and cash equivalents	28
	121
Total assets	706
Equity and liabilities	
Equity	
Ordinary share capital (£1 shares)	400
Share premium	60
Retained earnings	109
Total equity	569
Non-current liabilities	
5% Debentures	80
Current liabilities	
Trade and other payables	27
Tax	30
	57
Total liabilities	137
Total equity and liabilities	706

Accounting standards

15

Introduction

In order to attract shareholder investment a company must convince potential shareholders that it is worth the investment. This will usually mean that a company's financial statements should show that the company is profitable and is going to remain profitable. This will encourage the potential investor to believe that attractive financial returns can be gained from such an investment. Given that all investments of this form are a risk to investors, we need to ensure that even though risky, the financial statements of a company do not mislead. How do we ensure that the financial statements of a company are produced in a way which most accurately reflects the fair presentation of the company's position?

The rules and guidelines that govern best practice for compiling and presenting financial statements are collectively referred to as **accounting standards**. Each of these standards addresses a particular issue concerning an aspect of a company's accounting records and how they are to be recorded, measured and presented. Over the past century, many countries developed their own set of accounting standards. The particular set of standards, rules and regulations governing how accounting records and statements are to be maintained are referred to as **GAAP (Generally Accepted Accounting Principles)**.

UK GAAP

Each country or regime responsible for producing accounting regulations has its own version of GAAP. For example, there exists UK GAAP, US GAAP and so on. These principles have gradually evolved as the idea of the best way (or the least bad way) of recording and presenting financial data has changed over time and they have gradually been updated. These standards will normally be codified by the country's legislation, but there are also independent guidelines, often published by the accounting professional bodies. The UK GAAP has been formulated over a number years by the Accounting Standards Board (ASB).

The UK Accounting Standards Board (ASB)

The ASB is part of the **UK Financial Reporting Council (FRC)**. The role of the FRC is to support investor, market and public confidence in the financial accounting and financial reporting of business entities. The FRC attempts to achieve this through maintaining and improving the accounting standards used for the basis of financial reporting. The FRC is funded through financial levies placed on UK companies according to their size. The structure of the FRC is presented in Figure 15.1.

FIGURE 15.1 The Financial Reporting Council

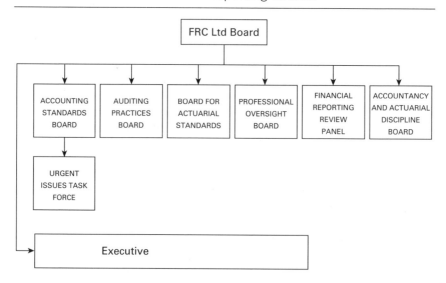

Although part of the FRC, the ASB is an autonomous body which can set accounting standards on its own. However, in reality, accounting standards are issued after wide consultation (at least two formal consultations are used for each new standard). In addition, the ASB will collaborate with its international equivalent – the **International Accounting Standards Board (IASB)**. The ASB is also supported in its role by the **Urgent Issues Task Force (UITF)**.

The **UITF** is a separate body that exists to support the work of the ASB when conflict or uncertainty exists concerning the interpretation of an accounting standard. Decisions made by the UITF are communicated by the publication of **UITF Abstracts,** which, to all intents and purposes, act as further accounting standards which must also be followed by companies.

The mechanism by which UK companies are meant to follow UK GAAP rules is through the individual accounting standards that have been published over time. These standards are a combination of relatively old and also fairly new standards. There are two main groups of standards in existence, known as:

- Statements of Standard Accounting Practice (SSAPs);
- Financial Reporting Standards (FRSs).

These standards are supported by the UITF Abstracts (as mentioned above) and also by **Statements of Recommended Practice (SORPs)**. These are statements that are meant to supplement existing standards. They are produced by industry bodies in response to special or unusual circumstances in that particular industry, which means that further guidance on how to interpret a particular accounting standard is necessary. A SORP must carry a statement which states that the guidance provided does not contradict any existing accounting standard. The industry body producing the SORP must agree to abide by the ASB's current code of practice. Further guidance for firms constructing accounting statements is provided by the Companies Act 2006.

Each accounting standard covers a different area of financial accounting in terms of matters such as accounting policy, presentation of financial statements and so on. The accounting standards were meant to apply to companies once they reached a certain size. Once through this size threshold, it would be taken as given that a company would prepare its accounts and produce financial statements in line with the most up-to-date accounting standards that existed at this time.

As mentioned earlier, these standards did not stand still. Standards were updated and modified as changes in the business environment developed, and problems and complications arose with the original standards. The SSAPs were the first 'phase' of widespread accounting standards to be published as part of the UK GAAP. These have been gradually replaced by FRSs. However, there is increasing recognition of the merits of producing a set of common accounting standards that would not be used by only one country but would be true set of global accounting standards.

International Accounting Standards

The task of producing a set of international accounting standards belongs to the **International Financial Reporting Standards (IFRS) Foundation**. This is an independent not-for-profit organization that exists to develop a set of globally acceptable financial reporting standards. These standards are produced through the standard-setting body of the IFRS Foundation, known as the **International Accounting Standards Board (IASB)**. The structure of the IFRS is presented in Figure 15.2.

FIGURE 15.2 The IFRS Foundation

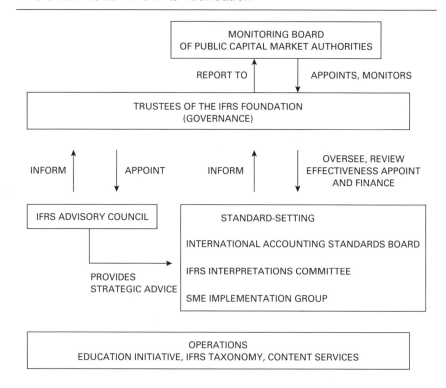

The IASB is responsible for the development and publication of the international accounting standards. The two main forms of international accounting standards produced by the IASB are as follows:

- International Accounting Standards (IAS);
- International Financial Reporting Standards (IFRS).

In order to move towards the goal of a globally utilized set of accounting standards, the IASB works with a range of interested parties (for example, national bodies responsible for setting the relevant national accounting standards, such as the UK's ASB, as well as investors, regulators and auditors). The benefits of having a set of common standards used by many countries would include:

- Comparability between the financial reports produced by UK companies and those from other countries would be improved, which would help potential investors and other user groups.
- A single accounting framework should make financial reporting simpler and less costly for companies.

- Trade between companies across national borders should be increased by the knowledge that companies have followed a common set of standards.

- Accountants would have to be familiar with only one set of accounting standards (though this does not preclude the possibility of differing standards for different types or size of organization within the same framework).

To develop a coherent set of common accounting standards, it helps if there are common underlying principles that can be established which will determine what directions any accounting standards are meant to follow. Without this broad set of principles or underlying philosophy it will mean that each new standard is developed without any unifying theme, which will make it harder for successive standards to be consistent with each other. In the same way that some countries have their own constitution which sets out the fundamental rules and guidelines on which the country's laws can be developed, there exists for international standards an underlying set of principles on which each new accounting standard can be based and developed. The IASB has attempted to achieve this through the publication of a document known as the '*conceptual framework*'.

IASB conceptual framework

The first attempt at a unified framework for accounting was published by the IASB in 1989 as the *Framework for the preparation and presentation of financial statements*. In conjunction with the US-based **Financial Accounting Standards Board (FASB)**, this document has been updated and the new version, the conceptual framework, was published in 2010. The original 1989 framework is being updated and parts replaced with newer versions. It is hoped that the joint work of the IFRS and the FASB will lead to a fully global framework.

The need for a conceptual framework

The IASB conceptual framework is a published document which, from the viewpoint of the IASB, sets out the purpose of accounting statements. The framework assumes that accounting statements are meant to provide useful and meaningful information to the various user groups of financial information, such as investors (current and potential), lenders to the firm and so on. In this case, the framework will attempt to provide the basis for which accounting standards can help to produce accounting statements which do provide useful and meaningful information.

The uses of the conceptual framework include the following:

- It assists the IASB in the development of future accounting standards.
- It seeks to reduce the ambiguity of accounting standards by reducing the number of alternative interpretations of individual accounting standards.
- It provides useful information, which is less prone to misunderstanding, to user groups of accounting statements.
- To help with the presentation of accounting statements where no standard currently exists to provide guidance.
- To ensure that existing standards are coherent and to flag up the need for an improved standard.

The conceptual framework is not an accounting standard in its own right. If the framework contradicts the content of an individual accounting standard (which should not really happen but may do with older accounting standards not yet updated), it is the accounting standards that should be followed.

Content of the conceptual framework

The conceptual framework covers a wide range of different topics which are all underlying concepts in the preparation and presentation of financial statements. The content of the framework includes the following.

Qualitative characteristics of useful financial information

There are six qualitative characteristics of useful information that are identified by the framework. Fundamental characteristics are that the information should be relevant and should possess faithful representation.

Relevance

Useful financial information should be relevant to the users of the information and be useful for decision-making purposes. Irrelevant information is not useful and therefore is not needed. The relevance of information can be judged by whether it helps users to make predictions of future outcomes. This is not to say that it is a direct forecast of future events but that a user may be able to make predictions of future business performance based on the information that is provided.

Relevance also refers to the **materiality concept**, which was covered in Chapter 5. Only material information of the business is considered to be relevant. For example, the omission of an immaterial amount from the financial statements will not seriously affect the user's ability to make predictions from the financial information provided. However, the omission of a material item will impair the ability to make predictions as to the future.

Faithful representation

In the same way that auditors may look for the statements to present a 'true and fair' view, it is believed that financial information will be useful if it faithfully represents the financial transactions that it is meant to represent. According to the framework, this will mean that the information provided has the following characteristics:

- It is neutral (ie it is free from bias).
- It is complete (ie all necessary information is provided so as to enable a user to understand the transactions that have taken place).
- It is free from error (by which we mean that no material errors are present which would serve to mislead).

In addition to these fundamental characteristics, there are also four characteristics that enhance the information provided. These are as follows.

Comparability

A user will find information more useful if comparisons can be made with information from earlier time periods or from similar businesses for the same period. The comparability of information will enable a user to identify similarities and differences between the businesses.

Verifiability

This means that the information can be verified by independent users of the data so that they would agree that the financial information faithfully represents the business transactions that have taken place.

Timeliness

The information should be presented in good time so that users can make decisions about the financial information that would not lead to out-of-date decisions. For example, publication of financial statements should be available early enough for relevant investment decisions to be made by investors.

Understandability

Information provided should be capable of being understood by the users of the information. Financial information that cannot be understood is no use to anyone. However, a distinction should be made such that when we say that financial information should be understood by the users of the data, we are not necessarily including the layperson. The information should be understood by those who already have a reasonable knowledge of business and economic activities and can analyse such information in a meaningful manner. Even with this condition, the information presented may still need the use of an analyst or adviser.

Elements of financial statements

In order to construct the financial statements of the business, the framework provides definitions of what it terms the five 'elements' of financial statements. These are divided as follows.

Construction of the balance sheet

- **Assets** are those resources which are controlled by the business as a result of past actions and from which future economic benefits are expected to flow to the business. These do not need to be owned by the business and must result from past actions (such as the purchase of the asset or the manufacture of the asset).
- **Liabilities** are an obligation of the business arising from past actions which will require an outflow of resources from the business. As with assets, the liabilities of the firm must result from past actions, such as obtaining a loan or taking advantage of trade credit.
- **Equity** is the residual interest in the assets of the business after deduction of the liabilities. This is based on the accounting equation covered in Chapter 1.

Construction of the income statement

- **Income** represents an increase in economic benefits flowing to the business during the accounting period. The income can take the form of either an inflow to the business or an increase in assets or a decrease in liabilities that results in an increase in equity.
- **Expenses** are decreases in economic benefits flowing out of the business during the accounting period. The expense can take the form of either an outflow from the business or a decrease in assets or an increase in liabilities that results in a decrease in equity.

Incomes can therefore be defined in two ways: in terms of revenue in the form of sales and other forms of operating income, and from a gain in an asset. Likewise, an expense can also be defined in two ways either involving the loss in the asset of cash to meet payments for items such as the cost of sales and other operating expenses, or losses in the value of an asset, such as the incidence of bad debts.

Recent progress towards a single set of accounting standards

Progress towards this goal of seeing all countries utilizing a single set of accounting standards has been made over recent years. There are now over one hundred nations that allow the use of the IFRS framework for companies listed on the respective stock exchanges. The majority of the G20 countries (leading 20 industrial nations) comply to some extent with the IFRS system.

Since 2005, all EU listed groups of companies have had to comply with the accounting standards published by the IASB rather than those specifically produced as part of UK GAAP. Strictly speaking, the UK ASB still helps to produce the international standards, but these now have to comply with EU requirements.

At present the United States does not require its companies to conform to IFRS and continues to follow its own standards in the form of the US GAAP. The US **Securities and Exchange Commission (SEC)**, which oversees the FASB (the US equivalent of the IASB), has expressed a desire to see a core set of accounting standards that could be used globally and, since 2002, the FASB and the IASB have committed to working together to develop a common set of accounting standards. The SEC is expected make a decision imminently as to when and how it aims to incorporate IFRS into the US GAAP system. This does not necessarily mean that the United States will replace US GAAP with IFRS but that it may seek to further develop common standards that can be applied by both regimes. Current IFRS have moved closer to the US GAAP but there still exist differences in standards.

By following the IFRS set of standards, companies will have to ensure that their accounting records and financial statements are produced in line with the full IFRS framework of accounting standards. In other words, in the case of the UK, these companies will no longer have to follow the UK GAAP set of accounting standards. There had been a belief that the IFRS set of standards would eventually replace the older UK GAAP standards. However, the burden of having to comply with the full set of IFRS standards was seen as overly excessive in terms of the reporting requirements that were made on some companies. Smaller companies and ones that operate on a national rather than an international basis might be currently best served by the existing UK GAAP. As a result a dilemma has developed: should we continue to persevere with UK GAAP or should we push for a set of international standards under the IFRS framework?

The future of UK GAAP

The solution to this dilemma has been to attempt to simplify the existing framework of accounting standards for all UK companies. Various proposals as to the way forward have been published. The current proposals are meant to be in place so as to take effect from 1 January 2015. This means that the financial year-end of 31 December 2015 would be following the new proposed framework for accounting standards.

The proposals have been through consultation and have been modified in the light of suggestions put forward by companies and also by those directly connected with the accounting profession. This has led to the development of new accounting standards which will be used within the UK. The proposed system will mean that there are three options for companies looking to apply a set of accounting standards. These are summarized in Table 15.1.

TABLE 15.1 Options for accounting standards

Accounting standards to be followed	Type of business organization
International Financial Reporting Standards (IFRS)	Companies listed on a recognized stock exchange (eg LSE and AIM)*
Financial Reporting Standard applicable for the UK and Republic of Ireland (draft FRS 102)	Private companies and individual listed companies
Financial Reporting Standard for Smaller Entities (FRSSE)	Small companies

* The London Stock Exchange and the Alternative Investment Market – a sub-market of the LSE used for small companies wishing to float shares.

Those companies already using the IFRS systems as required by company law – those producing consolidated accounts and having their share price listed on a recognized stock exchange – will continue to use the IFRS as their accounting standard framework. In addition, there is an option for certain parent company or subsidiary company accounts that would allow them reduced disclosure – that is, they would have to publish and produce less detailed reports if it was felt that duplication would be present in the group accounts of the group to which the company belongs.

A full list of the IASB accounting standards, and the existing UK GAAP standards, appears at the end of this chapter.

The financial reporting standard applicable in the UK and Republic of Ireland

A new draft standard has been produced for all other UK companies beyond a certain size (medium sized or larger). Those companies that have publicly traded equity on a stock exchange but are not producing group accounts, and private companies (ie whose shares are not publicly traded), will follow this new accounting standard produced by the UK ASB. Technically speaking, these companies can choose to follow the full IFRS if they so wish, but it is assumed that many will choose to adopt this new standard. The new standard, the FRS, is a self-contained standard which is meant to provide as much guidance on reporting requirements as possible but without the need for individually published accounting standards.

The **Financial Reporting Standard applicable in the UK and the Republic of Ireland** (known as **draft FRS 102**) will replace all FRSs and SSAPs that currently exist. The initial proposal was for these companies to follow the **International financial reporting standard for small and medium sized entities** (known as the **IFRS for SMEs**). However, it was felt that there were issues with the IFRS for SMEs that were not satisfactory for companies producing financial statements by following this standard. The IFRS for SMEs did not allow certain procedures that were allowed under the 'full' IFRS and were also allowed under the current UK GAAP standards. Therefore it was thought that this standard would mean less flexibility for those companies 'forced' to follow the IFRS for SMEs. The options that were not permitted under the IFRS for SMEs included the following:

- No revaluation of non-current assets was allowed, despite its being allowed under IFRS and UK GAAP.
- Borrowing costs could not be capitalized under the IFRS for SMEs but could be under IFRS and UK GAAP if certain conditions were met.
- Internally generated development costs could not be capitalized under IFRS for SMEs but were allowed under IFRS and UK GAAP.

The draft FRS 102 is based largely on the IFRS for SMEs but has been modified so that all UK companies have the ability to follow the policies mentioned above which were available to both large IFRS-based firms and small Financial Reporting Standard for Smaller Entities (FRSSE) firms.

A company that qualifies for the new FRS standards may still choose to follow the IFRS standards if it is in its interest to do so. An example where it may be advantageous to adopt the IFRS is where a company expects to become a listed company in the near future. In this case it may be easier to go straight for the IFRS standards, as this avoids having to undergo transition to the new FRS followed by a further transition to the IFRS.

Financial Reporting Standard for Smaller Entities (FRSSE)

Small, private companies that are not required to follow the new UK GAAP FRS or the existing IFRS would fall into the third category of accounting standards. The relevant standard for these companies is the **Financial Reporting Standard for Smaller Entities (FRSSE)**.

Small companies and small groups are defined as those which fulfil two or more of the following criteria:

1 net turnover   £6,500,000 or less;

2 balance sheet total   £3,260,000 or less;

3 number of employee   50 or fewer.

In this case, the company (or group) can use the FRSSE accounting standard for reporting and presenting financial statements. However, public limited companies that met the criteria would not be allowed to follow this standard.

This is, like the proposed FRS 102, a self-contained standard, that is, the requirements made on companies is contained within one overall standard. The current FRSSE was published in 2008.

The FRSSE makes fewer demands on a business in terms of what reporting requirements are made. For example, there is no requirement for a statement of cash flows to be produced. In addition, some smaller companies will be exempted from having an external auditor for their accounts if certain conditions are met.

The FRSSE sets out prescribed standards for the financial statements (one for the balance sheet and two for the profit and loss account) of the business, which are given as follows:

Balance sheet format for eligible small companies

A Called up share capital not paid

B Fixed assets

   I   Intangible assets

      1 Goodwill

      2 Other intangible assets

   II Tangible assets

      1 Land and buildings

      2 Plant and machinery, etc

  III Investments

      1 Share in group undertakings and participating interests

      2 Loans to group undertakings and undertakings in which the company has a participating interest

      3 Other investments other than loans

      4 Other investments

C Current assets
  I Stocks
    1 Stocks
    2 Payments on account
  II Debtors
    1 Trade debtors
    2 Amounts owed by group undertakings and undertakings in which the company has a participating interest
    3 Other interests
  III Investments
    1 Shares in group undertakings
    2 Other investments
D Prepayments and accrued income
E Creditors: amounts falling due within one year
  1 Bank loans and overdrafts
  2 Trade creditors
  3 Amounts owed to group undertakings
F Net current assets/liabilities
G Total assets less current liabilities
H Creditors: amounts falling due after more than one year
  1 Bank loans and overdrafts
  2 Trade creditors
  3 Amounts owed to group undertakings and undertakings in which the company has a participating interest
  4 Other creditors
I Provisions for liabilities
J Accruals and deferred income
K Capital and reserves
  I Called-up share capital
  II Share premium account
  III Revaluation reserve
  IV Other reserves
  V Profit and loss account

Profit and loss account format 1 for eligible small companies

1 Turnover
2 Cost of sales
3 Gross profit or loss
4 Distribution costs
5 Administrative expenses
6 Other operating income
7 Income from shares in group undertakings
8 Income from participating interests
9 Income from other fixed asset investments
10 Other interest receivable and similar income
11 Amounts written off investments
12 Interest payable and similar charges
12A Profit or loss on ordinary activities before taxation
13 Tax on profit or loss on ordinary activities
14 Profit or loss on ordinary activities after taxation
15 Other taxes not shown under the above items
16 Profit or loss for the financial year

Profit and loss account format 2 for eligible small companies

1 Turnover
2 Change in stocks of finished goods and in work in progress
3 Own work capitalized
4 Other operating income
5 **A** Raw materials and consumables
B Other external charges
6 Staff costs
A Wages and salaries
B Social security costs
C Other pension costs
7 **A** Depreciation and other amounts written off tangible and intangible fixed assets
B Exceptional amounts written off current assets
8 Other operating income
9 Income from shares in group undertakings
10 Income from participating interests
11 Income from other fixed asset investments

12   Other interest receivable and similar income

13   Amounts written off investments

14   Interest payable and similar charges

14A Profit or loss on ordinary activities before taxation

15   Tax on profit or loss on ordinary activities

16   Profit or loss on ordinary activities after taxation

17   Other taxes not shown under the above items

18   Profit or loss for the financial year

It is estimated that small and medium-sized businesses account for over 99 per cent of all UK business enterprises. However, the term 'small' can cover a wide range of businesses of varying sizes when measured in financial terms. As a result, it has become apparent that even with smaller companies, having to comply with the FRSSE still places to great a burden on certain companies. This has led to a further classification being provided for that of **micro-entities**.

Micro-entities

A micro-entity is defined as a business that has:

- turnover of less than £440,000;
- total assets of less than £220,000;
- fewer than 10 employees.

Most UK companies registered with the UK Companies House would meet these criteria, as well as over three million unincorporated businesses. It is currently being debated as to whether exemptions should be made for micro-entities as to financial reporting requirements.

It is proposed that there would be a reduction in the financial information that a micro-entity would have to prepare, and this might be pared down to the following.

A simplified trading statement

This would replace the income statement that is produced by larger companies. The trading statement would summarize the income and expenses of the business and could be produced on a cash basis rather than an accruals basis – meaning that incomes and costs would be recorded when they are paid and received rather than when they are generated.

A statement of position

This would replace the traditional balance sheet and would be simplified in what it contains – with just a simple list of assets, liabilities and shareholders' equity provided.

There is still debate as to how micro-entities would be expected to report in the future. The EU looks set to make recommendations on this topic over the next few years.

Current applicable accounting standards

International accounting standards

The following IFRS statements are currently issued.

International financial reporting standards

IFRS 1	First time Adoption of International Financial Reporting Standards
IFRS 2	Share-based Payment
IFRS 3	Business Combinations
IFRS 4	Insurance Contracts
IFRS 5	Non-current Assets Held for Sale and Discontinued Operations
IFRS 6	Exploration for and Evaluation of Mineral Resources
IFRS 7	Financial Instruments Disclosures
IFRS 8	Operating Segments
IFRS 9	Financial Instruments
IFRS 10	Consolidated Financial Statements
IFRS 11	Joint Arrangements
IFRS 12	Disclosure of Interests in Other Entities
IFRS 13	Fair Value Measurement

International accounting standards

IAS 1	Presentation of Financial Statements
IAS 2	Inventories
IAS 7	Cash Flow Statements
IAS 8	Accounting Policies, Changes in Accounting Estimates and Errors
IAS 10	Events After the Balance Sheet Date
IAS 11	Construction Contracts
IAS 12	Income Taxes
IAS 16	Property, Plant and Equipment
IAS 17	Leases
IAS 18	Revenue
IAS 19	Employee Benefits (2011)
IAS 20	Accounting for Government Grants and Disclosure of Government Assistance

IAS 21	The Effects of Changes in Foreign Exchange Rates
IAS 23	Borrowing Costs
IAS 24	Related Party Disclosures
IAS 26	Accounting and Reporting by Retirement Benefit Plans
IAS 27	Separate Financial Statements (2011)
IAS 28	Investments in Associates
IAS 29	Financial Reporting in Hyperinflationary Economies
IAS 31	Interests in Joint Ventures (will be superseded by IFRS 11 and IFRS 12 effective 1 Jan 2015)
IAS 32	Financial Instruments Presentation
IAS 33	Earnings per Share
IAS 34	Interim Financial Reporting
IAS 36	Impairment of Assets
IAS 37	Provisions, Contingent Liabilities and Contingent Assets
IAS 38	Intangible Assets
IAS 39	Financial Instruments Recognition and Measurement (will be superseded by IFRS 9 effective 1 Jan 2015)
IAS 40	Investment Property
IAS 41	Agriculture

UK GAAP standards

Financial reporting standards (FRS)

FRSSE (2008)	Financial Reporting Standard for Smaller Entities
FRS 1	Cash Flow Statements
FRS 2	Accounting for Subsidiary Undertakings
FRS 3	Reporting Financial Performance
FRS 4	Capital Instruments
FRS 5	Reporting the Substance of Transactions
FRS 6	Acquisitions and Mergers
FRS 7	Fair Values in Acquisition Accounting
FRS 8	Related Party Disclosures
FRS 9	Associates and Joint Ventures
FRS 10	Goodwill and Intangible Assets
FRS 11	Impairment of Fixed Assets and Goodwill
FRS 12	Provisions, Contingent Liabilities and Contingent Assets
FRS 13	Derivatives and other Financial Instruments Disclosures
FRS 14	Earnings per Share
FRS 15	Tangible Fixed Assets
FRS 16	Current Tax
FRS 17	Retirement Benefits
FRS 18	Accounting Policies

FRS 19	Deferred Tax
FRS 20	Share-based Payment
FRS 21	Events after the Balance Sheet Date
FRS 22	Earnings per Share
FRS 23	The Effects of Changes in Foreign Exchange Rates
FRS 25	Financial Instruments Presentation
FRS 26	Financial Instruments Recognition and Measurement
FRS 27	Life Assurance
FRS 28	Corresponding Amounts
FRS 29	Financial Instruments Disclosures
FRS 30	Heritage Assets

Statements of Standard Accounting Practice (SSAPs)

SSAP 4	Accounting for Government Grants
SSAP 5	Accounting for Value Added Tax
SSAP 9	Stocks and Long-term Contracts
SSAP 13	Accounting for Research and Development
SSAP 19	Accounting for Investment Properties
SSAP 20	Foreign Currency Translation
SSAP 21	Accounting for Leases and Hire Purchase Contracts
SSAP 24	Accounting for Pension Costs
SSAP 25	Segmental Reporting

Review questions

1   Why do you think it has been suggested that micro-entities might be allowed to produce their trading statement on a cash basis rather than on an accruals basis?

It is only a suggestion, so we are not yet sure if this will come to pass. However, there are certain reasons why this might be applicable to micro-entities.

It is likely that the number of shareholders in a micro-entity is small and nearly all of these will be connected with the running of the business (or will be related to those who run the business). As a result, the need for annual trading statements to reflect the accruals concept is less pressing given that most of the shareholders will already be aware of the trading position of the business. In addition, it is likely that the expense of hiring an accountant to produce a statement on the accruals basis is more significant for a micro entity. The chances of the accruals basis being used to hide poor trading positions are less pressing for these micro-entities, which means that a cash basis might be more appropriate.

2   What benefits are there in replacing all existing UK GAAP standards with one overall standard (draft FRS 102)?

A self-contained standard would be easier to use by those concerned with the presentation of the firm's financial statements. Details currently included within the array of standards might not be necessary for many of these companies. The vast majority of the companies to which UK GAAP applies are privately held companies, which means that the need to present statements to external shareholders is less pressing. The reduced complexity of FRS 102 and the up-to-dateness of a new standard would be useful. Improvements have been made to IFRS for SMEs in that FRS 102 is more in line with IFRS standards as well.

3   What purpose does the IFRS conceptual framework serve?

The framework acts to provide the underlying principles from which all IFRS accounting standards should be derived. In the same way that a country's laws may derive from its underlying constitution, the conceptual framework serves to provide a set of principles which should be applied in all standards. This means that standards drawn up must be coherent in the sense that they share the same set of principles. This should make future accounting standards more consistent and less likely to contradict each other (though it won't completely prevent that occurring).

Statement of cash flows

16

Introduction

The income statement provides information relating to the overall success of the business in the form of the profit earned. However, earning a profit does not guarantee business survival. Firms are known to have failed not because they were loss-making but because they did not have adequate cash flow available for the business to continue trading. There have been cases where a firm has appeared profitable but the increases in the profits were found to be due to creative window dressing of the firm's financial statements. For example, changing depreciation policy by extending the lifespan of non-current assets will reduce the depreciation charge in that year's income statement and, all other things being equal, lead to higher reported profits. Even without deliberate manipulation, the profit earned by a firm is subject to adjustments which may disguise poor cash flow.

As a result, adequate cash flow came to be seen as a further measure of business performance and assessment. The statement of cash flows became the third component of a set of financial statements at the end of a trading period. Since the early 1990s, it has been a legal requirement for large UK companies to produce one alongside the traditional income statement and balance sheet.

The differences between cash and profit

Cash and profit are related. As a firm earns profit through trading, we would eventually expect this to lead to cash being generated. However, there are differences which have led to the fact, mentioned above, that profitable businesses do fail and a very common cause of business failure is poor cash flow.

One fundamental difference between cash and profit is that cash is an asset which can be measured at a particular point in time, whereas profit can only be earned and measured over time. This means that it can be difficult to assess a firm's cash flow position. For example, taking a loan on the day before the balance sheet is constructed may give a false impression of the firm's underlying cash flow position. Further investigation may be warranted.

There are other differences between cash and profit and some of these have been mentioned in earlier chapters. The following are some examples of ways in which cash and profit differ and can, in some situations, move in opposite directions to each other.

Capital expenditure

The income statement will not include the purchase of non-current assets and other forms of capital expenditure. These, even if initially purchased on credit, will eventually involve an outflow of cash. However, the only reduction in profit will be through the depreciation of the asset which, if the expected lifespan is long, could be fairly small relative to the original cost of the asset. Therefore profit could decrease slightly, but this may hide a poor cash flow position if not monitored or planned for.

Overtrading

Firms can be lulled into a situation where they chase profitable sales without adequate checking of cash flow. A firm which over-expands and chases more sales than its cash flow can fund is said to be **overtrading**. In this situation the firm will be incurring outflows of cash as it pays for new goods and services to be produced. Some of these payments can be delayed, through the credit periods offered by suppliers, but other payments, such as wages and other expenses, will need immediate settlement. If the sales are made on credit terms, it may be some time before the cash is received from the sale. If a firm takes on further orders for sales, however profitable the sales may be, it can experience problems with cash flow as it will be making payments without having adequate receipts of cash if not managed carefully. Here profit and cash flow will give conflicting views of business performance.

Non-cash adjustments to profit

Profits will be affected by changes in items which do not generate an immediate movement in cash flow. The income statement is constructed using the accruals concept, which means that both incomes and expenses in the income statement may not yet correspond with a similar movement in cash.

Profits are also affected by changes in provisions. A reduction in a provision will actually boost profit but will not generate an inflow of cash.

Loans and other non-current liabilities

Obtaining external long-term finance can provide a useful source of cash flow for a firm. However, the repayment of these non-current liabilities will act negatively on the firm's cash flow balances. Repayment of non-current liabilities will not affect the income statement, so profit and cash flow, once again, can move in opposite directions.

The statement of cash flows

Given that there are differences between cash flow and profit, a statement showing the firm's ability to generate cash flows from its activities would be useful for those wishing to analyse a firm's financial position. The statement of cash flows is produced to highlight the sources of the firm's cash flow and how these have changed over the most recent accounting period.

When we talk about the firm's cash flow we are referring to what is known as cash and cash equivalents. Cash and cash equivalents refer not only to the firm's cash in hand (ie cash held on the business premises) but also to the firm's bank balances (including a subtraction if the bank balance is overdrawn). It will also include highly liquid investments held by the firm if they are easily convertible into cash without any significant risk of a change in value. An investment would be included in the cash and cash equivalents of the firm if the maturity (ie repayment) date of the investment is within the next three months from the date of the statement of cash flows.

The income statement provides a bridge between the previous and most recent balance sheets of the firm. The statement of cash flows will provide another bridge in that it shows the flows of cash into and out of the firm that have taken place over the most recent period. By comparing the cash and cash equivalents figures on the earlier and most recent balance sheets we should be able to see the reasons why cash has changed.

The statement of cash flows that we will examine is based on the guidance give in IAS 7. This stipulates that a statement of cash flows should categorize flows of cash under three separate headings:

- cash flows from operating activities;
- cash flows from investing activities;
- cash flows from financing activities.

The net sum of the totals of each individual cash flow (the net cash flow) should always be equal to the overall change in the cash and cash equivalents figures found on the previous and most recent balance sheets. In this sense, the statement of cash flows provides details as to why cash has altered between one period and the next. We will now consider the exact content of each of the three headings.

Cash flow from operating activities

Cash flows under this heading arise out of the firm's main revenue-producing activities, that is, the buying and selling of goods and services. This section will look at the cash flows that relate to those activities and will include the cash inflows relating to sales made and the cash outflows relating to the purchase of, or the production of, goods to be sold.

There are two different methods used to calculate the cash flow from operating activities – the direct method and the indirect method.

Direct method

The direct method looks at the operations of the business and the major classes of gross cash receipts and gross cash payments made resulting from its operations. The overall net cash from operations will be the total of the cash inflows less the total of the cash outflows and is likely to include the following calculations:

- Cash received from customers
- Cash paid to suppliers
- Cash paid to employees
- Cash paid for other operating expenses
  - *Equals cash generated from operations*
- Less cash paid for interest
- Less cash paid for income taxes
  - *Equals cash flow from operating activities.*

Cash received from customers and cash paid to suppliers can be derived from the sales and purchases figures. However, given that the income statements are produced on the accruals basis, the sales and purchases figures will requires adjusting for changes in the net balance of trade receivables and trade payables over the year. For example, if the balance on the trade receivables has increased between the start and the end of the year, the sales figure contained within the income statement will be higher than that of cash received in respect of sales.

Indirect method

This method begins with the operating profit of the business – the profit before deductions for interest and taxation. The profit would then be adjusted for any non-cash transactions that have been included within the profit calculation. For example, any non-cash transaction which has been deducted against that year's profit, such as depreciation, would have to be added back so that we arrive at the cash generated from the operating activities. Adjustments are also made to changes in the items appearing within the firm's working capital as these will indirectly affect the overall operating profit of the firm. The calculations required for the direct method would appear as follows:

- Operating profit.
- Add back depreciation and amortization of non-current assets.
- Add back any other provisions charged against profit (and subtract and provisions that add to profit).
- Add back losses on disposal of non-current assets (less any profits on disposal).
- Add decrease in trade receivables (less increase in trade receivables).
- Add increase in trade payables (less decrease in trade payables).
- Add decrease in inventory (less increase in inventory).
- Less Interest paid.
- Less Income taxes paid.

Example 16.1

From the following data, present an extract from the statement of cash flows showing the net cash flow from operating activities:

	31 December 2012 £	31 December 2013 £
Trade receivables	4,500	3,200
Inventory	2,750	3,950
Trade payables	1,890	2,740

Net profits for the year ended 31.12.13 were £15,690 and depreciation charged that year amounted to £1,120.

	£
Operating profits	15,690
Change in trade receivables	1,300
Change in inventory	(1,200)
Change in trade payables	850
Depreciation	1,120
Net cash flow from operating activities	17,760

The rationale for these adjustments is that we are trying to see by what amount the profit of the firm generates a corresponding inflow of cash. For example, adding back depreciation and any losses on disposals are attempts to redress the fact that these would both have been deducted against the profit, despite the fact that neither corresponds to a cash outflow.

The adjustments made for changes in the non-cash aspects of working capital are not as easy to understand. An increase in working capital (either an increase in current assets or a decrease in current liabilities) means that more cash has been tied up in working capital. However, these changes to working capital have not affected the profit of the business. Therefore we must 'correct' the profit to take this into account. For example, a reduction in trade receivables will reduce the firm's working capital. Given that this is probably caused by customers paying the business what they owe, this would appear as a cash inflow and is added to the profit figure. Similarly, a reduction in trade payables would increase the firm's working capital but is probably the result of the firm making payments for goods purchased on credit. Therefore the reduction in trade payables will appear as a cash outflow.

Both the direct and indirect methods will produce the same figure. According to IAS 7, firms are encouraged to use the direct method as it gives more detail on where exactly cash flows have arisen and where cash outflows were made. However, the direct method is less popular. In assessment-type questions, it is also less popular as it requires more information to be given out than that contained in the income statement and the balance sheet. The information relating to cash payments for expenses may not always be available for those outside the business. It has been suggested that the indirect method is more popular because the direct method is too costly. However, this has been countered by those who claim that the indirect method gives greater scope for businesses to manipulate the cash flow from operating activities through misclassification of items between the various headings in the statement of cash flows.

Interest and dividends

Interest paid and received, and dividends paid and received, would normally be found in the cash flow from operating activities section of the statement. However, it is permissible for firms to include these in either the investing activities or financing activities section if it is felt more appropriate that they appear in another section. If the firm chooses to include these under one of the other sections of the statement, it should be consistent in successive periods as to which heading they appear under.

Cash flows from investing activities

This section will include the cash inflows and cash outflows that relate to the acquisition and disposal of any non-current assets. For example, the purchase of a non-current asset will appear as a cash outflow (as long as the firm has paid for the asset; if it has not, this will not appear). Similarly, it is the selling price that a firm receives when selling a non-current asset that would appear in this section as a cash inflow. The income statement would show only the profit or loss on the disposal (and this profit or loss would be adjusted in the operating activities section of the statement of cash flows).

Any acquisitions and sales of subsidiaries, or joint ventures and associates, would also be included within this section as well as the purchase or sale of intangible assets, such as investments. The interest payments received on any investments, as well as the dividends received from any financial assets held, would also be included within this section.

Any revaluation of assets would not be included within this section as it does not correspond to a cash flow. This is important when constructing a statement of cash flows based on information obtained by comparison of balance sheets.

Cash flow from financing activities

The final section of the statement of cash flows deals with the cash flows arising out of changes in the long-term capital of the firm. This will focus mainly on changes in the equity of the firm and changes in the long-term borrowings of the firm. This will also include the dividends paid on the equity issued by the firm (keeping in mind that any dividends received by the firm would be included in the investing activities section).

Using balance sheets to calculate the cash from operating activities is usually straightforward. However, there are potential areas which could be misleading when attempting to calculate the cash flow generated from any share issue. For example, if shares are issued by the firm, the value of issued equity capital would indicate a cash flow. However, if these shares are issued at a premium (ie for a value in excess of their face value), more cash would have been received by the firm, which is simply the change in the share capital. Therefore, attention should be paid to any changes in the share premium reserve. Likewise, if a firm makes a bonus issue of shares, the value of issued share capital will increase. However, the increase in the value of the share capital is achieved purely by conversion of existing reserves into these 'free' shares. No cash inflow results from a bonus issue.

Foreign exchange transactions

For companies that engage in transactions with other currencies, the transactions must be converted back into the currency of the country in which the company prepares its report.

Foreign assets and liabilities converted at balance sheet dates back into the domestic currency value may give rise to differences which are caused by changes in the value of the currency. Foreign exchange gains or losses will be included in the relevant section of the statement of cash flows. For example, a change in exchange rate which results in either a gain or a loss on profits earned in another country once converted back into the 'home' exchange rate would appear in the cash flow from operating activities section.

Reconciliation of cash balances

Alongside the statement of cash flows, a firm should also present a reconciliation of the balances of cash and cash equivalents from the two most recent reporting periods on the statement of financial position. The difference between the two figures should be equivalent to the overall change in cash and cash equivalents as found on the statement of cash flows.

Example 16.2

When preparing statements of cash flow for assessment questions you are strongly advised that all your preliminary calculations are done first. It is highly likely that there will be plenty of adjustments to be made before you can begin to draw up the finished statement. This approach is shown in the following fully worked example.

The balance sheets of Fraser Ltd for the two most recent trading periods are presented below:

Fraser Ltd
Balance sheets as at 31 December

	Year ended 2015			Year ended 2016		
	£	£	£	£	£	£
Non-current assets	Cost	Dep.	NBV	Cost	Dep.	NBV
Property	500,000	25,000	475,000	750,000	–	750,000
Machinery	54,000	18,000	36,000	104,000	27,900	76,100
Vehicles	42,400	8,900	33,500	34,000	13,000	21,000
	596,400	51,900	544,500	888,000	40,900	847,100
Current assets						
Inventory		15,103			27,357	
Trade receivables		8,979			15,453	
Cash and cash equivalents		1,414			15,354	
		25,496			58,164	
Current liabilities						
Trade payables	15,454			6,477		
Tax owing	12,231	27,685	(2,189)	3,422	9,899	48,265
			542,311			895,365
Non-current liabilities						
Debentures			80,000			35,000
			462,311			860,365

Fraser Ltd
Balance sheets as at 31 December

	Year ended 2015			Year ended 2016		
	£	£	£	£	£	£
Equity						
Ordinary share capital			300,000			380,000
Share premium			40,000			50,000
account						
Revaluation reserve			–			275,000
Retained earnings			122,311			155,365
			462,311			860,365

An extract from the income statement for the year ended 31 December 2016 is presented below:

Extract from income statement
for year ended 31 Dec 2016

	£
Operating profit	74,454
Less Interest	3,500
Profit before interest	70,954
Taxation	25,400
Profit for the year	45,554

The following information has also been made available:

- Dividends paid for the year amounted to £12,500.

- A vehicle which cost £14,000 and has accumulated depreciation of £9,200 was sold during the year for £5,000 cash – which was received on the date of the sale.

The statement of cash flows would be constructed as follows.

Cash flow from operating activities

It is normal to show the adjustments to the profits made by the firm for changes in working capital as well as the adjustments made to profit during the year for non-cash movements, such as depreciation.

The changes in items of working capital can be ascertained from the balance sheets. These can be summarized as follows:

	Effect on cash flow (£)
Increase in inventories	(12,254)
Increase in trade receivables	(6,474)
Decrease in trade payables	(8,977)

The depreciation figure to be added back on to the profit figure can be calculated as follows.

The change in the depreciation figures on the balance sheet will help indicate how much depreciation was charged to the income statement.

The increase in the depreciation total on the balance sheets will indicate the amount that had been charged. However, a reduction in the depreciation on the asset of property arose during the year owing to the revaluation of this asset (notice how the increase in the net value of property is matched by an increase in the revaluation reserve under the equity section of the balance sheet).

The increase in the balance sheet values for depreciation would be as follows:

- Increase in depreciation on machinery: £9,900

- Increase in depreciation on vehicles: £4,100.

The figure for depreciation on vehicles would be higher still if there had been no disposal of vehicles during the year, so we will need to add this back on to the total. Therefore the total depreciation charged to the income statement will be £9,900 + £4,100 + £9,200 = £23,200.

We will also need to adjust for the profit or loss made on the vehicle disposal. The net book value of the vehicle sold was £4,800 (£14,000 – £9,200). This means the profit on disposal of £200 (£5,000 – £4,800) will be subtracted in the statement of cash flows.

Although the taxation charge for the year was £25,400, we can see from the balance sheets that this isn't the amount that was actually paid during the year as there are amounts owing for taxation under the current liabilities. Therefore the amount of taxation paid would be as follows:

Tax paid = Amount charged to income statement
+ Amount owing at start of year
– Amount owing at end of year

Taxation paid = £25,400 + £12,231 – £3,422 = £34,209

Interest paid will be equal to the amount appearing in the income statement as there is no evidence of amounts for interest remaining outstanding at either the start or the end of the year.

Therefore the cash flow from operating activities would be as follows:

	£
Operating profit	74,454
Change in inventories	(12,254)
Change in trade receivables	(6,474)
Change in trade payables	(8,977)
Depreciation	23,200
Profit on disposal	(200)
Interest paid	(3,500)
Taxation paid	(34,209)
Cash flow from operating activities	32,040

Cash flow from investing activities

The firm has certainly sold non-current assets during the year and the statement of cash flow will show the £5,000 received on the disposal of the vehicle as a cash inflow.

The amount of cash paid for acquiring non-current assets can be ascertained form the balance sheet totals.

We have already noted that the increase in the value of property is not a cash outflow as it represents an upwards revaluation of the value of this asset.

The increase in the cost value of machinery of £50,000 represents a cash outflow.

Although the cost value of vehicles has decreased over the year, we know that part of this is attributed to the asset disposal. If we add the cost value of the vehicle sold (£14,000) back on, we would find that the cost value of vehicles has risen to £48,000 (£34,000 + £14,000), so we can infer that the cash outflow for vehicles was £5,600.

The cash flow from investing activities will be as follows:

	£
Purchase of non-current assets (£50,000 + £5,600)	55,600
Sale of vehicle	5,000
Cash flow from investing activities	(50,600)

Cash flow from financing activities

We can see that the amount paid out in equity dividends represents a cash outflow for the firm of £12,500.

The value of debentures has decreased, which suggests that the firm has redeemed (ie paid back) some of the debentures it had issued. This will represent a cash outflow for the business. We can see the value of debentures has decreased by £45,000.

The value of the ordinary share capital has increased and this will represent a cash inflow for the business. We can see that the share capital has increased by £80,000. However, the cash inflow from this share issue was higher because we can see that the shares were issued at a premium. Therefore the cash inflow from the share issue will be the cost of the combined increase in the share capital and the share premium account, in this case a cash inflow of £90,000 (£80,000 + £10,000).

The cash flow from financing activities would be as follows:

	£
Issues of shares (including share premium)	90,000
Redemption of debentures	(45,000)
Equity dividends paid	(12,500)
Cash flow from financing activities	32,500

The full statement of cash flows will appear as follows:

Fraser Ltd
Statement of cash flows
for year ended 31 December 2016

	£	£
Operating activities		
Operating profit	74,454	
Change in inventories	(12,254)	
Change in trade receivables	(6,474)	
Change in trade payables	(8,977)	
Depreciation	23,200	
Profit on disposal	(200)	
Interest paid	(3,500)	
Taxation	(34,209)	
Net cash flow from operating activities		32,040
Investing activities		
Purchase of machinery and vehicles	(55,600)	
Sale of vehicles	5,000	
Net cash flow from investing activities		(50,600)
Financing activities		
Issues of shares	90,000	
Repayment of debentures	(45,000)	
Equity dividends paid	(12,500)	
Net cash flow from financing activities		32,500
Increase in cash and cash equivalents		13,940

Reconciliation of cash and cash equivalents

	£
Cash and cash equivalents at 1 January 2016	1,414
Increase in cash and cash equivalents	13,940
Cash and cash equivalents at 31 December 2016	15,354

Review questions

1 From the following data, present an extract from the statement of cash flows showing the net cash flow from operating activities:

	31 December 2014	31 December 2015
	£	£
Trade receivables	11,329	14,380
Trade payables	18,754	22,345
Inventory	9,986	10,101

Net profits for the year ended 31.12.14 were £56,890 and depreciation charged that year amounted to £7,500.

Solution

	£
Operating profits	56,890
Change in receivables	(3,051)
Change in payables	3,591
Change in inventory	(115)
Depreciation	7,500
Net cash flow from operating activities	64,815

2 The following are extracts from the balance sheets of a company:

	As at 31 Dec 2013		As at 31 Dec 2014	
	£000	£000	£000	£000
Non-current assets				
Land and property		800		1,000
Plant and equipment at cost	250		300	
Less depreciation	130	120	150	150
Motor vans at cost	50		64	
Less depreciation	18	32	22	42

- There were no purchases of land and property during the year.

- During the year, plant and equipment costing £60,000 and with a book value of £27,000 were sold for a loss of £5,000.

- Vans, which had cost £8,000, with a book value of £4,000, were sold for neither a profit nor a loss.

From the above data, calculate the amount to include in the statement of cash flows under the heading 'cash flow from investing activities'.

Solution

Given that there are no purchases to land and property, the increase in value must have arisen out of a revaluation. This generates no cash flow at all.

The amount purchased on plant and equipment can be calculated from the change in the 'cost' valuation on the balance sheet (adjusting for what was sold).

	£000
Plant and equipment at end of year	300
Less Plant and equipment at start of year	250
	50
Add Cost value of plant and equipment sold during year	60
Purchase of plant and equipment	110

The amount of plant and equipment sold can be calculated by reconstructing an asset disposal account for plant and equipment:

Plant and equipment disposal

	£		£
Plant and equipment at cost	60,000	Depreciation (*)	33,000
		Cash received from sale	22,000
		Loss on disposal	5,000
	60,000		60,000

(* if the cost value is £60,000 and the book value £27,000, then the accumulated depreciation on the plant sold must be £33,000)

The cash received from sale must be the figure needed to enable the account to balance, that is, £22,000.

	£000
Motor vans at end of year	64
Less Motor vans at start of year	50
	14
Add Motor vans sold during year	8
Net purchases of motor vans	22

The motor vans sold had a net book value of £4,000. If no profit or loss was generated in the sale, they must have been sold for the net book value, that is, £4,000.

The overall net cash flow from these activities is as follows:

	£000	£000
Plant and equipment		
Cash inflows	22	
Cash outflows	(110)	(88)
Motor vans		
Cash inflows	4	
Cash outflows	(22)	(18)
Net cash flow for investing activities		(106)

There was a net cash outflow of £106,000 with regard to investing activities.

3 The following extracts are taken from the balance sheet of Surridge Ltd:

	As at 31 December 2017 £000	As at 31 December 2018 £000
Taxation owing	65	43

The income statement for the year ended 31 December 2018 shows an entry for taxation as £187,000.

Calculate the amount of taxation actually paid out by Surridge Ltd in the year to 31 December 2018.

Solution

Reconstruction of the ledger account for taxation will enable us to see how much was actually paid during the year:

Taxation

2018		£000	2018		£000
31 Dec	Cash paid	?	1 Jan	Balance b/d	65
31 Dec	Balance c/d	43	31 Dec	Profit and loss	187
		252			252

The amount paid would be the figure needed to balance up the account, which is £209,000.

4 In the statement of cash flows, why do the following adjustments need to be made to the operating profit in order to calculate the cash flow from operating activities?

(i) Subtraction of any profit on asset disposal.

(ii) Adding back any deprecation.

(iii) Subtracting any increase in trade receivables.

Answer

(i) Profits on disposal are subtracted because this profit would have been added on to the operating profit in the income statement. However, they do not actually generate cash of this corresponding size, so we subtract. The income from the disposal is dealt with later on in the cash flow statement.

(ii) Depreciation is added back on because it would have originally appeared as a deduction from the operating profits. No cash was spent on this as depreciation is a provision, not an expense, therefore we add back the amount charged.

(iii) The increase in trade receivables implies that more money has been tied up in the sale of inventory. Think of it this way: if the trade receivables had decreased, this would mean that they were paying the firm back – which would be treated as an inflow. Hence, an increase in trade receivables is an outflow of cash and therefore is deducted.

5 Below are two balance sheets for Throup Ltd for the most recent and the previous year's trading periods.

Throup Ltd
Balance Sheets at financial year end

	Year ended 31 December 2015			Year ended 31 December 2016		
	£	£	£	£	£	£
Non-current assets	Cost	Dep.	NBV	Cost	Dep.	NBV
Property	180,000	10,000	170,000	180,000	14,000	166,000
Equipment and machinery	23,000	4,500	18,500	44,000	11,310	32,690
	203,000	14,500	188,500	224,000	25,310	198,690
Current assets						
Inventory		5,630			12,131	
Trade receivables		6,432			6,265	
Cash and cash equivalents		2,300			11,888	
		14,362			30,284	
Current liabilities						
Trade payables	11,991			1,321		
Tax owing	7,871	19,862	(5,500)	5,453	6,774	23,510
			183,000			222,200
Non-current liabilities						
10% Debentures			–			20,000
			183,000			202,200
Equity						
Ordinary share capital			100,000			100,000
Share premium account			20,000			20,000
Retained earnings			63,000			82,200
			183,000			202,200

The folioing extract from the income statement is available:

Extract from income statement
for year ended 31 Dec 2016

	£
Operating profit	34,950
Less Interest	2,000
Profit before interest	32,950
Taxation	11,250
Profit for the year	21,700

In addition, the following information is available:

- Dividends of £2,500 were paid during the year.

- There were no sales of non-current assets during the year.

From the above information, construct a statement of cash flows for the year ended 31 December 2016.

Solution

Throup Ltd
Cash flow statement for year ended 31 December 2016

	£	£
Cash flow from operating activities		
Operating profit	34,950	
Change in inventories	(6,501)	
Change in trade receivables	167	
Change in trade payables	(10,670)	
Depreciation	10,810	
Interest paid	(2,000)	
Taxation	(13,668)	
Cash flow from operating activities		13,088
Investing activities		
Purchase of equipment and machinery	(21,000)	
Cash flow from investing activities		(21,000)
Financing activities		
Issue of debenture	20,000	
Equity dividends paid	(2,500)	
Cash flow from financing activities		17,500
Increase in cash and cash equivalents		9,588

Reconciliation of cash and cash equivalents

	£
Cash and cash equivalents as at 31 Dec 2015	2,300
Increase in cash and cash equivalent during 2106	9,588
Cash and cash equivalents as at 31 Dec 2016	11,888

---

6 Below are two balance sheets for Stroish Ltd for the most recent and the previous year's trading periods.

Stroish Ltd
Balance sheets at financial year end

	Year ended 31 December 2018			Year ended 31 December 2019		
	Cost	Dep.	NBV	Cost	Dep.	NBV
	£	£	£	£	£	£
Land and buildings	500,000	40,000	460,000	500,000	45,000	455,000
Plant and equipment	72,000	22,000	50,000	98,000	39,500	58,500
Machinery	27,500	18,300	9,200	45,000	22,550	22,450
	599,500	80,300	519,200	643,000	107,050	535,950
Current assets						
Inventory		17,313			27,357	
Trade receivables		12,313			16,852	
Cash and cash equivalents		8,898			–	
		38,524			44,209	
Current liabilities						
Trade payables	9,780			4,980		
Bank overdraft	–			8,048		
Tax owing	6,935	16,715	21,809	3,422	16,450	27,759
			541,009			563,709
Non-current liabilities						
Loan (long-term)			100,000			100,000
			441,009			463,709
Equity						
Ordinary share capital			200,000			320,000
Share premium account			80,000			–
Revaluation reserve			40,000			–
Retained earnings			121,009			143,709
			441,009			463,709

Additional information is available:

1 An extract from the income statement appears below.

	£
Operating profit	54,500
Less Interest	11,000
Profit before interest	43,500
Taxation	11,800
Profit for the year	31,700

2 Dividends paid during the year totalled £9,000.

3 Machinery was sold during the year for £3,200. It had originally cost £22,000 and had accumulated depreciation on the machinery totalling £17,500.

4 A bonus issue of shares was made during the year on the basis of three ordinary shares for every five already held. The capital reserves were utilized in the creation of the bonus issue.

Construct a statement of cash flows for the year ended 31 December 2019 and a reconciliation of cash flow at the start and the end of the year.

Stroish plc		
Cash flow statement for year ended 31 December 2019		
	£	£
Cash flow from operating activities		
Operating profit	54,500	
Change in inventories	(10,044)	
Change in trade receivables	(4,539)	
Change in trade payables	(4,800)	
Depreciation	44,250	
Profit on disposal	1,300	
Interest paid	(11,000)	
Taxation	(15,313)	
Net cash flow from operative activities		54,354
Investing activities		
Purchase of non-current assets	(65,500)	
Sale of machinery	3,200	
Net cash flow from investing activities		(62,300)
Financing activities		
Equity dividends paid	(9,000)	
Net cash flow from financing activities		(9,000)
Net cash outflow for year		(16,946)

Reconciliation of cash and cash equivalents	
	£
Cash and cash equivalents at start of year	8,898
Net cash outflow for year	(16,946)
Cash and cash equivalents at start of year	(8,048)

Accounting ratios

17

Introduction

The main measure of business success is assumed to be the operating profit or net profit earned in a particular period, with higher profits assumed to indicate a better level of business performance. However, looking at profit figures in isolation will not tell us much at all. For example, we might know that a firm has a net profit of £50,000 for the most recent financial year, but we would need to know much more about the firm before we could judge the profit earned a success or a disappointment. Consider the following data:

	Firm A £000	Firm B £000
Sales	120	75
Cost of sales	40	30
Gross profit	80	45
Expenses	50	20
Net profit	30	25

Although firm A generates the highest net profit, we cannot say definitively that this firm is the better performer. Looking at the sales data for the two firms would help clarify matters: firm A's sales figures are significantly higher than those of firm B, so it is no surprise that firm A generates a higher net profit. The question we might want to ask is: why did the sales generated by firm A not generate an even higher level of net profit?

Profit and profitability are not the same thing. Profit represents an absolute figure which is, broadly speaking, revenue less expenses. Profitability is concerned with looking at the profits earned in relation to some other variable such as sales or capital. Analysing profitability will involve looking at the manner in which the firm is generating profit, or its potential to generate future profits.

We can use accounting ratios to help us assess how well a firm is performing. An accounting ratio is the comparison of two or more pieces of financial data which, once combined, aim to give much more meaningful and useful information about business performance.

In this chapter we will consider what each ratio indicates in terms of assessing business performance and how it is calculated.

Types of accounting ratio

There are many different accounting ratios which can be calculated and they all attempt to enable us to interpret business performance. The different ratios can be categorized according to what particular aspect of business performance they are designed to assess. Although there is no definitive method of classifying ratios, the following groupings are fairly typical:

- Profitability ratios: Assess measures of profits in relation to sales, capital and other financial variables.
- Efficiency ratios: Assess how well the firm manages its current and non-current assets and liabilities in terms of their efficient management.
- Liquidity ratios: Assess the ability of the firm to manage working capital and its ability to pay its short-term debts without running into cash flow and liquidity problems.
- Gearing ratios: Assess the long-term capital structure of the business in terms of the relative quantities of debt and equity capital.
- Investor ratios: Assess the performance of the business in terms of returns for shareholders.

Profitability ratios

For most businesses, especially limited companies which have one eye on shareholder satisfaction, the profit earned for a period is the key indicator of business success. However, as we saw in the introductory section to this chapter, the size of the profit does not always provide very useful information about overall performance unless we are furnished with more information about the business. Therefore the profitability ratios are designed to provide more insight into assessing whether the profit earned is an indicator of success. The following are commonly used profitability ratios.

Return on capital employed (ROCE)

Often seen as the most important ratio in assessing overall business perform-ance, this ratio compares the profit of the business to the capital employed figure found on the balance sheet. It is calculated as follows:

$$\text{Return on capital employed (ROCE) (\%)} = \frac{\text{Operating profit}}{\text{Average capital employed}} \times 100$$

This ratio expresses profit as a percentage of the amount of capital invested within the firm. This provides a rate of return based on the size of the finan-cial investment within the firm in terms of capital employed.

Operating profit is profit before interest and taxation. The profit before interest and tax is the preferred measure of profit as the ROCE ratio is aiming to analyse the profit made by the firm's operations. A firm that has financed more of its capital through debt rather than equity would, all other things being equal, have a lower ROCE owing to interest charges being a deduction made against profit, whereas the dividends paid on any equity capital would only be subtracted after the profit has been calculated. Net profit can also be used if operating profit is unavailable.

The average capital employed is calculated as the arithmetic mean of the capital balances at the start and end of the period. However, it is fairly commonplace to just use the final capital figure at the end of the period if the opening balance is not available.

Capital employed refers to the total of shareholders' equity (issued capital plus reserves) and the non-current liabilities issued by the firm. The rationale for including the non-current liabilities within the capital em-ployed total is that although this is borrowed capital, it is still long-term and has helped finance the operations of the firm (and hopefully has generated profit).

Return on equity (ROE)

$$\text{Return on equity (ROE) (\%)} = \frac{\text{Profit after tax}}{\text{Equity (Issued capital + Reserves)}} \times 100$$

This ratio expresses profit as a percentage of the firm's equity, that is, its issued share capital and any reserves. The profit figure used is the one after deductions for all operating expenses (including interest charges) and tax-ation. If the firm has issued preference share capital we would also deduct any preference dividend as well, given that in normal circumstances prefer-ence dividends are a compulsory payment out of the firm's profits (unlike ordinary dividends which are optional).

This ratio provides useful information in that it relates profits to the amount of actual investment belonging to the shareholders within the company by comparing profit to the overall equity (or shareholders' funds) rather than any debt capital which will be repaid at some point in the future. For the owner(s) of the firm this will provide a more useful yardstick to what the return is on their investment. This is why we use the profit after tax and after any preference dividends; this is the profit which is available for ordinary shareholders for either dividend payments or reinvestment within the firm.

Profit margins

Profitability focuses on the ability of the firm to generate profit. One way of assessing the firm's profitability is through the use of the profit margin ratios. Each of the profit margin ratios measures how much profit is earned from a unit of sales revenue. The profit margin ratios are calculated as follows:

Gross profit margin

$$\text{Gross profit margin (\%)} = \frac{\text{Gross profit}}{\text{Sales revenue}} \times 100$$

In effect, this shows how much profit is generated out of the sales revenue. For example, a gross profit margin of 40 per cent would mean that for every £10 of sales earned, £4 would be earned in gross profit (with the other £6 being accounted for by the cost of goods sold, or costs of production).

A rising gross profit margin will mean that the firm is turning more of its sales revenue into gross profit. This could be due to one or more of the following:

- higher selling prices – meaning that the gap between the costs of the goods sold and the revenue generated is increasing;
- lowered costs of production (through either greater efficiency in production or by the use of cheaper inputs into the production process), which mean that the firm will earn higher profits on each unit sold as long as the selling price is not also reduced;
- reduced competitive pressure in the market – which means that the firm is not forced to reduce its selling price.

Of course, the opposite would be true for the above explanations. One point worth noting is that a falling profit margin is not always a cause for concern. For example, a firm attempting to increase its market share may instigate a policy of deliberately undercutting its competitors by price discounting. This means that the gap between price and costs will narrow, thus reducing the gross profit margin. Similarly, a change in the firm's product mix may mean that the gross profit margin falls, if the new product line cannot be sold at a price which would generate a higher profit margin.

Profit margin is related to the overall level of profit. However, the level of sales in terms of physical volume will be the determinant of the overall level of profit. A firm can have a high profit margin but can still be experiencing disappointing overall profits if it is not managing to shift its output.

Profit margin

$$\text{Profit margin (\%)} = \frac{\text{Operating profit}}{\text{Sales revenue}} \times 100$$

The profit margin calculates the percentage of sales revenue that is converted into operating profit (profit before interest and tax deductions). For example, a profit margin of 10 per cent would mean that for every £100 of sales, £10 was earned in operating profit. The other 90 per cent would be accounted for by all costs associated with running the business, with the exception of the interest charges. Where the operating profit figure is not available, net profit is an adequate substitute.

An acceptable profit margin figure would depend on the industry in which the firm operated. Competitive industries are more likely to have lower profit margins owing to competitive pressures keeping a lid on price increases. Generally, a business would desire a high and rising profit margin (or at best, a profit margin that is not falling).

Comparisons of the two profit margins can provide useful information as they are obviously connected. If the gross profit margin falls, it is almost certain that the net profit margin will fall as well – a fall in the proportion of sales turned into gross profit will mean that, unless the firm can reduce other costs elsewhere within the business, the net profit as a proportion of sales will fall as well.

If the gross profit margin is reasonably constant but the (net or operating) profit margin is falling, this would be an issue of control of expenditure. In this situation it would appear that the firm is experiencing a disproportionate rise in expenditure such as general overheads. For example, a rise in output and sales may lead to a firm experiencing diseconomies of scale whereby costs begin to rise faster than the rise in output. This may be worth investigating. Many firms will see profit margins rise as output expands. This is due to the beneficial effects of economies of scale. For example, overheads that are fixed in nature, such as the costs involved in running a human resources department, will not rise over certain increases in output. This means that revenue will rise faster than costs and the profit margins will rise.

It may be the case that profit margins fall owing to circumstances beyond the firm's control and possible reasons are as follows:

- higher cost of materials or higher labour costs in production;
- lower selling prices – possibly owing to a promotional campaign or other special offer;

- increased competition forcing prices down;
- switch from profit maximization to sales maximization (ie price cuts).

Supermarkets operate with very low profit margins, but they are very profitable. This is because, although they earn very little profit on each 'unit' sold, the output is sold at a very rapid rate – thus the overall profits quickly build up.

An antique dealer would not expect sales to be achieved at such as rapid rate. This means that the antique dealer would probably have to charge high selling prices – which mean a higher profit margin – in order to compensate for the slower rate of sales. This means that profits build up at a slower rate, but in bigger steps.

Example 17.1

We will examine the profitability ratios of Buzz Ltd.

Buzz Ltd
Extracts from final accounts for year end

	2012 £	2013 £
Turnover	16,555	23,220
Cost of goods sold	12,345	18,650
Gross profit	4,210	4,570
Overhead expenditure	2,540	3,275
Net profit	1,670	1,295
Average capital employed	46,700	49,850

Return on capital employed

Using the data from Buzz Ltd, we arrive at the following results:

	2012	2013
Return on capital employed	$\dfrac{1,670 \times 100}{46,700} = 3.6\%$	$\dfrac{1,295 \times 100}{49,850} = 2.6\%$

What do these results tell us?

- A return of 2–4% as experienced by Buzz does not look too encouraging and the slight decline may be worrying. There are other factors, though, that should be explored before we pass judgement.

- External factors, such as an economic downturn, may be affecting the industry in which Buzz Ltd operates. Not all firms are affected in the same way by economic downturns and upturns. For example, the takeaway pizza market was always thought to be an industry that would perform better during an economic downturn (perhaps because people would resort to takeaways pizzas rather than restaurant pizzas). However, in the period of steady economic growth the demand for takeaway pizzas has increased as well, which was not expected.

- Profits may be low due to one-off factors (such as high research expenditure – which is only capitalized in the UK according to strict guidelines – meaning that many UK firms have to put a lot of their research expenditure into the income statement, rather than capitalizing the expenditure.

Profit margins

Both the gross profit margin and the net profit margin are calculated in a very similar way (the only difference is in the measure of profits used in the ratio – gross and net profits). It makes sense to consider these ratios together, as they will often be affected in the same way by changes affecting the firm.

Using the data from Buzz Ltd, we arrive at the following results:

Gross profit margin	
2012	**2013**
$\dfrac{4{,}210 \times 100}{16{,}555} = 25.4\%$	$\dfrac{4{,}570 \times 100}{23{,}220} = 19.7\%$

Net profit margin	
2012	**2013**
$\dfrac{1{,}670 \times 100}{16{,}555} = 10.1\%$	$\dfrac{1{,}295 \times 100}{23{,}220} = 5.6\%$

Gross profit margin – what does this tell us?

In 2012, 25.4 per cent of the sales revenue was made up of gross profit and this fell to 19.7 per cent in 2013. A fall in this ratio means that for every £1 of sales generated by the firm, less profit will be earned. It certainly does not mean that profits are falling – in fact, although the gross profit margin has fallen, the gross profits in 2013 are actually slightly higher than those of 2012.

Net profit margin – what does this tell us?

For Buzz Ltd, the net profit margin falls from 10.1 to 5.6 per cent over the two-year period. For every £1 of sales, 10.1p net profit was generated in 2012, but this fell by the next year to 5.6p in every pound. A falling net profit margin, as with the gross profit margin, does not mean that net profits have fallen. However, in this case, the net profits have fallen in 2013 compared with 2012. The reason for a falling profit margin is that the 'gap' between sales and the measure of profit has narrowed. This could be due to one or more of the following:

- selling prices have fallen;

- costs have increased.

As stated earlier, the fall in the profit margin may be the result of deliberate action by the business. A cut in the selling price should boost sales and the overall effect on the profits of the business should be examined.

Efficiency ratios

This group of ratios measures how efficiently the firm manages its assets and working capital. These ratios will include both current and non-current assets. The effective management of these assets will not boost the profits of the firm directly. However, failure to manage these efficiently will often lead to higher costs, meaning that profits will be directly reduced. The following ratios can be used to assess the firm's efficiency.

Asset turnover

This measures how efficiently the firm uses its net assets in order to generate sales. It is calculated as follows:

$$\text{Asset turnover} = \frac{\text{Sales revenue}}{\text{Net assets}}$$

The ratio is expressed as a factor – the amount of sales revenue that each unit of asset generated. For example, an asset turnover of '5' would indicate that each £1 of assets generated sales revenue of £5.

Given that the value of net assets should be identical to the value of the firm's capital employed, either figure, if available, may be used in calculating this ratio.

The objective of a firm should be to maximize its asset utilization, so a high and rising asset turnover ratio is desirable where possible. For firms operating in an industry which requires heavy investment in non-current assets, it is vital for achieving profits that the firm fully utilizes its assets For example, firms operating in the airline industry, such as Ryanair, have achieved higher levels of profits, despite deeply discounted ticket prices, by increasing the asset turnover ratio. Aeroplanes are utilized more effectively (ie the assets are 'turned over'), with gaps between each plane's flights (where it generates revenue) being significantly reduced.

Links between the asset turnover and the profit margin

The ROCE is often seen as the key ratio in assessing business performance. However, one issue with this ratio is that it does not really indicate how the firm is generating its profits. Consider the following extract from financial statements for two firms:

	Firm A £000	Firm B £000
Sales	500	600
Operating profit	100	40
Capital employed	1,000	400
Return on capital employed (%)	10%	10%

From this we can see that the ROCE for both firms is identical at 10 per cent. However, how these firms generated their profits is different. Consider the profit margins of both firms:

	£000	£000
Profit margin	100/500 = 20%	40/600 = 6.7%

We can see that firm A is more profitable, with a profit margin three times higher than that of firm B. However, if we consider the asset turnover ratio for both firms, we arrive at the following:

	£000	£000
Asset turnover	500/1,000 = 0.5	600/400 = 1.5

Here we can see that firm B uses its assets more efficiently in generating sales revenue. Assets generate a level of sales three times the rate for firm A. Although both firms have an identical return in the form of the ROCE ratio, we can see that they generate their profits quite differently. Firm A operates with high profit margins, so each sale contributes a relatively high amount of profit, whereas for firm B each sale generates a lower level of profit. However, firm B utilizes its assets such that it generates a higher amount of sales from a smaller asset base.

We can take this further by showing how the ROCE ratio can be thought of in the following calculation:

$$\text{ROCE} = \frac{\text{Operating profit}}{\text{Sales}} \times \frac{\text{Sales}}{\text{Net assets (or Capital employed)}}$$

In other words, ROCE = Profit margin × Asset turnover.

Inventory turnover

How a firm manages its inventory levels will also contribute to the firm's overall efficiency. In Chapter 11 we looked at how managing the level of inventory can minimize any costs associated with holding inventory. This ratio provides information about how long the firm holds its inventory, on average. It can be expressed in two different ways – by the number of days' inventory held on average and also the inventory turnover in terms of number of times per year.

The inventory turnover ratio is calculated as follows:

$$\text{Inventory turnover} = \underbrace{\frac{\text{Average inventory}}{\text{Cost of sales}} \times 365}_{\text{As number of days}} \quad \underbrace{\frac{\text{Cost of sales}}{\text{Average inventory}}}_{\text{Number of times per year}}$$

Example 17.2

For example, if average inventory was £10,000 and the cost of goods sold for the year was £120,000, the inventory turnover would be calculated as follows:

$$\text{Inventory turnover} = \underbrace{\begin{array}{c}£10,000/£120,000 \times 365 \\ = 31\ \text{days}\end{array}}_{\text{As number of days}} \quad \underbrace{\begin{array}{c}£120,000/£10,000 \\ = 12\ \text{times per year}\end{array}}_{\text{Number of times per year}}$$

Average inventory would be the arithmetic mean of inventory at the start and close of the period. However, it is also acceptable simply to use the closing balance for inventory where this is the only data available.

Each time a firm turns its inventory over, it is basically generating more profit from the sales of the inventory. An inventory turnover which is high in terms of number of days means that more resources are tied up in inventory and, as covered earlier in the book (see Chapter 11), we know that a high level of inventory imposes certain costs on the business.

A high inventory turnover would appear as a low number of days or a high number of times per year. A high inventory turnover is generally preferable but a firm with a high inventory turnover should be careful to ensure that it does not run out of inventory and miss out on potential sales.

Trade receivables days

This ratio measures how long a firm takes on average to collect the payments from trade receivables. This is part of the firm's management of working capital. The ratio is expressed in the number of days it takes for debts to be collected and it is calculated as follows:

$$\text{Trade receivable days} = \frac{\text{Trade receivables}}{\text{Credit sales}} \times 365$$

The higher the result of this ratio, the longer a firm is taking to collect monies outstanding in respect of credit sales made. Managing the credit period offered is important and is explored in Chapter 11. A rising ratio could indicate that the firm is losing control of the amounts offered under the credit control policy. Collecting debtors faster would mean that cash was being returned to the business at a faster rate. However, a rising ratio might also be the deliberate policy of the business in that it is offering more generous credit periods in order to hold on to or to attract new customers.

Trade payables days

This ratio measures how long a firm takes on average to settle the amounts owing to the creditors of the firm, the trade payables. The ratio is expressed in the number of days it takes for debt to be settled and it is calculated as follows:

$$\text{Trade payables days} = \frac{\text{Trade payables}}{\text{Credit purchases}} \times 365$$

The higher the number of days, the longer the time taken by the firm to pay the amounts due on its trade payables. This ratio is often examined in conjunction with the trade receivable days ratio. If the trade payables days are lower than the trade receivables days, it would mean that the firm is paying its debts faster than it is collecting cash from credit customers. This could indicate the potential for the firm to experience cash flow difficulties as money leaves the firm faster than it is received.

Using the two ratios together may help the firm to avoid overtrading. Overtrading occurs when a firm takes on too many apparently profitable sales but without adequate cover in terms of liquid resources. If the firm extends credit periods to customers or accepts orders for more credit sales, it will be using the firm's liquid resources in terms of inventory and trade receivables. If trade payables are paid more quickly than the trade receivables are settled, the firm will gradually run out of money. Therefore, firms should aim to ensure that the trade receivables days is at the very least no less than the trade payables days. Receiving money more quickly will give the firm breathing space in terms of ensuring that it has sufficient liquid resources.

Example 17.3

We will look at how a firm manages its trade receivables and trade payables with the following extract from the financial statements of a company:

	2010	2011
	£	£
Sales	225,000	310,000
Purchases	140,000	195,000
Trade receivables	18,500	38,000
Trade payables	12,400	13,200

Trade receivables collection period

2010	2011

$$\frac{£18,500 \times 365}{£225,000} = 30 \text{ days}$$

$$\frac{£38,000 \times 365}{£310,000} = 45 \text{ days}$$

Trade payables payment period

2010	2011

$$\frac{£12,400 \times 365}{£140,000} = 32 \text{ days}$$

$$\frac{£13,200 \times 365}{£195,000} = 25 \text{ days}$$

What do these results tell us?

The ratios are probably moving in the wrong direction as far as effective management of working capital goes. The firm is taking just over two weeks longer on average in 2011, when compared with 2010, to collect its debts from customers. At the same time it is paying its suppliers for credit purchases on average seven days faster in 2011 than in 2010. This could place a strain on the firm's cash flow as money is leaving the firm more quickly than the rate at which it is coming back into the firm.

This does not mean that a change in its working capital management has to be made. For example, paying trade receivables in a shorter period of time may mean that the firm is more likely to qualify for prompt payment cash discounts. Offering longer credit periods to customers may be a successful method of attracting more customers. However, the longer a debt remains outstanding, the more likely a bad debt will occur, so the firm should monitor this situation carefully. Consideration of these ratios should be made in conjunction with the liquidity position of the firm.

Liquidity ratios

Although profit is seen as the main measure of success of a firm, it is vital that a firm has sufficient liquid resources in order to ensure that it can pay what is expected of it in the form of expenses, wages, etc. Running out of cash is one of the commonest sources of business failure. Therefore, careful management of cash and working capital will help to avoid insolvency, where the firm literally runs out of cash. Ensuring that the firm has sufficient liquid assets – those that can be quickly converted into cash without any serious loss in value – can be monitored through the use of liquidity ratios.

Current assets consist mainly of inventory, trade receivables and cash balances. Likewise, current liabilities usually consist of any short-term debts, such as expenses owing and trade payables. The liquidity ratios are meant to act as a guide to ensure that the firm has enough cash and other liquid assets to pay what is owed. There are two main liquidity ratios.

Current ratio

The current ratio compares the relative size of the current assets to the size of the current liabilities. In this sense it is not the size of the current liabilities – debts that will need to be repaid in the near future – that matters but the size of them when compared with the firm's current assets. It is calculated as follows:

$$\text{Current ratio} = \frac{\text{Current assets}}{\text{Current liabilities}}$$

This ratio is expressed simply as a number or as a ratio, such as 1.5:1.

A rough guide is that the size of the current ratio should ideally be around 2:1, which would indicate that current assets are twice the size of current liabilities. In theory, the firm should have sufficient cover in its liquid assets to settle the debts that need paying. However, there are some problems with this reasoning.

Even if the liquid assets are twice the size of the current liabilities, the firm can still face liquidity problems. Inventory needs to be sold before it can be turned into cash and trade receivables may not be quickly recovered. In this case, an apparently safe figure for the current ratio may disguise a poor cash flow position.

Similarly, if a firm has a very low current ratio, this does not automatically mean that it will face liquidity problems. Large firms may be able to quickly arrange overdraft cover for any cash flow shortage and also delay payments to trade payables, ensuring that a liquidity crisis is avoided. However, the current ratio can indicate the potential for future cash flow issues.

Acid test ratio

As mentioned above, inventory is not always a very liquid asset. Apart from finished goods, inventory can consist of raw materials and work-in-progress. These cannot be converted into cash quickly at all, and would therefore not be very useful in assessing the firm's ability to cover its short-term debts. Even with the case of finished goods, retailers might be able to sell inventory quickly, but other firms may find that it takes time for inventory to be sold. In this case it would appear misleading to treat inventory as a liquid asset in the current ratio calculations. As a result, a second liquidity ratio, the acid test ratio, excludes inventory from the calculation. It is calculated as follows:

$$\text{Acid test ratio} = \frac{\text{Current assets} - \text{Inventory}}{\text{Current liabilities}}$$

As with the current ratio, the calculation will be expressed either as a number or as a simple ratio.

The result will always be lower than the current ratio (a firm that has no inventory would produce the same result for both the current and the acid test ratio). A rough guide is that the size of the acid test ratio should be around 1:1. This would mean that the firm has enough liquid assets to cover the short-term debts of the business.

However, if a firm's liquid assets consist mainly of trade receivables rather than cash, the firm will still have to ensure that it can collect the money quickly enough to cover its current liabilities. Therefore it is worth, when assessing the firm's liquidity position, to actually check the cash balances alongside the ratio analysis.

The ratios could be too high. A high current or acid test ratio (probably higher than 3 or 4, but this would depend on the type of firm and the situation it finds itself in) would also be a problem. There would be no danger of the firm experiencing liquidity problems, as it would have very 'safe' cover. However, the firm would be operating inefficiently. This is because it would have too many current assets to cover the current liabilities. This would be the result of one or more of the following:

- High stock levels would require storage costs and may lead to higher spoilage or theft.
- High debtors figure increases the chance of bad debts.
- High cash and bank balances are inefficient as higher returns could be obtained from long-term investments elsewhere.

However, we should be careful how we interpret the data. A high current ratio could be based on small absolute figures, for example if current assets totalled £700 and current liabilities £100, the current ratio would be 7:1, yet nobody would seriously suggest that the business needs to reinvest its excess cash.

Example 17.4

Tahoulan Ltd		
Balance sheet extracts as at 31 December		
	2013	**2014**
Current assets	**£**	**£**
Stock	6,780	11,456
Debtors	8,760	10,988
Cash	3,455	5,311
	18,995	27,755
Current liabilities		
Creditors	13,200	11,322

These are calculated as:

Current ratio	
2013	**2014**
$\dfrac{£18,995}{£13,200} = 1.44{:}1$	$\dfrac{£27,755}{£11,322} = 2.45{:}1$

Acid test ratio	
2013	**2014**
$\dfrac{£18,995 - £6780}{£13,200} = 0.93{:}1$	$\dfrac{£27,755 - £11,456}{£11,322} = 1.44{:}1$

What do these results tell us?

In both cases, the size of the current ratio and acid test ratio has increased, meaning that the liquidity position of the firm has improved. The increase in the current ratio is proportionately greater than the increase in the acid test ratio, which can be explained by the increase in the level of inventory.

For both years, it would appear that the firm has a fairly safe liquidity position. This should mean that the firm will not experience difficulties in meeting short-term debt repayment. However, we would need to know whether the balance sheet date was a typical date. In addition, it would make sense to looks at the data behind the results. Although the acid test ratio suggests that the firm has sufficient liquid assets to meet its obligations to meet trade payables, we can see that the actual level of cash balances is small relative to the size of trade receivables. This should not pose a problem if the firm can reliably collect the balances owed to it from the trade receivables. If the firm takes a relatively long time to collect what it is owed, or the industry has a higher than average incidence of bad debts, the firm may run into trouble. In this case it might be worth looking at the results of the trade receivables collection period.

Gearing ratios

Most firms will use a certain amount of debt to finance their operations. Non-current liabilities consist of external sources of finance such as loans, mortgages and debentures. In the case of external financing there is the risk attached to the finance that the firm is normally committed to interest payments on this debt. If a firm has relatively large amounts of external financing, there is the greater risk that cash flow and profits will be increasingly used to meet interest payments. The proportion of the firm's capital that consists of debt rather than equity is referred to as the firm's gearing position. A highly geared firm will have a large proportion of its long-term capital financed by debt.

The gearing ratio measures this proportion as a percentage of the firm's overall capital employed figure. It would be calculated as follows:

$$\text{Gearing ratio (\%)} = \frac{\text{Non-current liabilities}}{\text{Capital employed}} \times 100$$

Capital employed, as before, consists of both shareholders' equity and non-current liabilities. Some variations on this formula exist. For example, an alternative would add the value of issued preference share capital to the non-current liabilities in the numerator of the formula. This is due to preference dividends often being obligatory to pay. Similarly, another variation would also include current liabilities within the numerator of the formula. However, given that current liabilities frequently carry no interest charge, this variation is not as widespread.

One final variation which is reasonably commonplace is the Debt/Equity ratio which compares the size of the debt directly to the size of the equity. This would be calculated as follows:

$$\text{Debt/Equity ratio (\%)} = \frac{\text{Non-current liabilities}}{\text{Equity (Share capital plus Reserves)}} \times 100$$

This ratio will measure the same thing but will give a higher result than the gearing ratio as it does not include non-current liabilities in the denominator.

Example 17.5

The following are extracts taken from the summarized balance sheet of Carlin plc as at 31 December 2017:

	£000
Equity	
Ordinary share capital	500
Reserves	300
Non-current liabilities	
9% Debentures	700

The gearing ratios would be calculated as follows:

$$\text{Gearing} = \frac{\text{Non-current liabilities}}{\text{Equity + Non-current liabilities}} = \frac{700 \times 100}{1,500} = 46.7\%$$

$$\text{Debt/Equity} = \frac{\text{Non-current liabilities}}{\text{Equity}} = \frac{700 \times 100}{800} = 87.5\%$$

The ideal size of the gearing ratio

The particular combination of debt and equity finance utilized within the company is known as the capital structure of the company. A company with a high proportion of debt finance will have a high gearing ratio. However, we would be interested in finding out if one particular percentage for the ratio is better than another.

The cost of a firm's capital will consist of the cost of its debt finance and the cost of its equity finance. The combined cost of the debt and equity finance (as we saw in Chapter 12) is referred to as the weighted average cost of capital (WACC). The lower the WACC, the higher the market value of the company and, given that the objectives of the directors of the company are to maximize shareholder returns, deciding which capital structure gives the lowest WACC would be very useful to know.

The cost of debt finance is cheaper than equity finance. This is because debt is less risky than equity finance. First, any interest on the debt is likely to be fixed and will be compulsory, meaning it should always be paid back to the lenders – before any dividends can be paid. Second, the lenders to the business will, if the business is liquidated, receive their capital back before shareholders do, as they are deemed a higher priority in the pecking order of the firm settling with its creditors. The lower risks associated with debt will mean that lenders will be happy to be compensated with a lower interest rate in return for the risk of lending.

Debt is also a cheaper form of finance as interest payments are tax deductible, meaning that interest payments are made before tax is deducted, with the result that the tax charge will be lower. Dividends are not tax deductible, meaning that a firm that uses equity rather than debt finance will incur a higher tax charge for the period, even with profit levels similar to those of a firm that chooses debt finance.

So far, this would suggest that a high gearing ratio is preferable as the lower cost of debt finance will drive down the firm's WACC and will increase shareholder wealth. However, a higher gearing ratio means that more of the firm's profit will be used up in settling any interest payments and will leave fewer profits available for dividend payments. This means that equity holders will demand a higher return (ie the cost of equity will rise) in order to compensate them for the increased chance of less dividend being paid.

A higher gearing ratio will also increase the chance of bankruptcy as the firm may not be able to meet demand for interest payments by the lenders of capital to the firm. This will push up the riskiness of holding equity in the business and therefore shareholders will demand a higher return and the WACC will be pushed upwards.

As a result, a firm should aim for a gearing ratio which minimizes the WACC. A firm with a very low gearing ratio will not benefit from the low cost of debt finance. Likewise, a firm with a high gearing ratio would face higher WACC as equity holders demand a higher return to compensate for the risk of holding equity. Therefore, somewhere between the two extremes of low and high gearing is probably the norm. How risky the firm is perceived to be by lenders will directly affect the cost of both debt and capital, thus influencing the overall WACC.

Interest cover

Gearing is a useful ratio to assess the potential riskiness of a firm's capital structure. However, the ratio does not include the actual profits of the business. For example, comparable businesses may have similar gearing ratios, but if one of the businesses is consistently earning higher profits, the higher gearing may not be seen as too much of an issue. Additionally, periods of low interest rates may warrant less fear about excessive borrowing. For example, after the financial crisis of 2008, most central banks cut interest rates significantly, thus reducing the cost of servicing debt on variable-rate loans. Thus the gearing ratio cannot factor in the changing situation.

The interest cover ratio focuses on how much of the firm's profits are taken up by interest payments. This means that it takes into account both the level of profits and the actual interest rate. It is calculated as follows:

$$\text{Interest cover} = \frac{\text{Profit before interest and tax}}{\text{Interest payments}}$$

This ratio expresses the number of times over that the year's interest expenses could have been paid out of that year's operating profit. The higher the level of interest, the less the risk of the firm being unable to pay the interest costs out of the profits. For example, an interest cover of 4 would mean that the interest bill could have been four times higher before the firm ran out of profit to pay this charge. The lower the interest cover ratio, the greater the risk of the firm of not having sufficient profits available to cover that year's interest charges. In addition, a low interest cover increases the chances of a firm being unable to pay dividends to its ordinary shareholders. Therefore a high interest cover increases the profits available for redistribution.

Investor ratios

Ratios can be used by current and potential investors. The focus for an investor will be on the profits of the business and the returns that are generated to shareholders in the form of dividends. Obviously the operating profit of the business will be of interest to the investor. However, it is the profit after all deductions made for both interest and taxation that will be of more interest as it is this that is available for shareholders. Obviously these ratios are only to be used by limited companies.

Earnings per share

This ratio measures how much each share issued by the firm generates for the investor in terms of the profit earned. Although not all the profit is returned directly to the shareholder in the form of dividends, the profit which is not distributed to shareholders will be retained and will 'grow' the business, thus potentially leading to capital growth of the share price.

$$\text{Earnings per share (EPS)} = \frac{\text{Profit for year (after tax)}}{\text{Number of ordinary shares issued}}$$

Where a firm undertakes further share issues during the most recent period, an average of the number of shares in issue would be used.

Comparing the EPS over a number of years for the same company would allow an investor to see if this has been growing. Comparing between different firms will not necessarily give meaningful data as different firms may have significantly different capital structures (firms may have unusual profit levels but a firm that has relied heavily on debt rather than equity finance will have a much higher EPS). Therefore, comparing EPS results between firms is not particularly useful for comparing the profitability of the firms.

Dividends per share

Whereas the EPS measures the profit generated that is available for shareholders, the dividends per share calculates how much is actually returned to shareholders in the form of how much dividend is paid for each share in issue.

$$\text{Dividends per share (DPS)} = \frac{\text{Ordinary dividend}}{\text{Number of ordinary shares issued}}$$

Although a high dividend per share may be seen as preferable, the higher the proportion of profits which are distributed as dividends, the less there is available for reinvestment within the business. The directors of the company will have to make a decision on how much of the profits to distribute as dividends. One measure that can be used, in order to see how 'safe' a firm's dividends policy is, is the divided cover ratio.

Dividend cover

This ratio measures the number of times the current profit could have been used to make the dividend payment for that period. For example, if the profit for the year was £10m and the dividend payment was £5m, the dividend cover ratio would be 2. This means that the company could have paid the dividends twice over out of the profits.

$$\text{Dividend cover} = \frac{\text{Profit for year (after tax)}}{\text{Dividends}}$$

The lower the cover, the greater the risk that the current level of dividends will not be maintained into the future.

Given that profit and cash flow are not necessarily the same thing, a variation on the dividend cover ratio is sometimes used, where cash flow from operations is used instead of the profit figure. The rationale here is that cash flow provides more tangible evidence that the dividends can actually be paid.

Dividend yield

Knowing how much a firm pays out in dividends is one thing, knowing how this compares to an investment in the company is another. The dividend yield gives more meaning to the dividends per share ratio by comparing this to the current share price of the company. It is calculated as follows:

$$\text{Dividend yield (\%)} = \frac{\text{Dividends per share} \times 100}{\text{Current share price}}$$

The yield enables an investor to see, in clear percentage terms, how much of a return the purchase of shares in a particular business will generate in terms of dividends received. Of course, many investment decisions will also be made on the basis of capital growth in the share value, which may mean that the dividend yield gives only limited information.

Price/earnings ratio

The price/earnings (P/E) ratio relates the current earnings of the business to the current share price of the business. It is calculated as follows:

$$\text{Price/earnings ratio} = \frac{\text{Current share price}}{\text{Earnings per share}}$$

Given that the share price of a company is meant to reflect investors' current views of the future profitability of the company, the P/E ratio uses these expectations of the firm's future and relates them back to the current earnings. It provides a crude payback period for the time taken to repay the investment in terms of the current share price, with the number of years of earnings based on the current level of earnings. For example, a P/E ratio of 10 would indicate that it would take 10 years of current earnings in order to 'pay back' the amount needed to purchase the share.

The higher the P/E ratio, the greater the confidence in the firm's future prospects. This is because the higher the P/E ratio, the higher the share price, which, as stated earlier, represents the belief of investors in the firm's future profitability.

The P/E ratio is often interpreted in the context of industry averages. It is often published alongside share prices and firms in the same industrial sector can then easily be compared. A higher than average P/E ratio for one firm compared with other firms in the industry would indicate that investors are expecting this company to outperform other companies in the same industry.

Example 17.6

Simper plc
Extract from statement of changes in equity
for year to 31 December 2016

	£	£
Profit for year (profit after taxation)		105,000
Less:		
Transfers to general reserves	15,000	
Dividends	55,000	70,000
Retained earnings carried forward		35,000

The issued share capital of the company consists of 500,000 £1 ordinary shares. On 31 December 2016, the market price of each share was £1.85.

From the information, the following ratios would be calculated

- Earnings per share = £105,000/500,000 = £0.21 per share.

- Dividends per share = £55,000/500,000 = £0.11 per share.

- P/E ratio = £1.85/£0.21 = 8.8.

- Dividend yield = £0.11/£1.85 = 5.9%.

Limitations of ratio analysis

Although the ratios can indicate areas where correct treatment is needed, or areas in which the firm appears to be performing well, there are limitations regarding how much we can infer from the results of a ratio calculation. Some of the more common limitations are as follows:

1 Comparisons with other firms will lack meaning if the firms being compared are too dissimilar. Ideally, only similar firms should be compared, otherwise comparisons will largely lack significance. The type of firm should be considered along with the results from the ratio analysis. For example, the supermarket industry generally has low liquidity ratios. This is because the supermarkets are large enough to be able to survive with very few liquid assets – overdrafts can be quickly arranged and many supermarkets are quite capable of delaying payments to their suppliers. Therefore the poor liquidity position can be explained through the context of the particular type of firm.

2 One set of ratios from one year's worth of data is unlikely to allow a meaningful investigation into the firm's performance. Some ratios can be used as stand-alone figures and can identify potential issues, but other groups of ratios, such as profitability, only have meaning if we can analyse the changes in these over a period of time. Ideally comparisons should be made with ratios over a number of years for meaningful conclusions to be drawn.

3 The balance sheet date can often provide the explanation for a particular set of results, and the results of ratios using the balance sheet will have less validity if the date on which the balance sheet is constructed is an atypical day. For example, a firm's liquidity ratio may indicate issues with inventory levels being too high. However, if the balance sheet is drawn up just before a firm's main sales period, this would be understandable. If would be more of a worry if the inventory levels were high after the sales period was over.

4 When analysing the profitability ratios, care must be taken to see if the profits are earned in a sustainable manner and have not arisen out of creative accounting. This is not to say that the firm has acted illegally but that the profit figure may overstate the performance of the business. For example, profit can be generated through a profitable sale of the firm's non-current assets. Similarly, reductions in provisions can rescue an otherwise disappointing profit. Even if the ratios indicate that the firm is performing successfully, it is worth spending time to see if a surprisingly high profit figure is all that it seems.

5 Balance sheets will include only those assets that can be reliably measured. Many intangible assets that give the firm value may not be included on the balance sheet. The non-inclusion of the intangible assets when calculating ratios may give misleading or distorted views of business performance.

6 Similarly, the non-financial qualities of the business are often not apparent from financial ratio analysis. The skills and general morale of the workforce may not show up in the data and this may therefore give a misleading impression of the firm's performance. However, a well-skilled and motivated workforce should help generate higher than average profits for the firm, which would be apparent in the ratios calculated.

7 Ratios generally use historical data and provide no real basis for future predictions. It could be argued that the P/E ratio is forward looking, given the use of the share price in the calculation. However, all other ratios are looking at what has already happened. If they indicate a successful business or a cause for concern, the environment may have already changed. The speed at which the financial data becomes available will determine how dated the ratios are.
For internal users of accounting data, this may not be so much of an issue. However, for external users of accounting data, it could be a few months before the most recent financial statements are available.

Review questions

1   Waite runs a small antiques shop in Chichester. He has provided extracts from two years' final accounts. He would like you to analyse the accounts to assess the profitability of the firm. The balance sheet extracts are as follows:

	2018 £	2019 £
Sales	31,234	38,770
Cost of goods sold	17,970	23,133
Gross profit	13,264	15,637
Overheads	6,456	10,801
Net profit	6,808	4,836
Capital employed	90,940	102,013

(a)   Calculate for both years the following ratios:

i   return on capital employed;

ii   gross profit percentage;

iii net profit percentage.

(b)   Using your results from (a), analyse the profitability of the shop.

Solution

(a)

	2018 %	2019 %
Return on capital employed	7.49	4.74
Gross profit margin	42.47	40.33
Net profit margin	21.80	12.47

(b)   Relevant points to make would include:

● Profitability declining – given by fall in ROCE.

● Gross profit margin almost constant.

● Net profit margin falling – why is this? Rising overheads?

2 Preston runs a toy shop. She is concerned with the liquidity position of her firm as she has heard that liquidity problems are one of the most frequent explanations for failure. The following data are available:

	£
Inventory	14,500
Trade receivables	8,409
Bank	3,200
Trade payables	9,310

(a) Calculate the current and acid test ratio based on the above data.

(b) Give a brief evaluation of the liquid position of the business to Preston.

Answer

(a)

Acid test ratio	1.25
Current ratio	2.80

(b) Factors to mention:

- Both ratios seem reasonably 'safe'.

- Adequate cover for trade payables is available in both the acid test and the current ratio.

- However, we would need to know additional information:
  - Was the date of the data a 'typical' date?
  - How liquid is the inventory, especially in 'off peak' selling periods?
  - Are bad debts an issue?

3 A small audio equipment retailer has just completed the second year of trading. Profits are up, but the manager is slightly concerned. She feels that the firm could face liquidity problems in the near future. The data for this claim are as follows:

As at 31 December:	2015	2016
	£	£
Inventory	12,470	7,568
Trade receivables	6,662	10,121
Bank	3,200	
Trade payables	9,310	8,980
Bank overdraft		3,434

(a) Calculate the current ratio and liquidity ratio based on the above data.

(b) Should the manager be concerned with the liquidity position? Give a balanced argument.

Answer

(a)

	2015	2016
Current ratio	2.4	1.4
Acid test ratio	1.1	0.8

(b) Arguments which would support concern would include:

- Liquidity position has certainly declined over the year.

- Acid test ratio is now low enough that trade receivables would not cover the combined total of the trade payables and bank overdraft in 2016.

- Inventory may not be very liquid in January (unless sales were offered).

- The high trade receivables perhaps indicate sales over the Xmas period and this will generate cash over the next few months.

Arguments against concern would include:

- Firm may be able to extend overdraft if seen as a reputable firm.

- It is unlikely that all trade payables would want immediate settlement.

4 The following information is available for the past two years:

	For year ended 31 March 2013 £	For year ended 31 March 2014 £
Turnover	125,000	160,000
Purchases	80,000	128,000
	As at 31 March 2013	As at 31 March 2014
Trade receivables	13,500	31,000
Balance at bank	8,000	4,000
Trade payables	11,800	15,600

(a) Calculate both the trade receivables' collection period and the trade payables' payment period for each of the two years.

(b) Calculate the acid test ratio for each of the two years.

Answer

(a)

	For year ended 31 March 2013	For year ended 31 March 2014
Trade receivables collection period	39 days	71 days
Trade payables payment period	54 days	45 days

(b)

	For year ended 31 March 2013	For year ended 31 March 2014
Acid test ratio	1.82	2.24

5 The following data relates to extracts from the financial statements of Haxell Ltd for the year ended 31 December 2017:

	£000
Turnover	600
Gross profit	420
Net profit	95
Dividends	35

	£000	£000
Non-current assets		2,000
Current assets	380	
Current liabilities	270	
Net current assets		110
		2,110
Non-current liabilities		
Debentures		700
		1,410
Equity		
Ordinary shares of £1 each		800
Reserves		610
		1,410

The value of inventory as at 31 December 2017 was £180,000. The market price of an ordinary share on 31 December 2017 was £2.25.

From this data, calculate the following ratios:

- gross profit margin;

- net profit margin;

- return on capital employed;

- acid test ratio;

- current ratio;

- dividend yield;

- debt/equity ratio;

- gearing.

Answer

Gross profit margin	70%
Net profit margin	15.8%
Return on capital employed	4.5%
Acid test ratio	0.74
Current ratio	1.41
Dividend yield	1.94%
Debt/equity ratio	49.7%
Gearing	33.2%.

INDEX

NB: page numbers in *italic* indicate figures or tables